Free Will and the Law

This volume brings together many of the world's leading theorists of free will and philosophers of law to critically discuss the ground-breaking contribution of David Hodgson's libertarianism and its application to philosophy of law.

The book begins with a comprehensive introduction, providing an overview of the intersection of theories of free will and philosophy of law over the last fifty years. The eleven chapters that follow divide into two parts: the first five address libertarianism within the free will debate, with particular attention to Hodgson's theory, and in Part II, six contributors discuss Hodgson's libertarianism in relation to issues not often pursued by free will scholars, such as mitigation of punishment, the responsibility of judges, the nature of judicial reasoning, and the criminal law process more generally. Thus the volume's importance lies not only in examining Hodgson's distinctive libertarian theory from within the free will literature, but also in considering new directions for research in applying that theory to enduring questions about legal responsibility and punishment.

Allan McCay teaches at the University of Sydney Foundation Program and is an Affiliate Member of the Centre for Agency, Values and Ethics at Macquarie University.

Michael Sevel is Senior Lecturer in Jurisprudence at the University of Sydney Law School.

Free Will and the Law

New Perspectives

Edited by
Allan McCay and Michael Sevel

Routledge
Taylor & Francis Group
LONDON AND NEW YORK

First published 2019
by Routledge

2 Park Square, Milton Park, Abingdon, Oxfordshire OX14 4RN
52 Vanderbilt Avenue, New York, NY 10017

Routledge is an imprint of the Taylor & Francis Group, an informa business

First issued in paperback 2020

British Library Cataloguing-in-Publication Data
A catalogue record for this book is available from the British Library

Library of Congress Cataloging-in-Publication Data
A catalog record has been requested for this book

ISBN: 978-1-4724-8144-3 (hbk)
ISBN: 978-0-367-66144-1 (pbk)

Typeset in Galliard
by Apex CoVantage, LLC

Contents

Contributors

Bernard Berofsky is Professor of Philosophy Emeritus at Columbia University.

Christopher Birch is Adjunct Professor at Sydney Law School and Barrister in practice at the Sydney Bar and Senior Counsel.

Michael Louis Corrado is Arch T. Allen Distinguished Professor of Law and Adjunct Professor of Philosophy at the University of North Carolina at Chapel Hill.

RA Duff is Professor of Philosophy Emeritus at the University of Stirling, and Professor of Law and Russell M. and Elizabeth M. Bennett Chair in Excellence at the University of Minnesota.

Laura W. Ekstrom is Professor of Philosophy at the College of William & Mary.

Ishtiyaque Haji is Professor of Philosophy at the University of Calgary.

Robert Kane is University Distinguished Professor of Philosophy Emeritus and Professor of Law at the University of Texas at Austin.

Neil Levy is Professor of Philosophy at Macquarie University and Director of Research at the Oxford Centre for Neuroethics.

Allan McCay teaches at the University of Sydney Foundation Program and is an Affiliate Member of the Centre for Agency, Values and Ethics at Macquarie University.

Michael Sevel is Senior Lecturer in Jurisprudence at the University of Sydney Law School.

Nicole A Vincent is Senior Lecturer in the Faculty of Transdisciplinary Innovation at the University of Technology Sydney, and Honorary Fellow in the Department of Philosophy at Macquarie University.

1 Introduction

Allan McCay and Michael Sevel

Over the past half century, there has been an unprecedented number of major developments in both the philosophy of free will and the philosophy of law. On the one hand, the number, diversity, and sophistication of theories of free will and responsibility have risen sharply in recent years, and there has been greater appreciation of the connections between these debates and other areas of enquiry – in relation not only to perennial philosophical topics in, e.g., ethics and moral psychology, but also to ones in neuroscience, cognitive psychology, and theology. By the early twenty-first century, the relevant literatures on free will have accordingly become vast and increasingly technical. On the other hand, debates on a range of topics in the philosophy of law have flourished, regarding both general questions, such as the nature of law, coercion, and legal obligation, and more specific ones, such as the foundational principles of criminal law, torts, and contracts, the nature of legal responsibility, and the justification of punishment. While these developments have been concurrent, they have, to a large extent, proceeded in relative isolation from each other. While we cannot, and in any case need not, summarize all the twists and turns of these discussions,[1] we will aim instead to give a broad overview of the points of contact and interaction between theories of free will and the philosophy of law over the last several decades. That overview will provide some of the necessary context for our volume's eleven newly commissioned essays, authored by many leading philosophers of free will and law.

All of the essays engage in various ways with the libertarian theory of free will of philosopher and jurist David Hodgson (1939–2012). Hodgson is a unique figure in recent times, as he was both a well-respected appellate judge for nearly three decades, as well as an Oxford-trained philosopher of considerable skill and creativity, and over many years developed novel theories of free will, consciousness, rationality, and the justification of punishment. Our introduction will, therefore, conclude with an overview of Hodgson's career and philosophical views, as well as a summary of the structure and content of the eleven essays which follow.

1 For a concise summary of the free will debates in analytic philosophy over the past several decades, see Kane (2011). For an overview of the developments in the philosophy of law over roughly the same period, see Murphy (2007) and Postema (2011).

Free will and the criminal law

For much of the last century, discussions of the problem of free will in the context of the law have largely related to the responsibility, blameworthiness, and punishment of those who have committed criminal offences (Green 2014). In many legal systems, the criminal law often requires evidence of the *actus reus* (the criminal act) and the *mens rea* (the guilty mind) for an offence, which meets the requisite standard of proof to convict a person, and thereby hold them legally, and on many views morally, responsible for their crime. Theories of free will have informed normative views about the propriety of such practices. For example, it has been questioned whether the current practices of the criminal law in many, perhaps all, jurisdictions are morally justified if some purported general threat to free will turned out to be well-founded (Pereboom 2014).

To illustrate, consider one such purported threat in relation to the crime of murder. It is generally true of a person who has formed an intent to kill someone (*mens rea*) and then successfully acted on the intention (conduct constituting the *actus reus*) without any legally recognized defence that the person may be held responsible for this crime. They may then be sentenced and imprisoned for a substantial period of time. In some jurisdictions the person may even be sentenced to death. In most legal systems, part of the justification for the penalty lies in the need to protect the community; however, another part of the justification is normally retributive – that is, one aim of punishment is to give the murderer what they *deserve* for what they have done. But if we think of human beings as being part of a world in which all events (including human actions) are caused by prior events, one may then start to wonder whether the formation of intent and the act of killing are part of a long causal chain that began long before the birth of the offender, and are therefore ultimately caused by factors that are outside the offender's control. This sort of thought can easily begin to cast doubt on the offender's responsibility for what they have done, and likewise on the punishment rendered in light of it. In relation to the penalty, we may start to question whether the murderer really *deserves* to be jailed or killed. For many theorists, then, it is morally significant for the assessment of the offender's responsibility that the formation of an intent to kill and the act of killing resulted from the offender's *free* choice, and consideration of the causal history of the criminal behaviour, beyond the control of the offender, seems to call this freedom into question.[2]

The history of the free will debate includes consideration of various purported threats to human freedom. Concerns about fate, the powers or knowledge of a deity, and, particularly since the advent of modern science, a naturalistic picture

2 A focus on the remote causal history of behaviour has not been confined to theory. In 1924, the American attorney Clarence Darrow, in respect of one of his clients (Richard Loeb), famously referred to "the infinite forces that were at work in producing him ages before he was born". Darrow made this reference in his much-publicized plea in mitigation in the sentencing of Loeb and Nathan Leopold, for the murder of Bobby Franks. The plea also touched on the role of heredity and social environment in causing criminal behaviour. For the full text of Darrow's plea in mitigation, see Sellers (2006).

of the world in which all events are caused by earlier events have been thought by philosophers to threaten human freedom (Kane 2005). Much, but certainly not all,[3] of the contemporary free will debate responds to problems emanating from a naturalistic view of the world in which human action forms part of a web of cause and effect with all other natural events. A large portion of the contemporary debate has focused on deterministic causation and its compatibility with and consequences for the scope and significance of free will. Determinism has been defined in a number of different ways over the long history of the free will debate.[4] However, a useful working definition is as follows: given the causal antecedents of everything (including everyone) in the world, in conjunction with the laws of nature, there is only one possible future. So if determinism obtains, given the initial conditions of the Big Bang and the laws of nature, it was necessary, for example, that the cult leader Charles Manson and his followers to commit all their crimes in the precise manner they in fact did.

Within the free will debate, some are *compatibilists*, and, as will be seen in the next section, compatibilism has been influential in the development of much of the legal theory that addresses the issue of free will. Compatibilists argue that determinism is consistent with some or all of the following: free will, moral responsibility, blameworthiness, and retributive punishment (i.e., punishment that is deserved). Many compatibilists argue that the mere fact of deterministic causation does not justify withholding blame (or praise), and usually argue that what is significant in deciding whether an agent is free, morally responsible, or deserving of blame or punishment is features of the agent's psychological state, rather than metaphysical issues about the causal structure of the world. Thus, one influential compatibilist view, that of Fischer and Ravizza (1998), focuses primarily on the degree to which an agent is responsive to reasons for action in the demarcation of the line between those who are morally responsible and those who are not, rather than focusing on metaphysical issues concerning the nature of causation. On this compatibilist view the agent's mental capacities for choice are of primary significance.

For compatibilists, merely knowing that the Manson crimes were caused deterministically does not *ipso facto* ground a reason to exculpate the perpetrators; we would need to enquire into the psychological state, perhaps also the rationality, of those involved to know whether they were free, morally responsible, blameworthy,

3 For an example of some contemporary work that focuses on divine knowledge as a threat to free will, see Hasker (2011).

4 Perhaps the most famous historical exposition of determinism is that by the nineteenth century French mathematician, astronomer, and physicist Pierre Laplace:

> [A]n intelligence which could comprehend all the forces by which nature is animated and the respective situation of all the [things which] compose it – an intelligence sufficiently vast to submit these data to analysis – it would embrace in the same formula the movements of the greatest bodies of the universe and those of the lightest atom; for it, nothing would be uncertain and the future, as well as the past, would be present to its eyes.
>
> (Laplace 1951: 4)

and deserving of punishment. A compatibilist position has the potential to preserve much of what was purported to be under threat in the contemporary free will debate, including legal responsibility and retributive punishment. It is thus a view that is somewhat friendly to the law's status quo of presuming that persons are capable of being legally responsible for their actions, which may go some way to explaining its appeal to some legal philosophers.

By contrast, *incompatibilists* argue that if determinism is true, then we are *not* free, morally responsible, deserving of praise, blame, punishment, or reward.[5] For an incompatibilist, *if* it turned out that the world was deterministic, then no-one would ever be responsible for anything. So this would mean that those involved in the Manson killings would not have acted freely or been responsible for what they did. Nor would they deserve any punishment. In that case, for the criminal law to take morally justified action against them, it must rely on some other justification such as community protection or prevention of future offences.

Compatibilists are often agnostic about whether determinism is true; their core claim is often asserted conditionally (similar to that in the previous paragraph). In this regard, it is worth noting that since the advent of quantum theory in physics, many consider the plausibility of the claim that the world is deterministic to be either diminished or undermined entirely. The view that the universe is indeterministic, i.e., that causes do not determine their effects but somehow bring them about in an indeterministic way, has gained wider acceptance among scientists and philosophers (Kane 2011: 5–9).

While incompatibilists argue that determined choices cannot be free, can undetermined choices be free? Those who espouse *libertarianism* about free will (whether in response to the indeterministic picture of the world that some see as emerging from the sciences, or for other reasons) argue that the thesis of determinism is false.[6] Nonetheless, they argue, we can make undetermined choices that we somehow control, and are thus free. So, for example, in order for Manson and his followers to be responsible for their crimes they would need to have made at some point a libertarian choice or choices related to the formation of their character, or the commission of the offence. That is, they would need to have made one or more relevant undetermined choices that they control, to be responsible for their crimes.

Libertarian views have been less influential in legal philosophy than compatibilist views, and, as will be seen later, the main proponent of the view within such debates is David Hodgson (2012). If Hodgson is right, then libertarianism is friendlier to the legal status quo than has been previously thought. That is, if

5 Some philosophers take the view that some of the phenomena listed in this sentence are compatible with determinism but others are not. Thus one may be an incompatibilist with respect to some but not others. (Fischer and Ravizza's view, for example, although a form of compatibilism, is more precisely referred to as semi-compatibilism. See note 9 later in the introduction.) In this chapter, we use the term "incompatibilism" to refer to the view that *all* of these phenomena are incompatible with determinism.

6 When used in the context of the free will debate, the term "libertarian" therefore has nothing to do with the political philosophy of libertarianism.

legal subjects are libertarian free agents, they can be morally responsible for their conduct in a way that could preserve a link between legal and moral responsibility. According to Hodgson's view, the exercise of libertarian free will grounds the kind of responsibility that can make punishment deserved, thus preserving the retributive justification for punishment.

Thus, if one espouses some form of compatibilism or libertarianism, one may not be committed to either a major change to traditional legal practices or a radical shift in understanding of the point of those practices.[7] However, a notable minority of philosophers see the justification of the criminal law's responsibility and punishment practices as arising out of considerations that need not rely on any satisfactory account of free will, and so downplay or reject the significance of free will for justifying such practices. Some urge for radical change, seeing the role of the criminal law as being confined to protecting the community and prevention of harm to others, rather than imposing deserved punishment; these practices may be justified *even if* some sceptical position on free will is true (Pereboom 2014; Caruso 2016). In fact, a perhaps growing number of sceptics argue that there is no place for concepts such as free will, moral responsibility, blame, or deserved punishment in the law at all. Their general proposal suggests a radical reconception of the law's various frameworks for holding offenders responsible, or doing away with them altogether, while retaining some legal mechanisms for incarceration and in some cases rehabilitation (Waller 2011; Vilhauer 2013; Levy 2012; Corrado, Chapter 9, this volume). These views are revolutionary with respect to their prescriptions for the legal system in a way that compatibilism and libertarianism are not.

But compatibilist and libertarian views of free will and moral responsibility remain the primary approaches to justifying the criminal law's practices of holding responsible and imposing punishment (for retributive reasons) on those who commit crimes. Compatibilism has been, more generally, the most common way to respond to concerns about free will and responsibility in relation to other long-standing issues in legal theory. However, a greater diversity of views has now emerged; indeed, one purpose of this collection of essays is to contribute to that diversity. We turn now to examining these approaches in more detail, before turning to the distinctive contributions of the essays of this volume.

Compatibilism and legal theory

It is often said that compatibilism is the orthodox approach to free will in legal theory. Kaye (although not himself supportive of compatibilism) has asserted that "[a]ccording to the dominant view in contemporary criminal theory, we have a

7 Kolber (2016) has claimed that the "crafters of Anglo-American law" (those who over the centuries created the common law and legislation) are likely to have espoused a belief in a form of libertarian free will, which has "infused the law" (2016: 10). If this were true it might go some way in explaining why libertarianism is friendly to the status quo in common law systems.

compatibilist criminal law" (2005: 1158). Norrie (also not himself a compatibilist) has taken the most influential Anglophone legal philosopher of the twentieth century, H. L. A. Hart, to be a compatibilist (Norrie 1983: 62). And the most prominent contemporary theorist who has significantly engaged with the free will problem in the context of legal philosophy, Stephen Morse, contends that "only compatibilism can explain and justify our legal practices" (2004: 431). He states that compatibilism:

> is the approach that I and many other criminal lawyers explicitly or implicitly adopt. This approach accepts completely that we live in a thoroughly causal world, at least at the macro level, and that causal processes produce human action and all the other phenomena of the universe. But it also holds that genuine responsibility is possible. This approach best explains and justifies our moral and criminal law practices without endorsing the implausibilities of libertarianism. Even if mechanism is true, the law's concepts of moral responsibility and deserved blame and punishment are rationally defensible in the compatibilist view.
>
> (2004: 437–438)

More recently, Morse (2015) has reasserted a commitment to compatibilism in the face of a purported threat to the practices of the criminal law emerging from neuroscience. Here is not the place to survey the variety of compatibilist accounts,[8] but it is worth briefly mentioning one such account, that of Fischer and Ravizza (1998), which has perhaps been the most referenced form of compatibilism among legal philosophers (Hodgson 2012: 166–173; Morse 2000; Vincent 2015). Fischer and Ravizza's view focuses primarily on the agent's psychology, in particular their capacity for rationality, as a criterion for moral responsibility, rather than giving primacy to facts about the causal history of action. In their view, an important consideration in determining whether an agent is morally responsible for an act or omission is whether they are "moderately reasons-responsive". In order to be moderately reasons-responsive, one must have sufficient mental capacity to understand the reasons that bear on one's actions, and sufficient volitional capacity to control one's behaviour (1998: 62–91).

So to know whether someone is responsible for what they have done, one must enquire into these mental capacities. Of course, in a particular instance a person may not have actually exercised capacities that were adequate according to the view, in an appropriate way (perhaps in the context of compliance with the law), and if that is the case they did the wrong thing and are morally responsible for that wrong.[9]

8 For an overview of compatibilist accounts, independent of legal theory, see Levy and McKenna (2008).

9 Fischer and Ravizza's is a non-standard form of compatibilism which is more accurately described as semi-compatibilism, as it is an argument for the compatibility of moral responsibility with determinism, rather than for both free will and moral responsibility with determinism, as is often argued by compatibilists.

Fischer and Ravizza's view has perhaps held appeal in the context of discussions of the criminal law partly because of its significance and influence as one of the major positions in the free will debate, and, as suggested earlier, its potential to preserve the status quo. However, its focus on rationality as a criterion for the ascription of responsibility also seems to make something of a natural fit with some of the defences in the criminal law. Many criminal justice systems stipulate a form of rationality as a criterion of responsibility, excusing those who meet the criteria of their mental illness ("insanity") defences, and thus being regarded as having defects of rationality. Similarly, if one thinks of an accused person who claims to have been sleepwalking at the time of the offence and uses an automatism defence, they too seem to be highlighting issues related to their responsiveness to reasons. Thus there seems to be some common ground between Fischer and Ravizza's and the criminal law's approach to exculpation.

In his later work, the influential legal theorist Ronald Dworkin develops a compatibilist view that similarly focuses on the agent's mental capacities, in order to explain the kind of control required for free choice (2011: 219–252). For Dworkin, it is sufficient for an agent to act freely, and thus to be liable to blame and sanctions, when the agent makes a decision consciously, such that "no one else is making that decision through and for him", and so long as the agent "has the capacities to form true beliefs about the world and to match his decisions to his normative personality – his settled desires, ambitions, and convictions" (2011: 228). He argues that such a view explains and justifies the responsibility practices of the criminal law (such as the insanity defence) better than libertarian approaches (2011: 248–252).

Libertarianism and legal theory

While one can find historical traces of libertarianism in legal theory,[10] most contemporary proponents of libertarianism have not generally focused on questions at the intersection of theories of free will and the law. By the same token, legal theorists have not generally relied on libertarian moral justifications of legal practices. In fact, to the extent legal theorists have considered a libertarian view of free will, they have rejected it as a foundation for legal practices (Morse 2007; Moore 2009: 271).

And yet, the conception of libertarianism that these theorists have considered is arguably impoverished, given the growing diversity of views in recent debates about libertarian free will (Palmer 2014a). We can distinguish three different sorts of views, all of which are libertarian in that they include an indeterministic form of control over action (Palmer 2014b). First is the agent-causal approach. Chisholm advances a form of agent-causal libertarianism when he says

10 Lord Kames, Henry Home, the eighteenth century Scottish judge and important figure in the Scottish Enlightenment, developed a theory of free will which incorporates some libertarian themes, though Kames did little to extend the theory to address issues of legal responsibility and punishment (Harris 2005: 92–97).

"[i]n doing what we do, we cause certain events to happen, and nothing – or no one – causes us to cause those events to happen" (2005: 423). On this view, we are uncaused causers of our actions. Many philosophers think that causation is a relation between events (so, for example, the heavy rain caused the damage to the property), but on the agent-causal view, agents can cause events without being caused to do so by prior events. This capacity for agents to serve as the uncaused cause of their actions is put forth as an account of the sort of control requisite for freedom. One challenge for agent-causal libertarians is to fit their view of agency within a naturalistic view of the world that is consistent with our best scientific theories, but while indeterministic causation may now be palatable to many physicists, the *uncaused*-causation of agent-causal libertarians seems much less so.

However, on a second kind of view, event-causal libertarians (such as Kane and Ekstrom, in Chapters 2 and 3, respectively, this volume) argue that a form of libertarianism is possible which accounts for the choices of agents as undetermined, caused (indeterministically) by prior events, and yet still controlled by the agent. The indeterminism of quantum theory has a role in making such views more plausible by challenging the deterministic picture of the universe. Hodgson's theory (2012), which we introduce later and is discussed throughout the essays of this volume, represents a distinctive form of libertarianism which locates the requisite kind of agential control in the having of certain conscious ("gestalt") experiences of alternative possibilities leading up to action. According to Hodgson, we can make undetermined choices for which we are responsible, but his view is non-standard in the sense that it admits of both agent-causal and event-causal interpretations; nonetheless, Hodgson stands as one of the first philosophers to explore the consequences of such a view for central questions in legal theory. The third type of libertarian view is a non-causal account, according to which a person acts freely only if their action is not caused in any way (see Ginet 2007; Goetz 2008; Palmer 2016). Its implications for and prospects within legal theory have yet to be explored, so we set it aside here.

Scepticism about free will (and other related concepts), and legal theory

While compatibilism is the dominant approach in legal theory, and has not been displaced by libertarianism, there are a growing number of sceptical voices emerging in discussions of central issues of legal philosophy, in particular with regard to the justification of punishment. Such theorists doubt some or all of the following: that we have free will, are generally morally responsible for what we do, can be blameworthy, can be deserving of punishment, and can evaluate the blameworthiness of others with competency that is sufficient to justify engaging in retributive punishment. Such views raise doubts about the moral justification for many legal practices. Doubts about some or all of these claims have come both from philosophical arguments (e.g., Strawson 2011; Pereboom 2001) and in response to empirical studies (Greene and Cohen 2004).[11]

In terms of the potential for sceptical views to undermine aspects of the moral justification for the criminal law, there is an increasing group of philosophers who have voiced concerns, some of whom also consider what a criminal law that jettisoned some of these concepts might look like (Honderich 2006; Waller 2011; Oerton 2012; Caruso 2016; Pereboom 2013; Smilansky 2017). One of the contributors to this volume has elsewhere argued that criminal (and other) acts are too infused with luck to give rise to retributive punishment that is morally justified (Levy 2013b). Another considers an alternative justification for punishment that might have merit if retributivism were indeed thought to be discredited (Corrado, Chapter 9, this volume), and a further contribution raises doubts about the epistemic basis for judgements about retributive punishment (McCay, Chapter 11, this volume).

David Hodgson's libertarianism

A recurring focus of the eleven essays of this volume is the thought of jurist and philosopher David Hodgson, a unique figure in late twentieth century Anglophone philosophy. We will briefly discuss his biography and substantive views, and conclude with an overview of how each of the essays of the present volume engages with his work.

David Hodgson was born on 10 August 1939 in Sydney, New South Wales, Australia, the son of a solicitor.[12] He graduated in 1962 from the University of Sydney with honours in law. After serving briefly as an associate to Sir Victor Windeyer of the High Court of Australia, he took up a Rhodes Scholarship to Oxford University in 1964. He completed his DPhil in 1967 under the supervision of H. L. A. Hart, professor of jurisprudence, a towering figure in late twentieth century Anglophone jurisprudence (Lacey 2004). Hart remarked that Hodgson was the ablest DPhil student he'd ever had (Levy 2013a: 183). This praise is especially significant, given that many of Hart's other students, even during this period – for example, Brian Barry, John Finnis, Neil MacCormick, and Joseph Raz, among others – went on to become major figures in legal and political philosophy in the late twentieth century.[13]

11 Some have also drawn on empirical work to make arguments about the consequences of widespread adoption of a sceptical attitude toward free will (Morris 2018). For an overview of sceptical arguments, see Caruso (2013: 1–16).

12 Much of Hodgson's biography can be found in "Judge Blessed with Flawless Logic" (2012).

13 See ibid. We thank John Finnis, Leslie Green, Peter Hacker, former Justice Dyson Heydon of the High Court of Australia, Nicola Lacey, and Joseph Raz for sharing, in correspondence, their memories and observations regarding Hart's estimation of Hodgson's talent.

This was not, however, to be Hodgson's fate; in fact, Hodgson never held a full-time academic appointment. Instead, after completing the DPhil, he returned to Sydney and for the next four decades lived two, virtually parallel lives. On the one hand, he enjoyed a decades-long and distinguished career in legal practice, both at the bar and on the bench; on the other, over the same period, he produced a body of philosophical writings comparable to the lifetime creative output of a full-time academic philosopher. In 1967, his DPhil thesis appeared as a monograph, *Consequences of Utilitarianism*, a sustained critique of utilitarianism both on its own terms as well as with regard to how it fails to explain and justify legal reasoning and the imposition of punishment (Hodgson 1967). The book enjoyed a strongly positive reception,[14] and attracted the critical attention of some of the most distinguished utilitarian theorists and other philosophers across the Anglophone world (Singer 1972; Smart and Williams 1973: 153–154; Hoerster 1973; Lewis 1987).

Hodgson's interests then turned to topics that would preoccupy him for the rest of his life: free will and the nature of consciousness. His second monograph, *The Mind Matters: Consciousness and Choice in a Quantum World*, published in 1991, drew on the resources of quantum mechanics to argue against a computational model of the mind (Hodgson 1991). Here, he begins to develop a theory of "plausible" (non-deductive) reasoning, using examples of judicial reasoning in which incommensurate considerations often appear, as the basis of a critique of the limits of physicalist and functionalist theories of the mind. *The Mind Matters* was similarly well-received, though perhaps under-appreciated by academic philosophers.[15] In the twenty years following *The Mind Matters*, Hodgson published more than two dozen scholarly articles, further developing his theory of consciousness and its role in explaining free will. These lines of thought culminated in his last monograph, and the focus of many of the essays of this volume, *Rationality + Consciousness = Free Will* (2012).

In this last work, Hodgson develops a distinctive form of libertarian theory of free will, at the core of which is an account of what he calls "plausible

14 The influential economist and social theorist Friedrich Hayek remarked that Hodgson's book "for the time being ought to bring this discussion [of utilitarianism] to a close" (1976: 156). Joseph Raz said of the book that it "should convince everyone not already convinced of the importance of cross fertilization between ethics and jurisprudence" (1968: 616).

15 In a review of the book, the distinguished philosopher E. J. Lowe's assessment is striking in this regard (1993: 34): "It is extremely difficult to do justice to this densely and deeply argued book in a short review . . . Mainstream professional philosophers of mind should, however, perhaps feel humbled by the fact that while they have been satisfied for the most part with hanging on to the coattails of currently fashionable theories in cognitive science and artificial intelligence, it has largely been left to those outside the profession, like David Hodgson, to pursue the most profound metaphysical questions concerning the relations between mind and matter – questions which cannot even be begun to be addressed adequately without an understanding, such as Hodgson has taken so many pains to acquire, of the most successful theory of matter that humanity has ever devised, quantum mechanics".

reasoning", first introduced in *The Mind Matters*. Hodgson argues that such informal, and often practical, reasoning is at the foundation of scientific and other formalized kinds of reasoning (2012: 40) and so plays a fundamental role in human rationality and action, and in turn makes free choice possible. Central to plausible reasoning are what Hodgson calls conscious, feature-rich gestalt experiences, made up of unique informational content. Such content is partially shaped and limited by computational processes of the mind, and the agent's response to it is subject to some extent to laws of nature (which, by their operation, leave open a spectrum of possibilities of choice). And yet, the unified totality of the content of a given experience is unique and thus does not fully engage with, and so is not fully governed by, those laws. The precise combination of features in such gestalts cannot, Hodgson argued, be fully explained in terms of such laws. An agent's responses to the gestalts (as practical possibilities) is likewise not fully explainable by those laws. Such a response from the agent occurs as much in respect of artistic, creative contexts, such as composing the opening notes of *Tristan und Isolde* (2012: 83–84), as in contexts of practical deliberation and choice, both within and outside the law (2012: 136–137). In each of these contexts, the alternative possibilities of choice arise in a manner which involves causal consequences of antecedent events, but because of the uniqueness of the gestalts constituting each possibility, and their independence from the laws of nature, our choice among such possibilities is itself undetermined. Because Hodgson argues that such choices can also be rational this confers a form of control and thus a form of libertarian free will which extends to not only decisions about what to do, but decisions about what to believe (2012: 38).

Free will and the law: new perspectives

The eleven newly commissioned essays of this volume critically examine various aspects of Hodgson's view and explore the prospects of applying it to long-standing problems in legal philosophy. The essays, accordingly, divide into two parts. In Part I, five essays are devoted to critically examining Hodgson's libertarianism in the context of the broader free will debate. Hodgson acknowledges (2012: 159–161) that his theory has much in common with that of the leading defender of libertarianism, Robert Kane, but can be distinguished in several important ways. Kane (Chapter 2) contrasts Hodgson's views with his own, but in the end argues that he and Hodgson both endorse an event-causal version of libertarianism, though Hodgson's is a non-standard version which requires conscious experiences to be both efficacious and non-rule-governed. Kane argues that this aspect of Hodgson's theory, while intriguing, is unnecessary to defend libertarianism against critics. Laura W. Ekstrom (Chapter 3) agrees that Hodgson's is an event-causal theory, but argues against the view that conscious experiences play the distinctive role Hodgson claims; indeed there are good reasons to doubt that conscious experiences play the libertarian role in producing action which Hodgson claims. Neil Levy (Chapter 4) takes issue with

Hodgson's argument that the uniqueness of conscious experiences explains the role that they play in genuinely free action. Levy introduces alternative models of creativity that explain more parsimoniously the relationship between consciousness and free choice.

More generally, libertarian views have faced their own challenges, and it has been argued that if libertarian choices are undetermined *even by the agent*, then responsibility for them is undermined by luck. Bernard Berofsky (Chapter 5) considers several recent versions of "the luck argument" against libertarianism, and argues that while Hodgson's answers to the luck argument can be vindicated, his version of libertarianism does not thereby follow. Ishtiyaque Haji (Chapter 6) examines Hodgson's acceptance of both the principle of alternative possibilities (PAP) – that in order to be morally responsible for an action, one could have done otherwise – and the Guidance View – that it is a precondition of responsibility that one have the ability to grasp and be guided by reasons. Haji thinks that while "Frankfurt-style" examples against PAP are persuasive, and Hodgson's view is therefore flawed in accepting it, Hodgson's view is plausible insofar as it accepts the Guidance View about responsibility.

Part II comprises six essays that apply and extend Hodgson's libertarianism to a range of problems in legal philosophy, as well as examine how Hodgson himself applies his theory of free will to issues in the law such as justifying punishment. Michael Sevel (Chapter 7) extends Hodgson's libertarianism beyond issues of justifying punishment, to explain how judges are free to impose those punishments and to decide cases more generally. Sevel considers Hodgson's theory alongside several other major theories of judicial reasoning developed in the twentieth century, and concludes that Hodgson's represents a novel view in legal philosophy of the nature of judicial freedom. RA Duff (Chapter 8) agrees with Hodgson's position that retribution is central to justifying criminal punishment, but disagrees that incompatibilism about free will is required to vindicate the relevance of retribution. Duff, by contrast, sees retributive punishment is part of a social practice of holding wrongdoers responsible, and argues that such a practice can be explained and justified without endorsing libertarianism. Michael Louis Corrado (Chapter 9) considers Hodgson's arguments in favour of retributive punishment, and against treating people merely as instruments to be manipulated for the common good. Corrado agrees with this last claim, but argues, *pace* Hodgson, that we can endorse it while dispensing with the idea that punishment is justified only if a person deserves it.

Nicole A Vincent (Chapter 10) aims to answer Hodgson's challenge to compatibilists to explain how having the right psychological capacities makes a person a legitimate target of blame and punishment. Vincent argues that the relevance of capacities is the role they play in what she calls "fairness assessments", judgements about whether it is fair to impose a given punishment on a given person with a given set of capacities. She emphasizes that compatibilists in legal philosophy debates about the justification of punishment would make their views more cogent by attending to Hodgson's challenge. Allan McCay (Chapter 11) presupposes that blame and retributive punishment can be deserved, and constructs a theory that is intended to morally evaluate the mitigation practices of criminal justice systems, using insights about the assessment of degrees of blameworthiness found in the work of Dana Nelkin, in conjunction with Hodgson's views on self-formation. After using the theory to evaluate an actual mitigation practice, he notes that as a result of the complexity of any fully satisfactory theory, there is an epistemic problem inherent in the assessment of pleas in mitigation that means that even moderately competent evaluation of such pleas may be beyond the capacities of humans. Finally, Christopher Birch (Chapter 12) examines Hodgson's account of plausible reasoning, by considering a case of legal reasoning which Hodgson himself engaged in as an Australian judge. Birch argues that although such reasoning requires conscious creativity, it does not ultimately support a libertarian conception of free will. The success of such reasoning can be sufficiently explained by deterministic principles informed by theories in the philosophy of science.

While discussions of free will and the law have traditionally focused only on justification of punishment practices, a moment's reflection reveals that imposing punishment on those found to have committed an offence is a small part of the function and purposes of law, and the ways in which questions about freedom relate to those purposes. While further contributing to discussions about criminal responsibility and the moral justification of punishment, these essays aim to continue the expansion of discussions about free will as they relate to the law. And while the range of theories of free will that have been employed in legal philosophical debates has been rather narrow – confined mostly to compatibilist theories – the following essays also aspire to introduce a greater diversity of views about free will into those debates, and to begin to explore how libertarian theories of free will can suggest new avenues of enquiry within the philosophy of law.[16]

References

Caruso, GD 2013, 'Introduction: Exploring the Illusion of Free Will and Moral Responsibility', in GD Caruso (ed), *Exploring the Illusion of Free Will and Moral Responsibility*, Lexington Books, Lanham.

Caruso, GD 2016, 'Free Will Skepticism and Criminal Behavior: A Public Health-Quarantine Model', *Southwest Philosophy Review* 32(1): 25–48.

Chisholm, RM 2005, 'Human Freedom and the Self', in J Feinberg and R Shafer-Landau (eds), *Reason and Responsibility: Readings in Some Basic Problems of Philosophy*, Wadsworth Thompson Learning, Belmont.

Dworkin, R 2011, *Justice for Hedgehogs*, Harvard University Press, Cambridge, MA.

Fischer, J and Ravizza, M 1998, *Responsibility and Control: A Theory of Moral Responsibility*, Cambridge University Press, Cambridge.

Ginet, C 2007, 'An Action Can Be Both Uncaused and Up the Agent', in C Lumer and S Nannini (eds), *Intentionality, Deliberation, Autonomy*, Ashgate, Aldershot.

Goetz, S 2008, *Freedom, Teleology, and Evil*, Continuum, London.

16 We thank Neil Levy for useful comments on an earlier draft of this chapter.

Green, TA 2014, *Freedom and Criminal Responsibility in American Legal Thought*, Oxford University Press, Oxford.

Greene, J and Cohen, J 2004, 'For the Law, Neuroscience Changes Nothing and Everything', *Philosophical Transactions of the Royal Society B: Biological Sciences* 359: 1775–1785.

Harris, JA 2005, *Of Liberty and Necessity: The Free Will Debate in Eighteenth-Century British Philosophy*, Oxford University Press, Oxford.

Hasker, W 2011, 'Divine Knowledge and Human Freedom', in R Kane (ed), *The Oxford Handbook of Free Will*, 2nd edn, Oxford University Press, New York.

Hayek, FA 1976, *The Mirage of Social Justice*, Routledge and Kegan Paul, London.

Hodgson, DH 1967, *Consequences of Utilitarianism*, Clarendon Press, Oxford.

Hodgson, DH 1991, *The Mind Matters: Consciousness and Choice in a Quantum World*, Clarendon Press, Oxford.

Hodgson, DH 2012, *Rationality + Consciousness = Free Will*, Oxford University Press, New York.

Hoerster, N 1973, 'Is Act-Utilitarianism Truth-Telling Self-Defeating?', *Mind* 82: 413–416.

Honderich, T 2006, *Punishment: The Supposed Justifications Revisited*, Pluto Press, London.

'Judge Blessed with Flawless Logic' 2012, *Sydney Morning Herald*, 4 September, viewed 23 February 2018, www.smh.com.au.

Kane, R 2005, 'Introduction: The Contours of Contemporary Free Will Debates', in R Kane (ed), *The Oxford Handbook of Free Will*, 1st edn, Oxford University Press, New York.

Kane, R 2011, 'Introduction: The Contours of Contemporary Free Will Debates (Part 2)', in R Kane (ed), *The Oxford Handbook of Free Will*, 2nd edn, Oxford University Press, New York.

Kaye, A 2005, 'Resurrecting the Causal Theory of the Excuses', *Nebraska Law Review* 83: 1116–1177.

Kolber, A 2016, 'Free Will as a Matter of Law', in M Pardo and D Patterson (eds), *Philosophical Foundations of Law and Neuroscience*, Oxford University Press, Oxford.

Lacey, N 2004, *A Life of H.L.A. Hart: The Nightmare and the Noble Dream*, Oxford University Press, Oxford.

LaPlace, P 1951, *Philosophical Essay on Probabilities*, Dover, New York.

Levy, N 2012, 'Skepticism and Sanction: The Benefit of Rejecting Moral Responsibility', *Law and Philosophy* 31(5): 477–493.

Levy, N 2013a, 'Critical Notice of David Hodgson, *Rationality + Consciousness = Free Will*', *Australasian Journal of Philosophy* 91(1): 183–192.

Levy, N 2013b, 'Less Blame, Less Crime? The Practical Implications of Moral Responsibility Skepticism', *Journal of Practical Ethics* 3(2): 1–17.

Levy, N and McKenna, M 2008, 'Recent Work on Moral Responsibility', *Philosophy Compass* 43: 96–133.

Lewis, D 1987, *Philosophical Papers: Volume II*, Oxford University Press, Oxford.

Lowe, EJ 1993, 'Review of *The Mind Matters: Consciousness and Choice in a Quantum World* by DH Hodgson', *Philosophical Books* 34(1): 33–34.

Moore, MS 2009, *Causation and Responsibility: An Essay in Law, Morals, and Metaphysics*, Oxford University Press, New York.

Morris, S 2018, 'The Implications of Rejecting Free Will: An Empirical Analysis', *Philosophical Psychology* 31(2): 299–321.

Morse, SJ 2000, 'Rationality and Responsibility', *Southern California Law Review* 74: 251–268.

Morse, SJ 2004, 'Reason, Results, and Criminal Responsibility', *University of Illinois Law Review* 2: 363–444.

Morse, SJ 2007, 'The Non-Problem of Free Will in Forensic Psychiatry and Psychology', *Behavioral Sciences and the Law* 25: 203–220.

Morse, SJ 2015, 'Neuroscience, Free Will, and Criminal Responsibility', in W Glannon (ed), *Free Will and the Brain: Neuroscientific, Philosophical, and Legal Perspectives*, Cambridge University Press, Cambridge.

Murphy, MC 2007, *Philosophy of Law: The Fundamentals*, Blackwell, Oxford.

Norrie, A 1983, 'Freewill, Determinism and Criminal Justice', *Legal Studies* 3(1): 60–73.

Oerton, R 2012, *The Nonsense of Free Will: Facing up to a False Belief.* Troubador Publishing Ltd, Leicester.

Palmer, D (ed) 2014a, *Libertarian Free Will*, Oxford University Press, New York.

Palmer, D 2014b, 'Free Will, Libertarianism, and Kane', in D Palmer (ed), *Libertarian Free Will*, Oxford University Press, New York.

Palmer, D 2016, 'Goetz on the Noncausal Libertarian View of Free Will', *Thought* 5: 99–107.

Pereboom, D 2001, *Living Without Free Will*, Cambridge University Press, Cambridge.

Pereboom, D 2013, 'Free Will Skepticism and Criminal Punishment', in T Nadelhoffer (ed), *The Future of Punishment*, Oxford University Press, Oxford.

Pereboom, D 2014, *Free Will, Agency and Meaning Life*, Oxford University Press, Oxford.

Postema, G 2011, *Legal Philosophy in the Twentieth Century: The Common Law World*, Springer, Dordrecht.

Raz, J 1968, 'Review of *Consequences of Utilitarianism* by DH Hodgson', *Israel Law Review* 3(4): 616–617.

Sellers, AV 2006, *The Loeb-Leopold Case*, The Lawbook Exchange Ltd, Clark.

Singer, P 1972, 'Is Act-Utilitarianism Self-Defeating?', *The Philosophical Review* 81(1): 94–104.

Smart, JJC and Williams, B 1973, *Utilitarianism: For and Against*, Cambridge University Press, Cambridge.

Smilansky, S 2017, 'Pereboom on Punishment: Funishment, Innocence, Motivation, and Other Difficulties', *Criminal Law and Philosophy* 11(3): 591–603.

Strawson, G 2011, 'The Impossibility of Ultimate Responsibility?', in R Swinburne (ed), *Free Will and Modern Science*, British Academy, London.

Vilhauer, B 2013, 'Persons, Punishment, and Free Will Skepticism', *Philosophical Studies* 162(2): 143–163.

Vincent, N 2015, 'A Compatibilist Theory of Legal Responsibility', *Criminal Law and Philosophy* 9(3): 477–498.

Waller, BN 2011, *Against Moral Responsibility*, MIT Press, Cambridge, MA.

Part I

Libertarian free will

2 Making sense of libertarian free will

Consciousness, science, and laws of nature

Robert Kane

Introduction

In chapter 9 of his book *Rationality + Consciousness = Free Will*, David Hodgson compares and contrasts his view of free will with other views in the current literature.[1] The first view he discusses and compares to his own is my view of free will – a view I have been developing over the past forty years. Hodgson also compared our views in a number of previous writings (Hodgson 1999, 2002, 2005) – recognizing (rightly, I believe) that it is the closest view to his in the current philosophical literature. In this book (p. 160), he says "in many respects, Kane's position is similar to mine", and he goes on to list a number of key contentions that I have defended and he defends as well. In the earlier writings mentioned, he discusses additional similarities in our views as well as some differences.

In the next section of this chapter, I summarize some of the pertinent similarities between Hodgson's libertarian view and mine and then turn to the differences. A number of significant differences on which I focus concern a central and controversial feature of Hodgson's view – namely, the thesis that libertarian free choices result from "conscious gestalt experiences" that "do not engage with laws of nature or rules of any kind" (p. 80 and passim). This feature of his view has been questioned by many of Hodgson's critics;[2] and I share their suspicions. It is not that conscious experiences do not have a role to play in an account of free will. I think they do. Though I also believe (as does Hodgson) that unconscious neural processing is also crucial for understanding free will, including libertarian free will. (I have more to say about this later.)

What is problematic is the assumption that some processes that may be involved in free will, *whether* conscious or unconscious, must fail to engage with laws of nature or rules of any kind, if we are to make sense of libertarian free will. This assumption has often been made, to be sure, in the history of free will debates. It has often been assumed that if we are to make sense of libertarian free

1 Page references in the text hereafter will be to this work, unless another date or author is indicated.

2 See, for example, Clark (2005), Gomes (2005), Jaswal (2005), Maxwell (2005), Smart (2005), Capes (2012). Other contributors to this volume, including Neil Levy and Bernard Berofsky, are also critical of this thesis of Hodgson's.

will, we must postulate some unusual forms of agency or causation that somehow or other "escape the clutches" of scientific laws of nature.[3] Hodgson's view is a more sophisticated version of this traditional strategy, but it is a version of it.[4] And I think the strategy is misguided.

I will offer criticisms of it when I discuss the differences in our views in the latter sections of the chapter. First, I argue that the appeal to conscious gestalt experiences that do not engage with laws of nature or rules of any kind leads to problems that remain unresolved in Hodgson's view. Second, and more importantly, I will argue that this problematic feature of his view is unnecessary. I believe one can give an account of libertarian free will that has many of the features Hodgson argues for without assuming that the sources of free choices, including conscious gestalt experiences, do not engage with laws of nature or rules of any kind. One can also answer important objections often made against libertarian free will without appealing to this problematic assumption. I discuss how this might be done in the following sections. But I begin with the equally important agreements in our views.

Convergences

(i) First and foremost among these agreements is that Hodgson and I both defend a distinctive kind of *libertarian* view of free will, a view according to which there is an important form of human freedom (historically designated "freedom of the will") that is *incompatible* with determinism and could not exist in a fully determined world. While this is an obvious point of agreement, it is worth dwelling on. For the significant similarities in our views include the reasons we share for holding such a view.

Doctrines of determinism have taken many historical forms. People have wondered at various times whether their actions might be determined by fate or by God, by the laws of physics or the laws of logic, by heredity or environment, by unconscious motives or, in the latest neuroscientific versions (discussed by Hodgson in chapter 8 of his book), the physical processes of their brains. But there is a core idea running through all these historical doctrines that shows why they have

3 I have argued against such views in many writings, including Kane (1985) (chapter 4), 1989, 1996 (chapters 7 and 10), 2002e, 2004.

4 Hodgson explicitly rejects the usual versions of this strategy in the current literature, namely, "noncausalist" views and "(non-event) agent-causal" views. Hence he regards his view as "event-causal", like mine (event-causal views being usually regarded as the third option in current debates). But he also holds that free choices or actions are the causal results of conscious gestalt experiences and/or the apposite responses to such experiences in a manner that "does not engage with laws of nature of any kinds", either statistical or probabilistic (quantum) laws or deterministic laws. And that suggests his view, though event-causal, is nonetheless a version of the traditional strategy of postulating unusual forms of agency or causation that somehow "escape the clutches" of scientific laws of nature. Much depends, of course, on how one interprets the expression "does not engage with laws of nature of any kinds", and there are some ambiguities in what is meant by this expression, to which I will return.

been thought to be a threat to free will. They all imply that, *given the past and the laws governing the universe at any time, there is only one possible future.* Whatever happens is therefore inevitable (it cannot but occur), given the past and the laws.

There are a number of reasons why Hodgson and I both believe that free will is not compatible with determinism so understood. I'll mention one reason here that is important for later discussions. To explain it, one must first make clear that the issue is not whether *freedom* in any sense is incompatible with determinism. For there are many meanings of "freedom" (as one would expect from such a much-used term), and many of them *are compatible with determinism.* Even in a determined world, we would want to distinguish persons who are free from such things as physical restraint, addiction or neurosis, coercion, compulsion, covert control, or political oppression from persons who are not free from these things. And we can affirm that these freedoms would be preferable to their opposites *even in a determined world.*

Libertarians about free will, such as Hodgson and me, need not and do not deny that there are many kinds of freedom worth wanting that are compatible with determinism. What we insist upon is that there is at least one important kind of freedom worth wanting that is incompatible with determinism. I call this freedom the "freedom *of the will*" and distinguish it from the other freedoms (as does Hodgson) in the following way: The other (compatibilist) freedoms mentioned, freedoms from physical restraint, coercion, compulsion, and the like, all involve an *absence of constraints* that prevents agents from realizing *what they will to do* in action. Freedom of the will, by contrast, involves issues about how agents *came to have the will* to act as they do and to what degree they are ultimately responsible for having the wills (characters, motives, and purposes) they do in fact have.

To illustrate, consider an example I have previously used.[5] Suppose a young man is on trial for an assault and robbery in which the victim was beaten to death. Let us imagine that we attend his trial and listen to the evidence in the courtroom. First, our attitude toward the defendant is one of anger and resentment. What the young man did was terrible. But as we listen daily to how he came to have the mean character and perverse motives he did have – a sad story of parental neglect, child abuse, sexual abuse, and bad role models – some of our resentment against the young man is shifted over to the parents and others who abused and mistreated him. We begin to feel angry with them as well as with him. Yet we aren't quite ready to shift all the blame away from the young man himself. We wonder whether some residual responsibility may not belong to him. Our questions become: To what extent is *he* responsible for becoming the sort of person he now is? Was his behaviour *all* a matter of bad parenting, societal neglect, etc., or did he have any role to play in choosing it?

These are crucial questions about free will, and they are questions about what may be called the young man's ultimate responsibility. We know that parenting, society, genetic makeup, and upbringing have an influence on what we become and what we are. But were these influences entirely *determining*, or did they

5 Kane (2005: 4–5).

"leave anything over" for us to be responsible for? That is what we want to know about the young man. The question of whether he is merely a victim of bad circumstances or has some residual responsibility for being what he is – the question, that is, of whether and to what degree he became the person he is *of his own free will* – seems to depend on whether these other factors were or were not *entirely* determining.

(ii) There is much evidence that Hodgson thinks of free will in this way as well, both in his general comments about responsibility and in his often astute discussions of criminal law and punishment later in his book. Consider, for example, his response (pp. 165–166) to John Fischer, who is a compatibilist about moral responsibility and determinism: "The philosopher John Fischer has written that 'our behavior may well be "in the cards" in the sense that we simply have to play the cards that are dealt us'". Hodgson responds that this is true up to a point. But the cards that are dealt us need not determine exactly what we do. They may limit our options to "spectra of possibilities", and "our capacity for conscious decision-making can combine flexibly with our other cards so that the whole hand can steer a course within these spectra of possibilities" (p. 166).

This idea of "spectra of possibilities" as essential to free will is a second point on which we agree. Spelling out its implications further, Hodgson says the following:

> So long as our other cards are not seriously deficient, for example because of mental abnormality or senility or immaturity, [we are able] to make reasonable albeit fallible decisions about what to believe (including what to believe about right and wrong) and about what to do, for good or ill. And these decisions in turn can (like Kane's self-forming actions) affect what particular cards come . . . to constitute us for the future, for better or worse. [To the extent that we have this capacity we have] some ultimate responsibility for what we do and for how we turn out, again so long as our other cards are not too seriously deficient.
>
> (p. 166)

I agree with these statements and have also argued for them in different ways in many writings.[6] (I'll have more to say shortly about my "self-forming actions", to which Hodgson refers in this passage, and how I believe such actions enter the picture.) And given all that has been said in the preceding text, other agreements follow.

(iii) Hodgson and I also consequently agree that the responsibility we finite humans have for forming our own wills in this way is not unlimited, but is a *matter of degree*; and it *develops* over time as we form and *reform* our characters, motives, and purposes by making free (self-forming) choices. As a judge immersed in real world cases, Hodgson was all too aware that responsibility is not an "all-or-nothing" matter, as some libertarians of the past have mistakenly believed.

6 See the references in note 3, plus Kane (1988, 1994, 1999, 2000b, 2007).

To say such responsibility is "ultimate" is to say only that at some points the "buck stops with us", with our free decisions. It is *not* to say that such responsibility is *unlimited* by circumstances. We both accept, as I put it earlier, that parenting, society, genetic makeup, and upbringing have an influence (indeed a profound influence) on what we become and what we are. But the question is whether these influences (the "cards we are dealt") are entirely *determining*, or whether, in Hodgson's terms, they sometimes leave us (within limits) with a "spectrum of possibilities" from among which we may choose. (Of course, explaining how we can freely and responsibly choose from among this undetermined spectrum without the outcome being merely random or merely a matter of luck or chance is the challenge that any libertarian view must face.)

(iv) As a result, we also both reject the more extravagant claims and theories that have been proposed historically and in recent times in defence of libertarian free will.[7] We both reject, for example, the idea that libertarian free decisions must be "*uncaused* causes" (Hodgson, p. 166).[8] We grant that such free decisions are in fact causally influenced by many factors, and not just the general ones mentioned earlier, such as genetic makeup and upbringing. They are also causally influenced more immediately by the agent's accumulated character traits, desires, beliefs, preferences, intentions, and other mental states at the time they choose or act, as well as by the unconscious physical processes in their brains (Hodgson, p. 98). What we deny is that our free decisions must always be *determined* by the confluence of all of these factors which causally influence us – that these factors always limit the available options for rational choice *to one only*, rather than to a "spectrum of possibilities".

(v) In addition to rejecting libertarian views which claim that free decisions must be *uncaused causes* – so-called *noncausalist* libertarian views[9] – Hodgson and I both also reject views that appeal to a special kind of *agent causation* to explain libertarian free will. Such *agent-causal* libertarian views, as they are called, postulate a metaphysically primitive form of causation by an agent or substance that cannot in principle be explained in terms of states, processes, or events involving the agent of any kinds, mental or physical.[10] After citing my own objections to such agent-causal views on pp. 163–164, Hodgson says "I take a similar view. . . . An important feature of agent-causal views is that they seek to establish agents as originators of decisions ('uncaused causes'), by

7 For my own arguments against these views see the references in notes 3 and 6, plus Kane (1999a, b, 2009, 2011a).

8 Such "noncausalist" views, as they are called, are defended by Ginet (2002), Goetz (1988), and Pink (2011).

9 Noncausalists insist not only that free choices or actions are not determined by any prior events, they are also not caused by any prior events, even indeterministically or probabilistically. They typically argue as well that such choices or actions can be explained by motivating reasons, while insisting that reasons for actions need not be causes of actions.

10 Agent-causal views have been defended by Taylor (1966), Campbell (1967), Chisholm (1976), O'Connor (2000), Botham (2008), Griffith (2010), among others.

assuming that *as substances* they . . . can be causes" of other events, but cannot be caused themselves by other events. Hodgson finds this assumption problematic, as do I, for similar reasons.

(vi) Hodgson and I thus share a view that in contemporary free will debates is customarily called an *event-causal* libertarian view of free will. This designation is meant to distinguish the view from other libertarian views common in historical and contemporary debates. These other views include the two just mentioned, *noncausalist* views (according to which free choices or actions *themselves* are uncaused causes) and *agent-causal* views (according to which *agents* are uncaused causes of their free actions), as well as traditional *substance dualist* views (according to which free actions are caused by immaterial minds or substances outside of the natural order and not subject to its laws), which still have some advocates.[11]

Event-causal libertarian views are comparatively new on the scene. They were not even on the philosophical map when I first began thinking about free will in the 1960s. If you were a libertarian about free will at that time, believing it to be incompatible with determinism, it was assumed that you must appeal to some kinds of unusual or mysterious forms of agency or causation to make sense of it – uncaused causes, immaterial minds, noumenal selves, non-event agent causes, prime movers unmoved, and the like. P. F. Strawson in his influential 1962 essay "Freedom and Resentment" famously referred to all such traditional appeals as the "panicky metaphysics" of libertarianism.

The possibility of an alternative event-causal libertarian approach to free will that would avoid such traditional appeals was noted by several philosophers in the 1970s, but my view was the first developed view of this kind. Event-causal views have gained more currency and further advocates, including Hodgson, in the past couple of decades for several reasons.[12] They are motivated by the perceived

11 E.g., Foster (1991), Moreland and Rae (2000).

12 My event-causal (EC) view is sometimes called a "centred" EC view because it places the indeterminism at the moment of choice itself. Other more recent defenders of centred EC views include Balaguer (2010), Patarroya (2009), Franklin (2011), and Lemos (2007). Rogers (2008) argues that features of my centred EC view were foreshadowed by the mediaeval philosopher Anselm, and she defends a modified version of his view. There are also non-centred EC views which place the indeterminism at earlier stages in the deliberative process. Doyle (2011), who defends such a non-centred view, calls it a "two-stage" view of free will and provides an informative history of figures who suggested or defended such a view. They include more recently McCall and Lowe (2005) and Ekstrom (2000). Dennett (1978) and Mele (1995) had earlier suggested the possibility of such of view without endorsing it. As Doyle points out, I also put forward a two-stage view early in the development of my view of free will. But I did not believe it could be the whole story about libertarian free will for a number of reasons relating to responsibility and other issues. (In his contribution to this volume, Levy offers criticisms, with which I agree, showing the limitations of this non-centred or two-stage view. He calls it, following Dennett, a "Valerian" view.) I therefore made it a *part* of my theory of free will in subsequent books (1985, 1996, chapter 9), though only a part. A full theory of libertarian free will, I argued, would have to include "centred" as well as "non-centred" features, if it was to capture all that we need to hold about free agency and moral responsibility.

inadequacies of other alternatives, but more importantly, by the desire to give more *science-friendly* accounts of libertarian free will.[13]

Finally, I'll mention a couple of further similarities in our views that Hodgson himself mentions (pp. 160–161) and that have special relevance to my later arguments.

(vii) The first of these is the contention that, as he puts it, "prior to a choice being made, an agent‘s reasons are characteristically inconclusive, inter alia because they are incommensurable; and that it is the agent's choice or decision which resolves the issue. Kane endorses the idea that, in situations where an agent has to choose between alternative courses of action and has reasons or motives supporting each alternative, the agent *makes* one set of reasons or motives prevail over the others by *deciding*" (p. 160). Hodgson notes agreement with this contention.

(viii) And it is related to another that is central to Hodgson's view and that I share, namely, the contention (to which chapter 3 of his book is devoted) that *plausible reasoning* is crucial for understanding our rationality and for making sense of free will. Plausible reasoning, according to Hodgson, is reasoning in which premises or data do not logically entail the conclusions, but rather provide support for them "as a matter of reasonable albeit fallible judgment" (p. 5). This notion of plausible reasoning is crucial for free will on my view as well, for reasons that will become clear in subsequent sections.

Hodgson makes an important contribution here by showing that such plausible reasoning is not a mere gimmick that helps make sense of libertarian free will. Rather it is an essential feature of our rationality and plays a fundamental role in much of our *theoretical* as well as our *practical* reasoning in everyday life, where we often have reasons for making judgements about what to believe or what to do that are reasonable, though fallible and not conclusive. His lifelong experience as a judge shines through here in making a convincing case for the centrality of such reasoning in everyday life.

Contrasts: apposite reasons, engagement with laws, and other topics

In the "Introduction" section of this chapter, I said that many of the significant differences between Hodgson's view and mine on which I would focus concern a

13 The designation of these views as "event-causal" is unfortunate in some ways, however, though it is now well entrenched. For it may suggest that event-causal theorists about free will believe that free actions are caused only by events, *but not by agents*. And this is far from the truth, as Hodgson emphasizes (p. 164) and I have long emphasized in my writings. One does not have to choose between causation by events and causation by substances or agents. One can believe in both, as Hodgson and I do. What event-causal descriptions do is spell out *how* and *why* agents or substances cause what they cause by describing the specific states and changes of the agents or substances that play causal roles in their producing what they produce. There is no inconsistency in saying that agents cause things and saying that the *lives* of agents, including the exercise of their capacities, must be spelled out in terms of states, processes, and events involving them.

central feature of his view – namely, the thesis that libertarian free choices result from "conscious gestalt experiences" that "do not engage with laws of nature or rules of any kind" (p. 80 and passim). The appeal to this thesis, I will now argue, (i) leads to problems that remain unresolved in Hodgson's view and (ii) is unnecessary. One can give an account of libertarian free will that has all of the features mentioned in the previous section that Hodgson and I share without assuming that the sources of free choices, including conscious gestalt experiences, do not engage with laws of nature or rules of any kind.

I address the first of these two criticisms in this section and the second in the remaining sections. The first step in addressing both is to ask what exactly Hodgson *means* by saying that conscious gestalt experiences "do not engage with" laws of nature or rules of any kinds. The expression "do not engage with" is used in this context over and over throughout the book, and a number questions arise about its meaning. It clearly implies, for example, that conscious gestalt experiences are not subject to and do not conform to *deterministic* laws of nature, such as those of classical mechanics on the usual interpretations. But does it also imply that such experiences are not subject to and do not conform to nondeterministic or *statistical* laws, such as those of quantum mechanics (QM) on standard interpretations of it? Hodgson comes closest to directly answering this question in chapter 8, where he says that, on his view:

> Feature-rich gestalts of conscious experience, can have an input into what happens; and this input cannot be fully accounted for by QM, *or indeed by any system of physical laws of general application*. . . . Accordingly, while I cannot altogether exclude the possibility that rational choices could conflict with the statistics prescribed by QM, I say that this would not in any event amount to violation of physical law, because QM can prescribe statistics only for the general and quantitative features of the world with which its laws can engage [and conscious gestalt experiences do not have such general and quantitative features]. . . . Even if it were the case that the statistics of rational decision-making (if it were possible to calculate them) did not completely accord with those indicated by QM, this would not be a violation of physical law, but an indication of a limitation on its applicability.
>
> (pp. 147–148)[14]

To say therefore that conscious gestalt experiences "do not engage with" laws of nature of any kinds means that such experiences are beyond the scope of applicability of such laws, whether deterministic *or* statistical, and therefore may not accord with them. The laws simply do not apply to them.

Hodgson argues elsewhere (pp. 79–85) that the reason this is the case is that conscious gestalt experiences are unique and have qualitative features that cannot be accounted for by scientific laws of any kinds, which deal only with general and quantitative features of events. His primary examples of such unique experiences

14 Italics here are mine.

are aesthetic experiences, such as hearing a pleasing melody or seeing a beautiful painting *for the first time*. (Gershwin's "The Man I Love" is a favourite example.) He concedes that "once this melody had been composed and heard by its composer and others" so that it becomes a *type* (p. 83), the cognitive processing involved in subsequent hearings might engage with laws and computational rules, but this would not be the case the first time.

Yet, as a number of critics of Hodgson's view have argued, and I agree, he does not give convincing arguments for why the cognitive processing involved in the experience of hearing this melody, even for the first time, *could* not conform to computational rules or laws of *any* kinds, deterministic or statistical.[15] His arguments on this score are especially weak in view of the fact that he elsewhere concedes (p. 98) that "any information contained in our experiences must be contained or encoded in the physical processes" of our brains, "that there is no experiential change without a corresponding physical change", and that laws of nature *are* applicable to information that is encoded in the physical processes of our brains (p. 98).

Additional difficulties attend his claim that such conscious gestalt experiences, despite not engaging with any laws or rules, can nonetheless have a causal influence on reasoning and choice "because subjects of experience can respond appositely to them" (p. 80). On this matter, Hodgson himself concedes that his theory is incomplete. "I accept", he says (p. 111), "that my account of how conscious processes that are not rule-determined can contribute to reasonable decision-making is far from complete, and that it leaves many questions unanswered. In particular, I have not gone far in explaining how and why these contributions can be apposite".

Elaborating on this point, he notes that a question which naturally arises in this connection is the following:

> If conscious processes are not determined by laws or rules of any kind, exactly what is it about them that can make their contributions apposite? . . . I have suggested that conscious experiences assist conscious subjects in making judgments about such things as significance of information . . . and resolution of inconclusive reasons. [But] it may be said that I've given no account of *how* conscious experiences can give this assistance: how is significance detected and assessed, how *are* approximations appraised, how *are* incommensurable reasons resolved? Indeed, it may be asked, why, if conscious experiences can do things as sophisticated as making these kinds of contributions, do they need physical and/or computational underpinnings at all?
> (pp. 111–112)

15 See the critics of his view cited in note 2, including other contributors to this volume who are cited there. In his chapter for this volume, Levy, for example, says that Hodgson's "account leaves too much downright mysterious to generally constitute a solution to the problem". "Moreover", he adds, "Hodgson's claim that conscious experience plays a special role in enabling plans is also somewhat mysterious".

Hodgson responds to the last of these questions by saying that he is not suggesting that the conscious aspect of the relevant cognitive processes can "achieve anything on its own . . . independently of their physical (non-conscious) aspect" (p. 112). He is merely suggesting that the conscious aspect adds some "extra" influence that "the physical and/or computational underpinnings" do not supply.

But surprisingly, while he answers this last question in this way, he does not answer the other questions in the quoted passage: *How* exactly do conscious experiences assist conscious subjects in making judgements that are relevant to rational decision-making *in ways that* do not conform to any applicable laws or rules? "How *is* significance detected . . . how *are* approximations appraised, how *are* incommensurable reasons resolved?" About these questions he says that "there is little more I can say on questions such as these; satisfactory answers will indeed require greater understanding of consciousness than is available at present" (p. 112). By his own admission, then, many unresolved questions remain in Hodgson's view about just how conscious gestalt experiences contribute to reasonable decision-making in ways that "do not engage with laws of nature or rules of any kinds", questions that he hopes a greater understanding of consciousness will answer.

As a result, Hodgson notes that a common objection made to his view by critics is that he is "proposing an extravagant form of emergentism, in which emergent wholes are governed neither by the laws governing their constituent features nor by laws of their own" (p. 95).[16] He "pleads guilty" to this charge. "I accept that, in suggesting" such a view, "I am making a proposal that could be considered extravagant" (p. 96). His response is to invite readers to assess the strength of his arguments for this proposal in previous chapters of the book. Though his arguments, he says, are not conclusive, he believes they are "strong enough to make the view I am proposing preferable to alternative views" (p. 96). And he adds that, while there are unanswered questions about the view, he thinks it is *necessary* to hold such a view, *if* we are to make sense of libertarian free will. I question these claims in the remaining sections of the chapter.

Making sense of libertarian free will: an alternative

I noted in the "Introduction" section of this chapter that it has often been assumed in the history of debates about free will that if we are to make sense of libertarian free will, we must postulate some unusual forms of agency that are not

16 Hodgson is not always clear about whether it is the emergent wholes (the conscious gestalts) that are the things which are not governed by laws or rules, or whether it is the *responses of appositeness* to those gestalts or wholes which are not governed by laws or rules. Michael Sevel has suggested to me that Hodgson's examples of conscious responses to aesthetic experiences suggest the latter interpretation; and this seems right about such examples. But other things Hodgson says throughout the book suggest the former interpretation. In any case, it seems to me that the objections discussed in this section apply on either interpretation. These objections apply whether the gestalt experiences themselves or the responses to them (or both) are not governed by laws or rules of any kinds.

subject to scientific laws of nature – uncaused causes, immaterial minds, noumenal selves, and the like. The common idea behind all such traditional views was to look for something that might explain how agents could exercise voluntary control over events that were otherwise physically undetermined and might therefore happen merely randomly or by chance. Hodgson's view, I suggested, is a more sophisticated version of this traditional strategy, but a version of it nonetheless. On his view, some processes (conscious gestalt experiences or the responses to them) that may be involved in free will must fail to engage with laws of nature or rules of any kind, if we are to explain how agents could exercise voluntary control over events that would otherwise occur merely randomly or by chance.

I long ago became disenchanted with all such appeals to special factors of varying kinds, not subject to scientific laws, to account for libertarian free will. But where to go if one is to avoid such appeals? This question cannot be answered in one fell swoop. What is required, I believe, is a series of complex steps that must be fitted together like the pieces of an intricate puzzle and that involve a thorough rethinking of the relationship of indeterminism to freedom, choice, and action. Some of these steps are also a part of Hodgson's view, but many of them are not.

(i) First, let us be clear that it is an empirical and scientific question whether any indeterminism *is* there in nature in ways that are appropriate for free will – in the brain, for example. No purely philosophical theory can settle the matter. As the Epicurean philosophers said centuries ago, if the atoms don't "swerve" in undetermined ways, and in the right places, there would be no room in nature for free will. Christoph Koch is a distinguished neuroscientist and a tough-minded one at that. Like the vast majority of neuroscientists he is sceptical of claims of some scientists and philosophers that quantum indeterminism could influence human decision-making by way of large-scale quantum collapses of the wave packet in the brain. And he adds that "there is no evidence that any components of the nervous system – a warm and wet tissue strongly coupled to its environment – display quantum entanglement" (2009: 40). But Koch goes on to say that "what cannot be ruled out is that tiny quantum fluctuations deep in the brain are amplified by deterministic chaos" so that they might have non-negligible effects on neural processing and thereby affect human decision-making (ibid.). Koch does not endorse this idea, but says that it cannot be ruled out, given what is currently known about the brain.

In the most recent edition of *The Oxford Handbook of Free Will*, Robert Bishop agrees and cites a number of other neuroscientists and philosophers who have made similar suggestions to Koch's.[17] If minute quantum indeterminacies occurred at the intra-neural or synaptic levels of the brain, affecting the timing of firing of individual neurons, these indeterminacies, however minute, could be chaotically amplified, due to sensitivity to initial conditions, so that they had non-negligible effects on neural processing. Bishop goes on to point out that one

17 Bishop (2011: 91–92). He cites Baker and Gollub (1990), Hilborn (2001), Hobbs (1991), and Kellert (1993). Others who have made similar suggestions include Glimcher (2005), Shadlen (2014), and Brembs (2011).

need not even have to appeal only to chaos to get these effects. For, as he notes "the exquisite sensitivity needed for both the sensitive dependence arguments and the normal amplification of quantum effects is a general feature of nonlinear dynamics and is present whenever nonlinear effects are likely to make significant contributions to the dynamics of the system" (p. 91). Moreover, it is generally agreed, as he notes, that nonlinear dynamics is pervasive in the functioning of human brains.

But, of course, a serious question arises about this and all other suggestions about a possible role for indeterminism in the functioning of the brain, a question that has boggled people's minds since the time of the Epicureans: What could one *do* with indeterminism, assuming it *was* there in nature in the right places, to make sense of free will as something other than mere chance or randomness and without appealing to mystery? Suppose that minute quantum indeterminacies in the timing of firings of individual neurons were magnified in this way, so that they introduced some indeterminism into the larger scale neural processing involved in deliberation and decision-making. How could such indeterminism enhance the voluntary control agents are supposed to have over their free choices? Indeed it would seem that such indeterminism would diminish the agent's voluntary control over choices and actions and hence the agent's freedom and responsibility with respect to them.

One can see here why the tendency has been so strong in the history of free will debates to look at this point for some special factors not subject to physical laws to fill the causal gaps in the natural order that "mere indeterminism" leaves unfilled. The question we are now asking is this: Can this tendency be resisted? Can we explain how the presence of indeterminism in the neural processing of agents as described earlier, *if* it were present, might be consistent with and even enhance the agents' voluntary control over choices and actions, *without* appealing to any such special factors, including conscious experiences that do not engage with laws of nature or rules of any kinds? For that, many further steps are needed.

(ii) The first of these further steps is to note that *indeterminism does not have to be involved in all acts done "of our own free wills"* for which we are ultimately responsible. Not all of them have to be such that we could have done otherwise in a manner that was undetermined, but only those choices or acts in our lifetimes by which we make ourselves into the kinds of persons we are, namely, those referred to earlier as "*self-forming actions*" (*SFAs*). Often we act from a will already formed, but it is "our own free will", by virtue of the fact that we formed it by other choices or actions in the past (SFAs) for which we could have done otherwise in a manner that was not determined. If this were not so, I argue, there would be nothing we could have *ever* done differently in our entire lifetimes to make ourselves different than we are – a consequence, I believe, that is incompatible with our being (at least to some degree) ultimately responsible for being the way we are.

(iii) A third step then involves giving an account of how these SFAs arise and what they may involve. I argue that such self-forming actions occur at those difficult times of life when we are torn between competing visions of what we should do or become; and they are more frequent in everyday life than one may think. Perhaps we are torn between doing the moral thing or acting from ambition, or between powerful present desires and long term goals, or we are faced with difficult tasks for which we have aversions. In all such cases, we are faced with competing motivations and have to make an effort to overcome temptation to do something else we also strongly want. At such times, the tension and uncertainty we face about what to do, I suggest, would be reflected in some indeterminacy in our neural processes themselves (in the form of chaotically amplified background neural noise, as suggested in step (i)) – "stirred up" one might say, by the conflicts in our wills.[18] The uncertainty and inner tension we feel at such soul-searching moments of self-formation would thereby be reflected in some indeterminacy of our neural processes themselves. The experienced uncertainty would correspond physically to the opening of a window of opportunity that temporarily screens off complete determination by the past.[19]

(iv) When we do decide under such conditions of uncertainty, the outcome would not be determined because of the preceding indeterminacy – and yet it can be *willed* (and hence *rational* and *voluntary*) either way the agents choose owing to the fact that, in such self-formation, the agents' prior wills are divided by conflicting motives. Consider a businesswoman who faces a conflict of this kind. On her way to an important meeting, she observes an assault taking place in an alley. An inner struggle ensues between her moral conscience, to stop and call for help, and her career ambitions, which tell her she cannot miss this meeting. She has to make an effort of will to overcome the temptation to go on to her meeting. If she overcomes this temptation, it will be the result of her effort, but if she fails, it will be because she did not *allow* her effort to succeed. And this is due to the fact that, while she wanted to overcome temptation, she also wanted to fail, for quite different and competing reasons. When agents, like the woman, decide in such circumstances, and the indeterminate efforts they are making become determinate choices, they *make* one set of competing reasons or motives prevail over the others then and there *by deciding*.[20]

(v) Now add a further step. Just as (in the manner of (iv)) indeterminism need not undermine rationality and voluntariness, so indeterminism, in and of itself, need not undermine *control* and *responsibility*. Suppose you are trying to think through a difficult problem, say, a mathematical problem, and there is some indeterminacy in your neural processes complicating the task – a kind of chaotic background. It would be like trying to concentrate and solve a problem with background noise or distraction. Whether you are going to succeed in solving the problem is uncertain and undetermined because of the distracting indeterministic noise. Yet, if you concentrate and solve the problem nonetheless,

18 Kane (1996: 130ff).

19 Whether the requisite indeterminacy is there in the brain is an empirical question, of course. On this empirical question there is much recent discussion. See, e.g., Balaguer (2010), Heisenberg (2013), Glimcher (2005), Hameroff and Penrose (1996), Shadlen (2014), Brembs (2011), Stapp (2007), Tse (2013), Maye et al. (2007).

20 Kane (1996: 126 ff).

we have reason to say you did it and are responsible for it *even though it was undetermined whether you would succeed.* The distracting neural noise would have been an obstacle that you overcame by your effort.

(vi) There are numerous examples supporting this point (first suggested by J. L. Austin (1961), Elizabeth Anscombe (1971), and others) where indeterminism functions *as an obstacle to success without precluding responsibility.* Consider an assassin who is trying to shoot an official with a high powered rifle, but might miss because of some undetermined events in his nervous system that might lead to a wavering of his arm. The indeterministic wavering of his arm is an obstacle to his success. But if he did succeed in hitting his target nonetheless, he could obviously be held responsible because he would have succeeded in doing what he was *trying* to do. Here is another example. A husband, while arguing with his wife, in anger swings his arm down on her favourite glass table-top in an effort to break it. Imagine there is some indeterminism in the nerves of his arm making the momentum of his swing indeterminate so that it is literally undetermined whether the table will break up to the moment when it is struck. Whether the husband breaks the table or not is undetermined; and yet he is clearly responsible if he does break it. It would be a poor excuse for him to say to his wife, "Chance did it [broke the table], not me". Though there was a chance he would fail, chance didn't do it, *he* did.

Such examples, to be sure, do not amount to genuine exercises of free will in SFAs, such as the businesswoman's, where the wills of the agents are divided between conflicting motives. The businesswoman wants to help the victim, but she also wants to go on to her meeting. By contrast, the will of the assassin is not equally divided. He wants to kill the official, but does not also want to fail. (Thus, if he fails, it *will* be *merely* by chance.) Yet these examples, of the assassin, husband, and the like, do provide important clues. To go further one has to add further steps.

(vii) Imagine in cases of conflict characteristic of SFAs, like the businesswoman's, that the indeterministic noise which is providing an obstacle to her overcoming temptation (and doing the moral thing) is not coming from an external source, but has its source in her own will, since she also deeply desires to do the opposite (go on to her meeting). To understand how this could be, imagine that two competing recurrent neural networks are involved, each influencing the other and representing her conflicting motivations. (These are complex networks of interconnected neurons in the brain circulating impulses in feedback loops that are generally involved in higher-level cognitive processing.)[21] The input of one of these networks consists in the woman's desires and motives for stopping to help the victim. If the network reaches a certain activation threshold (the simultaneous firing of a complex set of "output" neurons), that would represent her choice to help. For the competing network, the inputs are her ambitious motives for going

21 Accessible introductions to the role of neural networks in cognitive processing which bring out the relevant features of recurrent networks include P. M. Churchland (1996) and Spitzer (1999).

on to her meeting, and its reaching an activation threshold represents the choice to go on.

Imagine further that the two networks are connected so that the indeterminism that is an obstacle to her making one of the choices is present because of her simultaneous conflicting desire to make the other choice – the indeterminism thus arising from a tension-creating conflict in the will, as noted. Under such circumstances, when either of the pathways reaches an activation threshold which amounts to choice, it would be like your solving the mathematical problem by overcoming the indeterministic background noise generated by the presence of the other pathway. And just as when you solved the mathematical problem despite the presence of this indeterminism, one could say you did it and are responsible for it, so one can say this as well, I would argue, in the present case, *whichever one is chosen*. The network through which she succeeds in reaching a choice threshold will have succeeded *despite* the indeterminism present because of the existence of the competing network.

(viii) Note that, in these circumstances, the choices either way will not be "inadvertent", "accidental", "capricious", or "merely random", because they will be *willed* by the woman either way, when they are made, and done for *reasons* either way (moral convictions if she turns back, ambitious motives if she goes on) which she then and there endorses. And these are the conditions usually required to say something is done "on purpose", rather than accidentally, capriciously, or merely by chance.

(ix) To be sure, with "self-forming" choices of these kinds, agents cannot determine which choice outcome will occur *before* it occurs or the outcomes would be predetermined after all. But it does not follow that, because one does not determine which of a set of outcomes is going to occur before it occurs, one does not determine which of them occurs, *when* it occurs. When the preceding conditions for self-forming choices are satisfied, agents determine their future lives *then and there* by deciding.[22] Indeed, they have what I have called "*plural voluntary control*" over their options in the following sense: They are able to

22 To be more precise, agents exercise an important kind of *control* in these circumstances over the choice they make at the time they make it. One has this kind of control *at a time* t over *whether or not* an event (e.g., a choice) occurs or does not occur when one has the power (ability plus opportunity) at the time t to *make* the event *be* at that time and the power at the time t to make it *not be* at that time. And in an SFA, one exercises just this kind of control over the choice one makes (e.g., the choice of A rather than B) at the time one makes it. For, one not only has the power at that time to make that choice be, one also has the power at that time to make it not be *by making the competing choice* (of B rather than A) *be*. One has both these powers because either of the efforts or endeavours in which one is engaged might succeed in attaining its goal (choosing A or choosing B) at that time, despite the probability or chance of failure because of the interfering effects of indeterminism. And if either effort or endeavour, which is a goal-directed activity of the agent, does succeed in attaining its goal, one can be said to have *brought about* the choice thereby made *by* endeavouring or attempting to bring it about. To have the power at a time to make an event be at that time and the power to make it not be at that time is what it commonly means to say that one has *control* over the event.

bring about *whichever* of the options they will, *when* they will to do so, for the *reasons* they will to do so, *on purpose* rather than by mistake or accident, without being coerced or compelled in doing so. Each of these conditions can be satisfied in cases like the businesswoman's, whichever choice she makes, despite the indeterminism involved, given the preceding steps, as I have shown elsewhere.[23] Satisfying them amounts in common parlance to the claim that the agents can choose either way "at will".

(x) Note further that this account of self-forming choices amounts to a kind of "doubling" of the mathematical problem. It is as if an agent faced with such a choice is *trying* or endeavouring to solve *two* cognitive problems at once, or to complete two competing (deliberative) tasks at once – in our example, to make a moral choice and to make a conflicting self-interested choice (corresponding to the two competing neural networks involved). Each task is being thwarted by the indeterminism created by the presence of the other, so it might fail. But if it succeeds, the agents can be held responsible because, as in the case of solving the mathematical problem, they will have succeeded in doing what they were trying or endeavouring to do. Recall the assassin and the husband once again. Owing to indeterminacies in their neural pathways, the assassin might miss his target or the husband fail to break the table. But if they *succeed*, despite the probability of failure, they are responsible, because they will have succeeded in doing what they were trying or endeavouring to do.

(xi) And so it is, I suggest, with self-forming choices, except in their case, *whichever way the agents choose*, they will have succeeded in doing what they were trying to do because they were simultaneously trying to make both choices and

23 E.g., Kane (1999, 2002b, 2007, 2011a). This notion of plural voluntary control (PVC) is related to a particularly important difference between my view and Hodgson's. I have argued in many writings that we must be able to exercise such plural voluntary control over at least some undetermined free choices (SFAs), if we are to be ultimately responsible to some degree for the formation of our own wills. (For arguments supporting this point, see especially Kane 1997, 2000a, 2002d: 409–414, but also 1996, chapter 7, and 2007: 17–22). Hodgson's view does not give us such plural voluntary control over undetermined free choices, which is a serious problem. This becomes especially clear in his response to the Replay Argument (pp. 177–179), which he says captures the "essence" of all arguments against libertarian free will regarding luck. Hodgson's answer to this crucial argument shows only that we could have made such choices voluntarily, intentionally, and rationally, but not that we could have also done *otherwise* voluntarily, intentionally, and rationally. Had we done otherwise in the scenarios Hodgson presents in answer to the Replay Argument (p. 177), the doing otherwise would have been irrational. As a result he does not adequately answer this argument and other related arguments from luck against libertarian free will. (Levy, in his chapter for this volume, also argues that Hodgson fails to adequately answer this Replay Argument.) To adequately answer these objections, one must show that agents can sometimes have plural voluntary control over undetermined free choices. For, as I have argued in the previously cited works, if it were always the case that we could only do otherwise involuntarily, unintentionally, or irrationally, we would lack freedom of *will*. While we would sometimes be able to do otherwise in this limited and unsatisfactory sense (involuntarily, unintentionally, or irrationally), we would never be able to *will* otherwise, and hence never be able to *do* otherwise *willingly*.

one is going to succeed. Their failure to do one thing is not a *mere* failure, but a *voluntary succeeding in doing the other.* Does it make sense to talk about the agent's trying to do two competing things at once in this way, or to solve two cognitive problems at once? Well, we know that the brain is a parallel processor; it can simultaneously process different kinds of information relevant to tasks such as perception or recognition through different neural pathways. Such a capacity, I believe, is essential to the exercise of free will.[24]

(xii) Putting these steps together, one can say that in cases of self-formation (SFAs), agents are simultaneously trying to resolve plural and competing cognitive tasks (represented by the distributed neural processes involved). They are, as we say, "of two minds", yet they are not two separate persons. They are not dissociated from either task. The businesswoman who wants to go back to help the victim is the same ambitious woman who wants to go on to her meeting. She is a complex creature, torn inside by different visions of who she is and what she wants to be, as we all are from time to time. But *this is the kind of complexity*, I argue, *that is needed for genuine self-formation and free will.* And when she succeeds in doing one of the things she is trying to do, she will endorse that as *her* resolution of the conflict in her will, voluntarily and intentionally, not by accident or mistake.

Objections and responses: luck and chance

Note that in none of these twelve steps is the assumption made that any of the processes or events involved in making such self-forming free choices (including conscious gestalt experiences) must fail "to engage with laws of nature or rules of any kind". It *is* necessary to assume that there is *some* relevant indeterminism in the neural processing of the brain, if we are to make sense at all of libertarian or indeterminist free will; and this assumption is a part of the preceding steps.[25] I believe some such assumption of indeterminism in the brain would have to be made by *any* libertarian view, even those that postulate "extra factors", such as immaterial minds or non-event agent causes. If there was no such indeterminism, there would be no "causal gaps" in nature where these extra factors might insert themselves.

24 Another commonly made objection at this point that I have addressed elsewhere (e.g., Kane 2007, 2011a) is that it is irrational to make efforts to do incompatible things. I concede that in most ordinary situations it is. But I contend there are special circumstances in which it is not irrational to make competing efforts. These include circumstances in which (i) we are deliberating between competing options; (ii) we intend to choose one or the other, but cannot choose both; (iii) we have powerful motives for wanting to choose each of the options for different reasons; (iv) there is a consequent resistance in our will to either choice; so that (v) if either choice is to have a chance of being made, effort will have to be made to overcome the temptation to make the other choice; and (vi) we want to give each choice a fighting chance of being made because the motives for each are important to us. But these I argue are just the conditions for self-forming actions.

25 On the question of whether the indeterminism might be there in the brain in places relevant to free choice, see the references in notes 17 and 19.

The preceding twelve steps do not assume any such extra-natural agencies, to be sure. But more importantly, with regard to Hodgson's theory (which also does not assume immaterial minds or non-event agent causes), these twelve steps also do not assume that any relevant indeterminism that might occur in the brain fails to accord with the statistical laws of quantum physics. Nor, we might add, do they fail to accord with what we know of the nonlinear neural processing of the brain.

Nor do these steps rule out a role for *conscious* experiences, including conscious gestalt experiences, in the deliberative processes leading up to such self-forming choices (though unconscious neural processing plays an important role as well). The businesswoman's conflict begins when she consciously *perceives* the assault taking place in the alley. Consciously experienced images may then flit through her mind as she tries to decide what to do. The image of the angry face of her boss, if she misses the meeting, inclines her to ignore the assault. The image of her mother reminds her of the moral and compassionate person she was taught to be, and inclines her to stop and help. Unconscious processing of these and other conscious experiences plays a role as well.[26] But what is *not* required, and is not assumed in these twelve steps, is that any such experiences or events which may be involved in her deliberative processes, *conscious or unconscious*, must fail to engage with laws of nature or rules of any kind.

Nonetheless, as one might guess, there are many objections that can be, and have been, made against the preceding view, objections that I have attempted to address in many writings over the past three decades. I cannot obviously address all these objections here and must refer you to other writings for responses to

26 These remarks about conscious and unconscious processing leading to SFAs are relevant to a criticism Hodgson makes of my view on p. 162 of his book. He says that "conflicting reasons do not merely support each alternative between which a choice is to be made, but operate in the selection itself by way of the agent's apposite" responses to those reasons. And he adds that, by pointing this out, his approach "fills a gap" in my view regarding the experiential dimension of free self-forming choices. I think he is correct in pointing out that apposite responses to conscious experiences relevant to conflicting reasons for one or another choice play an important experiential role in deliberations leading to SFAs. But I do not deny this and have made it an explicit part of my view from Kane (1996) onward. Consider the description given here of the businesswoman's deliberation. In this example and others I have used, consciously experienced images come to mind as she tries to decide what to do (images of her mother, her angry boss, etc.). Her apposite responses to these conscious experiences support her reasons for making one choice or the other, depending on the content of the conscious experiences and her apposite responses to them. What I insist upon, however, and what Hodgson must insist upon as well, given his overall view, is that these apposite responses to conscious experiences in the course of deliberation, while they influence the choice finally made, do not *determine* which choice will be made. And, relatedly, the reasons these experiences support, while they contribute to making the choice finally made a rational choice, are not *conclusive* reasons. They are not such that they render any alternative choice that might have been made irrational. In short, the reasoning involved in such deliberations is, as Hodgson argues, and I concur, *plausible reasoning*. The ultimate choice made, as he puts it, is "a matter of reasonable, albeit fallible judgment". I have also explained elsewhere (e.g., 2002e: 425, 2011b: 400–401) how choices satisfying these conditions might be reasonable without being merely arbitrary, something Hodgson insists upon as well.

them.[27] But I want to conclude by addressing several important objections concerning luck and chance that highlight further differences between my view and Hodgson's.

The first is a particularly powerful form such objections about luck and chance have taken: If the occurrence of a choice depends on the occurrence of some undetermined quantum events in the neural processing of the brain over which the agent lacks voluntary control, then whether the choice occurs one way rather than another would appear to be a matter of luck or chance. Such thoughts, as noted, send us scurrying around looking for special factors to "tip the balance" to one choice or the other. But there is an alternative way to think about how indeterminism might be involved in free choice that first occurred to me thirty years ago, a way that avoids such familiar stratagems and requires a transformation of perspective.

(xiii) Think, instead, of the indeterminism involved in free choice as an *ingredient* in larger *goal-directed* or *teleological* processes or activities, in which the indeterminism functions as a *hindrance* or *obstacle* to the attainment of the goal. Such is the role of indeterminism in the "efforts" or "endeavours" preceding undetermined SFAs. Each of these efforts is a temporally extended goal-directed activity, whose goal is a particular choice and whose input consists in the motives for making that choice, in which indeterminism is a hindering or interfering

27 See especially Kane (1996, 1999a, b, 2000b, 2002b, c, 2007a, b, c, 2008, 2011a). See notes 13 and 24 for my response to two of the more frequently made of these objections. Notes 22 and 23 address some further objections regarding the notion of control. My response to another frequently made objection is also worth noting. This objection is that we are not introspectively or consciously aware of making dual efforts or performing multiple cognitive tasks in self-forming choice situations. But I am not claiming that agents are introspectively aware of making dual efforts. What persons are introspectively aware of in SFA situations is that they are trying to decide which of two options to choose, and either choice is a difficult one because there are resistant motives pulling them in different directions that will have to be overcome, whichever choice is made. In such introspective conditions I am theorizing that what is going on underneath is a kind of distributed processing in the brain that involves separate attempts or endeavours to resolve competing cognitive tasks. There is a larger point in this response that I have often emphasized: *Introspective evidence cannot give us the whole story about free will.* Stay on the introspective surface and libertarian free will *is* likely to appear obscure or mysterious, *as it so often has in history.* What is needed is the theory about what might be going on behind the scenes when we exercise such a free will, not merely a description of what we immediately experience. And in this regard new scientific ideas can be a help rather than a hindrance to making sense of free will. It is now widely believed that parallel processing takes place in the brain in such cognitive phenomena as visual perception. Suppose someone objected that we are not introspectively aware of such distributed processing in ordinary cases of perception. That would hardly be a decisive objection against this new theory of vision. For the claim is that this is what we are doing in visual perception, not necessarily that we are introspectively aware of doing it. And I am making a similar claim about free will. If parallel distributed processing takes place on the input side of the cognitive ledger (in perception), then why not consider that it also takes place on the output side (in practical reasoning, choice, and action)? That is what I am suggesting we should suppose if we are to make sense of libertarian free will.

element. The choices or SFAs that result from these temporally extended activities thus do not pop up out of nowhere, even though undetermined. They are the *achievements* of goal-directed activities of the agent that might have failed due to the indeterminism, but did not.

But isn't it the case, one might further object, that whether agents succeed in making one choice, say, A, rather than another, B, in such circumstances (i) depends on whether certain neurons involved in their cognitive processing fire or do not fire (perhaps within a certain time frame); and isn't it the case that (ii) whether or not these neurons fire is undetermined and hence a matter of chance, so that (iii) the agent does not have voluntary control over whether or not they fire? But if these claims are true, it seems to follow after all that the choice merely "happened" as a result of these chance firings and so (iv) the agent did not *make* the choice of A rather than B (or vice versa) and (v) hence was not *responsible* for making it. To many persons, this line of reasoning clinches the matter. It looks like the outcome *must* be merely a matter of chance or luck after all.

(xiv) But they reason too hastily. For the really astonishing thing is that, even if claims (i)–(iii) are true, claims (iv) and (v) do not follow *when* the following conditions obtain: (a) the choosing of A rather than B (or B rather than A, whichever occurs) was something the agents were endeavouring or trying to bring about, (b) the indeterminism in the neuron firings was a hindrance or obstacle to the achievement of that goal, and (c) the agents nonetheless succeeded in achieving the goal despite the hindering effects of the indeterminism.

For, consider the husband swinging his arm down on the table. It is *also* true in his case that (i) whether or not his endeavouring or trying to break the table succeeds "depends" on whether certain neurons in his arm fire or do not fire; and it is *also* true in his case that (ii) whether these neurons fire or not is undetermined and hence a matter of chance and therefore (iii) not under his voluntary control. Yet, even though we *can* say all this, it does not follow that (iv) the husband did not break the table and that (v) he is not responsible for breaking the table, *if* his endeavouring or trying to do so succeeds. Astonishing indeed! But this is the kind of surprising result one gets when indeterminism or chance plays an *interfering* or *hindering* role in larger goal-directed activities of agents that may succeed or fail.

(xv) It is well to meditate on this: We tend to reason that if an action (whether an overt action of breaking a table *or* a mental action of making a choice) depends on whether certain neurons fire or not (in the arm *or* in the brain), then the agent must be able to *make* those neurons fire or not, if the agent is to be responsible for the action. In other words, we think we have to crawl down to the place where the indeterminism originates (in the individual neurons) and *make* them go one way or the other. We think we have to become originators at the microlevel and "tip the balance" that chance leaves untipped, if we (and not chance) are to be responsible for the outcome. And we realize, of course, that we can't do that. But we don't have to. It is the wrong place to look. We don't have to micro-manage our individual neurons one by one to perform purposive actions, and we do not have such micro-control over our neurons *even when we perform ordinary actions* such as swinging an arm down on a table.

(xvi) What we need when we perform purposive activities, mental or physical, is *macro-control* of processes involving many neurons – processes that may succeed in achieving their goals despite the *interfering* or *hindering* effects of some recalcitrant neurons. We do not *micro*-manage our actions by controlling each individual neuron or muscle involved. But that does not prevent us from *macro*-managing our purposive activities (whether they be mental activities, such as practical reasoning, or physical activities, such as arm-swingings) and being responsible when those purposive activities attain their goals.

Behind these steps is a peculiarly modern scientific way of understanding human agency. Agents, according to this modern conception, are to be conceived as *information-responsive complex dynamical systems.* Complex dynamical systems are the subject of "dynamical systems theory" and also of what is sometimes popularly called "complexity theory". They are systems (which are now known to be ubiquitous in nature, and include living things) in which novel capacities arise as a result of greater complexity, or as the result of movement away from thermodynamic equilibrium toward the edge of chaos.[28] When these novel capacities arise in complex dynamical systems, the systems as a whole impose novel constraints on the behaviour of their parts that did not constrain the parts before the new complexity was achieved. In such complex dynamical systems there is thus a reciprocal causal influence of wholes to parts and parts to wholes.[29]

Notice here that Hodgson is right in suggesting that emergent capacities characteristic of rational agents are necessary for free will. But the "emergence" involved need not be the "extravagant" form of emergence he suggests. There is no requirement here that any experiences, processes, or exercises of capacities involved in free, rational decision-making must fail to engage with laws of nature or rules of any kind. The emergence of novel capacities is the result of greater complexity and is consistent with contemporary scientific understanding of complex dynamical systems generally, which are now known to be ubiquitous in nature. A greater understanding of such complex systems is an important

28 There are a number of important recent works explaining how such complex dynamical systems may be used to account for human agency and action, including among others McKay (1991), Juarrero (1999), Usher (2006), and Murphy and Brown (2007).

29 Thus in the account of free will I have proposed, it is a conflict in the larger motivational system of the agent taken as a whole – the "will", as it was traditionally called – that stirs up chaos and amplifies indeterminism at the neuronal and synaptic levels; and the resulting amplified indeterminism in turn interferes with the goal-directed activities of the larger network. There is thus a mutual influence of wholes to parts and parts to wholes characteristic of complex dynamical systems. And novel capacities thereby arise. Only when creatures attain *the kind of inner complexity capable of giving rise to conflicts in their wills* does the capacity for self-formation characteristic of free *will* arise. So we are talking about a special kind of complex dynamical system that is information-responsive in highly complex ways, not seen in non-rational animals. The businesswoman, as I said, is torn inside by different visions of whom she is and what she wants to be, as we all are from time to time; and this is the kind of complexity needed for genuine self-formation or free will.

development in contemporary sciences. But rather than involving any departures from scientific laws of nature, it is a testament to the remarkable fecundity of such laws.[30]

References

Anscombe, GEM 1971, *Causality and Determinism*, Cambridge University Press, Cambridge.

Austin, JL 1961, 'Ifs and Cans', in JO Urmson and G Warnock (eds), *Philosophical Papers*, Clarendon Press, Oxford.

Baker, G and Gollub, J 1990, *Chaotic Dynamics: An Introduction*, Cambridge University Press, Cambridge.

Balaguer, M 2010, *Free Will as an Open Scientific Problem*, MIT Press, Cambridge, MA.

Bishop, RC 2011, 'Chaos, Indeterminism, and Free Will', in R Kane (ed), *The Oxford Handbook of Free Will*, 2nd edn, Oxford University Press, Oxford.

Botham, T 2008, *Agent-Causation Revisited*, VDN Verlag Dr. Muller, Saarbrücken.

Brembs, B 2011, 'Towards a Scientific Concept of Free Will as a Biological Trait', *Proceedings of the Royal Society B: Biological Sciences* 278(1707). doi:10.1098/rspb.2010.2325.

Campbell, CA 1967, *In Defense of Free Will*, Allen & Unwin, London.

Capes, JA 2012, 'Review of *Rationality + Consciousness = Free Will*', *Notre Dame Philosophical Reviews* 3 June: 1–4.

Chisholm, R 1976, *Person and Object*, Open Court, LaSalle.

Churchland, PM 1996, *The Engine of Reason, the Seat of the Soul*, MIT Press, Cambridge, MA.

Clark, TW 2005, 'Hodgson's Black Box', *Journal of Consciousness Studies* 12: 23–32.

Dennett, DC 1978, *Brainstorms: Philosophical Essays on Mind & Psychology*, MIT Press, Cambridge, MA.

Doyle, R 2011, *Free Will: The Scandal in Philosophy*, I-Phi Press, Cambridge.

Ekstrom, L 2000, *Free Will: A Philosophical Study*, Westview Press, Boulder.

Foster, J 1991, *The Immaterial Self*, Routledge, London.

Franklin, C 2011, 'Farewell to the Luck (and Mind) Argument', *Philosophical Studies* 156: 199–230.

Ginet, C 2002, 'Reasons Explanations of Actions: Causalist Versus Noncausalist Accounts', in R Kane (ed), *The Oxford Handbook of Free Will*, 1st edn, Oxford University Press, Oxford.

Glimcher, PW 2005, 'Indeterminacy in Brain and Behavior', *Annual Review of Psychology* 56: 25–56.

Goetz, S 1988, 'A Non-Causal Theory of Agency', *Philosophy and Phenomenological Research* 49: 303–316.

30 One other difference between Hodgson's view and mine that I have not had the space to discuss here is that he regards free will as important in deciding what to believe as well as what to do. I had not explicitly considered this possibility in my own prior writings on free will. But I realized after reading Hodgson that my own view could be extended to deciding to believe as well and that such an extension would be a worthwhile addition to a comprehensive account of free will. His bringing out this point is one of many reasons why Hodgson's writing on free will is worth reading and pondering.

Gomes, G 2005, 'What Should We Retain From A Plain Person's Concept of Free Will?', *Journal of Consciousness Studies* 12: 32–40.

Griffith, M 2010, 'Why Agent-Caused Actions Are Not Lucky', *American Philosophical Quarterly* 47: 43–56.

Hameroff, S and Penrose, R 1996, 'Conscious Events as Orchestrated Space-Time Selections', *Journal of Consciousness Studies* 3: 36–53.

Heisenberg, M 2013, 'The Origin of Freedom in Animal Behavior', in A Suarez and P Adams (eds), *Is Science Compatible With Free Will?*, Springer-Verlag, New York.

Hilborn, R 2001, *Chaos and Nonlinear Dynamics: An Introduction*, 2nd edn, Oxford University Press, Oxford.

Hobbs, J 1991, 'Chaos and Indeterminism', *Canadian Journal of Philosophy* 21: 141–164.

Hodgson, D 1999, 'Hume's Mistake', in B Libet, A Freeman, and K Sutherland (eds), *The Volitional Brain*, Imprint Academic, Thorverton.

Hodgson, D 2002, 'Quantum Physics, Consciousness, and Free Will', in R Kane (ed), *Free Will*, Blackwell, Oxford.

Hodgson, D 2005, 'Responsibility and Good Reasons', *Ohio State Journal of Criminal Law* 2(2): 471–483.

Jaswal, L 2005, 'Isolating Disparate Challenges to Hodgson's Account of Free Will', *Journal of Consciousness Studies* 12: 43–46.

Juarrero, A 1999, *Dynamics in Action: Intentional Behavior as a Complex System*, MIT Press, Cambridge, MA.

Kane, R 1985, *Free Will and Values*, State University of New York Press, Albany.

Kane, R 1988, 'Libertarianism and Rationality Revisited', *The Southern Journal of Philosophy* 26: 441–460.

Kane, R 1989, 'Two Kinds of Incompatibilism', *Philosophy and Phenomenological Research* 31: 219–254.

Kane, R 1994, 'Free Will: The Elusive Ideal', *Philosophical Studies* 75: 25–60.

Kane, R 1996, *The Significance of Free Will*, Oxford University Press, New York.

Kane, R 1997, 'Free Will, Responsibility and Will-Setting', *Philosophical Topics* 24: 67–90.

Kane, R 1999a, 'On Free Will, Responsibility and Indeterminism: Responses to Clarke, Haji and Mele', *Philosophical Explorations* 2: 105–121.

Kane, R 1999b, 'Responsibility, Luck, and Chance: Reflections on Free Will and Indeterminism', *Journal of Philosophy* 96: 217–240.

Kane, R 2000a, 'The Dual Regress of Free Will and the Role of Alternative Possibilities', *Philosophical Perspectives* 14: 57–80.

Kane, R 2000b, 'Precis of *The Significance* of *Free Will* and "Responses to Bernard Berofsky, John Martin Fischer, and Galen Strawson"', *Philosophy and Phenomenological Research* 60: 129–34; 157–167.

Kane, R 2002b, 'Free Will: New Directions for an Ancient Problem', in R Kane (ed), *Free Will*, Blackwell, Oxford.

Kane, R 2002c, 'Determinism, Indeterminism and Free Will', in H Atmanspracher and RC Bishop (eds), *Beyond Chance and Choice: Interdisciplinary Perspectives on Determinism*, Imprint Academic, Thorverton.

Kane, R 2002d, 'Some Neglected Pathways in the Free Will Labyrinth', in R Kane (ed), *The Oxford Handbook of Free Will*, Oxford University Press, Oxford.

Kane, R (ed) 2002e, *The Oxford Handbook of Free Will*, Oxford University Press, Oxford.

Kane, R 2005, *A Contemporary Introduction to Free Will*, Oxford University Press, Oxford.
Kane, R 2007a, 'Responses to Fischer, Pereboom and Vargas', in JM Fischer, R Kane, D Pereboom, and M Vargas (eds), *Four Views on Free Will*, Blackwell, Oxford.
Kane, R 2007b, 'Libertarianism', in JM Fischer, R Kane, D Pereboom, and M Vargas (eds), *Four Views on Free Will*, Blackwell, London.
Kane, R 2007c, 'Free Will: New Directions for an Ancient Problem: A Reply to Allen and Rogers', *Proceedings of the American Catholic Philosophical Association* 18: 291–302.
Kane, R 2008, 'Three Freedoms, Free Will and Self-formation: A Reply to Levy and Other Critics', in N Trakakis and D Cohen (eds), *Essays on Free Will and Moral Responsibility*, Cambridge Scholars Press, Newcastle-upon-Tyne.
Kane, R 2009, 'Free Will and the Dialectic of Selfhood', *Ideas y Valories* 58: 25–44.
Kane, R 2011a, 'Rethinking Free Will: New Perspectives on an Ancient Problem', in Kane 2011b, 381–404.
Kellert, S 1993, *In the Wake of Chaos*, University of Chicago Press, Chicago.
Koch, C 2009, 'Free Will, Physics, Biology, and the Brain', in N Murphy, G Ellis, and T O'Connor (eds), *Downward Causation and the Neurobiology of Free Will*, Springer-Verlag, Berlin.
Lemos, J 2007, 'Kantian Freedom and the Problem of Luck', *Southern Journal of Philosophy* 45: 515–532.
Maxwell, N 2005, 'Science Versus Realization of Value, Not Determinism Versus Choice', *Journal of Consciousness Studies* 12: 53–58.
Maye, A, Hsieh, CH, Sugahara, G, and Brembs, B 2007, 'Order in Spontaneous Behavior', *PLoS ONE* 2: e443. doi:10.1371/journal.pone.00066443.
McCall, S and Lowe, EJ 2005, 'Indeterminist Free Will', *Philosophy and Phenomenological Research* 70: 152–164.
McKay, DM 1991, *Behind the Eye*. Gifford Lectures, ed. Valerie McKay, Oxford: Blackwell Publishers.
Mele, A 1995, *Autonomous Agents*, Oxford University Press, New York.
Moreland, JP and Rae, SB 2000, *Body and Soul*, Intervarsity Press, Downer's Grove.
Murphy, N and Brown, WS 2007, *Did My Neurons Make Me Do It?*, Oxford University Press, Oxford.
O'Connor, T 2000, *Persons and Causes: The Metaphysics of Free Will*, Oxford University Press, New York.
Patarroya, C 2009, 'Libertarismo & Error Categorial', *Ideas y Valores* 58: 141–168.
Pink, T 2011, 'Freedom and Action Without Causation: Noncausal Theories of Freedom and Purposive Agency', in R Kane (ed), *The Oxford Handbook of Free Will*, 2nd edn, Oxford University Press, Oxford.
Rogers, K 2008, *Anselm on Freedom*, Oxford University Press, Oxford.
Shadlen, M 2014, 'Comments on Adina Roskies, "Can Neuroscience Resolve Issues About Free Will?"', in W Sinnott-Armstrong (ed), *Moral psychology*, Volume 4, MIT Press, Cambridge, MA.
Smart, JJC 2005, 'Comments on Hodgson', *Journal of Consciousness Studies* 12: 58–64.
Spitzer, M 1999, *The Mind Within the Net*, MIT Press, Cambridge, MA.
Stapp, H 2007, *The Mindful Universe*, Springer, Berlin.
Strawson, PF 1962, 'Freedom and Resentment', *Proceedings of the British Academy* 48: 1–25.

Taylor, R 1966, *Action and Purpose*, Prentice-Hall, Englewood Cliffs.

Tse, PU 2013, *The Neural Basis of Free Will: Criterial Causation*, MIT Press, Cambridge, MA.

Usher, M 2006, 'Control, Choice and the Convergence/Divergence Dynamics: A Compatibilistic Probabilistic Theory of Free Will', *Journal of Philosophy* 304: 188–213.

3 Conscious gestalts, apposite responses, and libertarian freedom

Laura W. Ekstrom

According to David Hodgson, the criminal justice system in Australia – along with the similar systems in the United Kingdom and the United States – serves two broad types of purposes, which jointly justify imposing restraints and other disadvantages on offenders: (i) retributive, backward-looking purposes, and (ii) consequentialist, forward-looking purposes. The retributive purposes are based on the idea, Hodgson writes, "that a person who has acted criminally *deserves* to be punished for this conduct, and that it is *just* that appropriate detriment be inflicted on that person" (2012: 210). Further, the idea that a person deserves punishment for criminal conduct "presupposes that the person is truly *responsible* for it, and is not deprived of that responsibility because the conduct was the inevitable outcome of things outside the person's control, such as genes and environment" (2012: 210). Hodgson argues that there are good reasons for "retaining retribution as a guiding purpose of criminal law" (2012: 212).

Hodgson's views about what is required for responsibility in the desert sense are, on the face of it, somewhat surprising. It may seem natural to think that a judge, of an Australian supreme court or otherwise, would be a compatibilist concerning, on the one hand, the sort of free will required for moral responsibility of the desert kind and, on the other hand, the thesis that every event, including every human action, is causally necessitated by prior events given the laws of nature. It may seem natural to think this given the regularity with which one in such a position needs to make assessments concerning responsibility of the sort grounding desert and so needs to make discernments between those who are and those who are not liable, at fault, or to blame for various outcomes. For one to think that metaphysical intricacies are tied up with the matter of responsibility – and to think, in particular, that the workings of the physical universe must involve causal indeterminism of an appropriate sort in the process of human decision-making – would seem to encumber one's making such discernments concerning who is, and who is not, responsible in the desert sense. After all, if responsibility requires the falsity of causal determinism and if one of the purposes of the criminal justice system is retributive, then it would seem that a judge's pronouncements of guilt and innocence should await the findings of science: We would need yet to know if quantum indeterminacy magnifies and plays an appropriate role in the processes leading to human action.

Hodgson, however, does not think that our assessments of responsibility in the desert sense must be put on hold, awaiting conclusive scientific discovery. Some theorists who maintain that free will of the sort required for responsibility is incompatible with causal determinism merely offer pictures of what such free will would look like, without committing to the claim that the world actually conforms to the contours of that picture. Hodgson, however, offers us not just a vision of what things would have to be like in order for us to be able to act freely in the sense required for moral responsibility. In addition, he offers us an argument for why it is reasonable to believe that we are in fact free in the indeterminist sense he specifies. Hodgson is thus not only an incompatibilist concerning free will and causal determinism, but also a metaphysical libertarian, in that he argues that we do sometimes act freely and in ways for which we are genuinely morally responsible.

My own work has also developed and defended an event-causal indeterminist account of free will. I do not claim to be sure that we are in fact free in the libertarian sense, however, as the conditions of the account may not be met in the world. I agree with Hodgson, nonetheless, that we would need to be free in an event-causal indeterminist sense in order for us to be morally responsible for our actions in the desert sense. Thus we share common opponents. Major opponents of event-causal indeterminists about free will include compatibilists, free will sceptics, and agent-causal libertarians. (They also include non-causal libertarians (e.g., Ginet 1990) and revisionists (e.g., Vargas 2013), but I will not discuss these latter two.)

In what follows I set out both Hodgson's reasons and my own for declining to rest in one of the other camps in the free will debate. Although I am in the event-causal indeterminist corner with him and am sympathetic to his fascinating view, I will make three critical points. (i) I believe that neither our conscious experiences nor our responses to them would need to be, as Hodgson posits that they are, non-law-governed and non-rule-governed in order for our decisions and other actions to be free. (ii) To my mind Hodgson does not provide convincing evidence that we are in fact free in his libertarian sense. (iii) I do not think that Hodgson's particular event-causal theory provides, upon close examination, an illuminating account of something that he alleges that other libertarian accounts fail to provide.[1]

Why not compatibilism

Hodgson makes clear that his main project in his recent book *Rationality + Consciousness = Free Will* is not to develop arguments against compatibilism but rather to make his positive case for indeterministic free will and responsibility. Indeed, he writes, "I accept that positions such as Fischer's semi-compatibilism are plausible positions, and I do not claim to have a knock-down argument

1 Hodgson's critique is focused specifically on the account of Robert Kane.

against them" (2012: 171). He does, however, give his general reasons for declining to join the compatibilist camp.

His reasons are these. (i) Determinism is "almost certainly false" (2012: 172), and the best account we can give of rational human decision-making is indeterministic because not rule-determined. (ii) A chess-playing computer can recognize and respond to good reasons and control its conduct accordingly, but "no one would suggest that such a computer has free will and responsibility", (2012: 172) so this compatibilist ability is not sufficient, and compatibilism owes an explanation of the capacity that human beings have but chess-playing computers do not have. Hodgson thinks that the idea that we can be in control and responding to reasons as we decide what to do "depends for its plausibility on an assumption that this control and response is provided consciously; but compatibilists give no account of how, consistently with determinism, this is plausible or even possible" (2012: 172). (iii) He contends that "compatibilism cannot deal in a satisfactory way with the relationship between *luck* and responsibility, and particularly cannot deal in a satisfactory way with questions of *degrees of responsibility* or *mitigation of responsibility* by reason of the causal influence of factors outside the control of the agent" (2012: 173).

The first two of Hodgson's reasons are not ones that I see as compelling. Compatibilists can give quite plausible accounts of rational human decision-making (e.g., Nelkin 2011), and they have resources for addressing the case of computers. With regard to the third of Hodgson's points, the potential mitigation of responsibility by reason of the causal influence of factors outside the agent's control is a matter with which accounts of responsibility of various stripes have to deal. Libertarians and compatibilists alike must face the question of degrees of responsibility – perhaps to the point of complete undermining of responsibility – by factors such as manipulation, compulsion, genetic and environmental disadvantage, and coercion. I do not see good reason for thinking that this matter affects compatibilist views especially negatively.

My own perspective is that compatibilists depict valuable agential abilities and show grounds for making distinctions between inferior and superior forms of agency. However, the lack of a requirement for moral responsibility (in the desert sense) of a categorical ability to do otherwise at some relevant point in the process leading to an agent's act seems to me a mistake. It seems unfair to blame people who can never do otherwise than they do and unfair to praise people who can never do otherwise than they do. This may be what concerns Hodgson in his reference to a problem of luck for compatibilism – the idea may be that it is wrong to hold persons responsible if there is luck in the way they are causally determined to be and luck in how they are causally determined to act by prior events and the laws of nature.

Why not agent-causal libertarianism

Hodgson rejects all views that characterize our free agency by appeal to agents as substances that cause our choices and actions, maintaining that such views are "mysterious and objectionable" (2012: 164). He takes there to be a general difficulty with agent-causal views, "namely the *inscrutability* of the origins of decisions and actions" (2012: 163). He also wonders why, if agents as substances are causes, then they are not also effects, remarking, "I do not believe any justification for asymmetry in this respect has been shown by proponents of agent-causation" (2012: 164). Furthermore, Hodgson comments that he cannot see how substances can reasonably be considered to make a contribution to the causation of events that is additional to the contribution made by events involving the substance. "How can the sculpture make some causal contribution to the lump appearing on the person's head that is additional to the effects of the sculpture falling on the person?" he asks. "By the same token, how can an agent make a contribution to the occurrence of one choice rather than another, that is additional to the agent's activity giving rise to the choice?" (2012: 164). Moreover, Hodgson believes it is not necessary to find an uncaused cause because we can account for free decisions without making an appeal to such a thing.

I agree with Hodgson that agent-causal libertarianism is problematic in making an appeal to uncaused causes or prime movers unmoved. Event-causal libertarian accounts have no need to invoke uncaused causes, can be straightforwardly naturalistic, have no need to appeal to any unusual metaphysical entities, and fit with a natural way of looking at causal relations as obtaining between events. I find it puzzling how an enduring substance can bring about an event at a particular time without changing to do so. A substance does not take place at a time, as an event does. It seems to me that, in an instance of causation, something happens, which brings about the occurrence of something else. The postulation of a substance standing in a causal relation to an event, I agree with Hodgson, is opaque. If we were to say that a substance brings about an event by exerting its causal powers at a time, then that exertion of causal power is an event, which causes the subsequent event. In addition, it is natural to think that a person's having reasons for making one decision or another contributes causally to her making the decision. It is hard to see how causation of a decision by a substance that is an uncaused cause makes room for the natural thought about reasons as causally connected to decisions.

Why not free will scepticism?

Some theorists take a sceptical view toward the idea that persons are free with respect to, and morally responsible in a desert sense for, some of their actions. Hodgson's perspective is that there is no good reason to be a free will sceptic, because his own account of free will is coherent and persuasive, and there is good reason to think that its conditions are realized, in fact. The free will sceptic Galen Strawson, for instance, Hodgson thinks, is wrong to say that luck swallows everything, and so we are neither free nor responsible. Hodgson responds to Strawson's argument in this way:

> The sense in which it is true that we do what we do because of the way we are is that (a) the way we are plus our circumstances plus laws of nature provide

> alternatives, inconclusive reasons, and unconscious tendencies, and also the capacity to decide between the alternatives on the basis of the reasons; and (b) what we do is what we decide in exercise of that capacity. That leaves us at least partly responsible for what we do, even if we were not responsible for the way we are. . . . And I also contend: We do become partly responsible for the way we are, as our decisions, for which we are partly responsible, come to supplement the effects of genes and environment on the way we are.
> (Hodgson 2012: 176–177)

An assessment of Hodgson's response to Strawson's sceptical argument turns on evaluation of the merits of his own theory of free and responsible action, along with his case for its being realized in fact. This is because Hodgson claims that we *do* have the capacity to decide between genuinely available alternatives and thus that we are partially responsible for what we do (and hence partially responsible for the way we are, as we shape ourselves by way of our free choices). Evaluation both of Hodgson's account and of his confidence that its conditions are met is undertaken in subsequent sections. I do think that Hodgson could give a stronger response to Strawson and that others' arguments for free will scepticism, for instance, Derk Pereboom's argument, founder on the assessment of event-causal libertarianism. Pereboom (2014) thinks that event-causal libertarianism succumbs to problems with luck and with a "disappearing agent". I think that an event-causal libertarian can give successful responses to these problems concerning luck, disappearing agents, and chance (Ekstrom 2003, 2011, forthcoming; Franklin 2013; Kane 1996; Mele 2006).

The requirement of non-law-governed and non-rule-governed responses

In this section, first, I will situate Hodgson's view among other event-causal libertarian theories, and then I will argue that, contrary to Hodgson, neither our conscious experiences nor our responses to them would need to be non-law-governed and non-rule-governed in order to be free. Other event-causal libertarian theories on offer do not make this presumption of lawlessness, including my own account and the accounts of Alfred Mele (1995 and 2006), Daniel Dennett (1981: 286–299), and Robert Kane (1996).

On the view defended in Ekstrom (2000), one acts freely in acting from a preference that could have been otherwise – more specifically, one that was non-coercively formed or maintained and that has an indeterministic causal history, with its causes being various considerations that occur to a person as she is contemplating the question of what she prefers to do (Ekstrom 2000, 2003). A preference, as the term is used on this account, is by stipulation a desire that has survived scrutiny with respect to an agent's conception of the good. This notion results from discussion of problems with the Frankfurtian model of free action on which second-level desires – desires concerning other desires, which Frankfurt takes to be (unlike first-level desires for action) internal to the self – can be formed and maintained on any basis whatsoever and even on no basis. The idea is to capture the fact that our free acts derive from our selves, where preferences are arguably key components in the identity of the self (Ekstrom 1993, 2005).

On the model Dennett (1981: 286–299) sketched as the best available to a libertarian (without himself endorsing the model), in the case of a free action it is causally undetermined which particular considerations occur to an agent as she is deliberating over what to do. Similarly on Mele's model of modest libertarianism (Mele 1995, 2006), it is causally undetermined which of an agent's non-occurrent beliefs will become occurrent and function in his deliberation; the beliefs that occur happen to occur when they do, but they might not have, given the past and natural laws. Once the thoughts occur and the last of them has occurred in practical deliberation, on both Dennett's model and Mele's modest libertarian model, there is a deterministic causal relation between the particular pattern of beliefs that has happened to occur and the outcome of the deliberative process.

On the newer Ekstrom account (Ekstrom forthcoming), in a case of directly free action (an action the freedom of which does not derive from an earlier free action), the act is caused non-deviantly and indeterministically by certain kinds of agent-involving events – that is, attitudes of hers, such as preferences, convictions, desires, values, and beliefs – and the act is not the result of compulsion, manipulation, or coercion for which the agent herself has not freely arranged. A decision to act, conceived as the active formation of intention to act, is free in virtue of having this sort of causal history. The directly free act, so conceived, counts as self-governed in virtue of its being caused by the agent's reasons, which on this model include any of the agent's psychological or motivational attitudes, not only certain ones such as preferences; and it counts as meeting the alternative possibilities condition of freedom in virtue of the fact that, at the time the agent performed the act, she could have done otherwise in a categorical sense. The self-direction component of freedom is broadened over that of the Ekstrom (2000) account described earlier, in order better to connect with our intuitions concerning moral responsibility in the desert sense. The specialized notion of preference might be better suited for capturing cases of autonomy, rather than free will, as well as for helping to illuminate autonomy-related phenomena such as alienation, identification, and wholeheartedness (Ekstrom 1993, 2005, 2011).

On this newer view, then, a decision or an act is free just in case it is caused non-deviantly and indeterministically by attitudes of the agent's and so long as other reasonable compatibilist conditions on free action are met. On Randolph Clarke's (2003) classification of libertarian theories, this is an unadorned event-causal libertarian account. Mele's "daring libertarian" proposal is also a view of this sort, on which the indeterminism required for what Mele terms "basically* free acts" (2006: 115) lies between one's considered best judgement concerning what to do and one's decision to act.

Robert Kane's view (discussed in detail in Chapter 2 of this volume) contains a number of inventive and intriguing details, including a focus on competing efforts of will, which he argues helps to address concerns about luck and arbitrariness. Kane speculates on how causal indeterminacy might work in the human decision-making process; concerning times when there are powerful competing motivations, he writes, "there is tension and uncertainty in our minds about what to do, I suggest, that is reflected in appropriate regions of our brains by movement away from thermodynamic equilibrium – in short, a kind of stirring up of chaos in the brain that makes it sensitive to micro-indeterminacies at the neuronal level" (Kane 2011: 387).

On any of the preceding event-causal libertarian theories, free decisions may be made in light of rules of rational reflection and, indeed, may be guided by and governed by them. On any of the preceding event-causal libertarian theories, as well, free decisions may be governed by natural laws, so long as those laws are not deterministic, and the processes that lead to our free decisions may, as well, be law-governed and rule-governed.

What is different and especially interesting about Hodgson's event-causal libertarian account is his emphasis on the notion of a conscious gestalt experience. Hodgson suggests that, in making decisions, "persons respond appositely to gestalt experiences that are too feature-rich to engage as wholes with laws of nature and generally do not engage with computational rules, so that the response is not determined by laws or rules of any kind" (2012: 153). He maintains, too, that the person, "the *subject* of the experiences, can also as a whole contribute to the response" (2012: 153). This may sound like an appeal to agent causation as causation by a substance, but, again, Hodgson makes clear that he is not an agent-causalist: "I say that agents do cause free decisions, because they cause one thing rather than another to happen. . . . However, I do not see that any contribution to this process *by the agent* is additional to the contribution by *events involving the agent*" (2012: 164). The law-governed physical realm leaves room, he suggests, for an agent to "steer" among "spectra of alternatives" as she responds to non-law-governed and non-rule-governed conscious experiences.[2] Hodgson writes: "The picture I am suggesting is of rational decision-making by conscious subjects (persons), which cannot be broken down into component parts, but which occurs within constraints prescribed by the combination of the physical aspect, considered in isolation, and the laws of nature" (2012: 153–154).

Hodgson's reason for contending that natural laws and computational rules do not govern or engage with gestalt experiences is because laws and rules "apply over a range of circumstances, and must engage with *types or classes* of things or features that different circumstances have in common, and/or *variable quantities* that can engage with mathematical rules" (2012: 81). Our feature-rich conscious experiences, such as perceiving a scene or hearing a new piece of music, Hodgson says, are "too complex and rarely occurring" for them "to engage as a gestalt whole with laws of nature".

2 Hodgson writes: "from the point of view of the conscious subject, there are (1) spectra of alternatives . . . and also (2) consciously felt pros and cons of these alternatives. *The conscious subject steers within* those spectra, for example by doing or not doing something, or shaping an action, or deciding upon an answer to a consciously addressed problem" (2012: 157).

These seem to me to be problematic claims. Whether a conscious experience is rare, unique, or new, it might well fall under a general deterministic law, in virtue of the physical processes that give rise to it. I do not see any convincing argument in Hodgson's work for thinking that it could not. The contention that such an experience could not be law-governed is especially problematic given Hodgson's view that "that there is no experiential change without a corresponding physical change" and that "there is accordingly a sense in which any information contained in our experiences must be contained or encoded in those physical processes" of our brains (2012: 98).

It also seems to me that decisions made in light of our conscious experiences can be free while at the same time making use of, following, or falling under rational rules of thumb, guidelines, or rules which specify permissible alternative moves, manoeuvres, or choices. Furthermore, our experiences and the free decisions we make as we respond to them could be governed by probabilistic natural laws. The libertarian maintains that our free decisions and other actions are not causally determined by the past and natural laws. On any of the various plausible and defensible event-causal libertarian views set out previously other than Hodgson's, the processes leading to our free decisions and free actions may be governed by laws of nature, so long as those laws are nondeterministic ones. There is, then, no need to posit something like emergent wholes that transcend the laws of nature in order to account for free will, and doing so seems to generate more questions than answers.[3]

Does Hodgson show that we actually have libertarian freedom?

In my view philosophers and legal theorists would do best to set out accounts of what the sort of freedom required for moral responsibility in the desert sense would look like, remaining neutral on the matter of whether or not it is instantiated, since it seems unlikely that we could establish the fact of our having indeterminist free will in the absence of relevant and compelling scientific data.

Hodgson, however, has reasons for thinking that we need not wait on science to tell us about how human decision-making works in detail. His estimation that the doctrine of causal determinism is almost certainly false (2012: 172) would not settle the matter, as he recognizes, since even if it is not the case that every event is causally necessitated by prior events given the natural laws, theoretically it could be the case that human decision-making proceeds deterministically. Hodgson, though, is convinced that it does not. As we've seen, he takes the nature of conscious experience itself to rule out our responses to that experience being either natural law-governed or rule-governed, and thus, he thinks, given our rationality, our consciousness implies that we do in fact have libertarian free will.

3 Hodgson himself admits that, in suggesting a kind of emergentism, "I am making a proposal that could be considered extravagant" (2012: 96).

Hodgson's argument relies not only on the claim about the nature of conscious experience we have examined – namely, that our conscious experiences are too feature-rich, unified, and unique to be governed either by natural laws or by computational rules – but also on the claim that our responses to our conscious experiences, although not rule-governed, nonetheless are not random because they are fitting responses made by us. Each of these claims – the first concerning the nature of conscious experiences and the second concerning the rationality of our responses to our experiences – plays a key role in the case for Hodgson's conviction that we are actually free in his sense.

Certainly it would be nice to know if we are free in a libertarian sense, and if we could indeed prove just by thinking about things that we are, this would be quite something! In that case we would have made an empirical discovery about ourselves by way of reflection. However, we have seen reason to question the first key claim in Hodgson's case for our being libertarian free, the claim concerning consciousness. In the subsequent section we'll look more closely at the second claim, concerning apposite responses.[4]

Notice that Hodgson contends that we have free will in a robust sense "because (1) alternatives *are truly open*, albeit limited by the engagement of prior conditions . . . with the laws of nature, (2) the occurrence of one of the alternatives is not random but the result of our selection between them on rational grounds, and (3) we put our selection into effect by voluntary actions" (2012: 157). But, again, it is not clear that we really know, in the absence of good scientific data, whether or not alternatives are genuinely open to us as we face the future. The matter seems not accessible to us either by reflection (such as Hodgson's reflections on the nature of conscious experience) or by way of introspection alone. Hodgson is confident that "conscious decisions and actions are caused indeterministically by the totality of the relevant conscious and unconscious processes" (2012: 165). In my view it would be better to say that, *in order to be free*, actions would need to be caused indeterministically by relevant agent-involving events.

Apposite responses

In this section, I'll argue that Hodgson does not himself provide an account of something that he alleges that other libertarian accounts fail to provide. Hodgson writes: "what my approach does, that I think no other approach has done, is to identify something specific about the process that is both indeterministic and rational, namely *the person's apposite response to feature-rich gestalts of conscious experience*" (2012: 179, italics added). It is not clear how the italicized phrase provides something missing in Kane's account, Mele's account, or Ekstrom's account. The "response" to which Hodgson refers might be an interpretation of the experience, or it might be a decision concerning what to believe or what to

4 Neil Levy's chapter in this volume argues that Hodgson's principal evidence for his claim that consciousness enables libertarian free choice is better explained by existing models of creativity that are consistent with causal determinism.

do. An "apposite response" is one that is fitting, appropriate, pertinent, or apt in the circumstances. It is apt, it seems on Hodgson's view, because it is made for reasons. Hodgson alleges that what is missing from Kane's account is "a developed account of how the choice between alternatives is made, from the experiential perspective" (2012: 162). But to say that a choice or decision between alternatives is "apposite" does not provide what is allegedly missing. Suggesting that our conscious experiences are gestalts says something about what it is like to have conscious experiences of the world, but it does not provide an account of how the choice between alternative ways of responding to those experiences is made. To call our responses apposite is insufficient to illuminate the matter.

Hodgson alleges that Kane's theory "falls short in relation to the *selection* between the alternatives open to the agent. . . . Certainly, he makes no suggestion as to how the agent's reasons could explain *which way* the judgment goes". Hodgson argues that his approach "fills this gap" (2012: 162). He says that in the case of a free choice, the selection among alternatives "is not arbitrary, because *the conflicting reasons do not merely support each alternative between which a choice is to be made, but operate in the selection itself by way of the agent's apposite non-rule-determined response to them*" (2012: 162, italics added).

It is not clear what the italicized portion of the previous sentence means. It sounds as if Hodgson is suggesting that, in addition to an apposite non-law-governed and non-rule-governed response to conscious perceptual experiences, an agent has an apt non-rule-determined response *to the reasons* that support various decision outcomes. On the other hand, the term "them" in the phrase "apposite non-rule-determined response to them" might refer to the alternatives rather than to the reasons supporting each alternative. The alternatives in a case of deciding what to believe are different beliefs, and in a case of deciding what to do the alternatives are different actions. So perhaps Hodgson is suggesting that reasons operate in the agent's selection of one alternative belief or of one alternative action over another by way of the agent's "apposite non-rule-determined response" to the alternatives. Again, something is apposite if it is appropriate or fitting, which presumably means it is reasonable or adopted for reasons. I do not see something here that is "gap filling" or an improvement on other event-causal libertarian models, which also depict free decisions as made for reasons.

Hodgson continues to describe his view of freely made decisions in this way: "the choice is not inscrutable: although it is not uniquely determined by pre-decision circumstances and laws, or indeed by the agent's reasons, it is understandable as a rational decision by the agent" (2012: 165). I think that any plausible event-causal libertarian view makes the same claim: that is, that a free choice is not inscrutable but rather understandable as a rational decision by the agent. This is not unique to Hodgson.

Hodgson's subsequent discussion of the analogy of a hand of cards – on which we ourselves are the hand of the usual playing cards plus the joker – is difficult to follow. He again denies agent causation in the uncaused cause or unmoved mover sense. But then the reference to "whatever is playing the cards" is mysterious. It seems he might think of "the joker" as what one would naturally call "the will", in the faculty or power sense. He does call the joker, at one point, our capacity for conscious decision-making. But it is odd that a capacity or power for decision-making is a card, on the analogy, as are our various psychological attitudes including desires and beliefs, since the latter are mental states rather than abilities or powers.

There is an interesting addition into the equation of "what a person makes of her experiences" at one point in the exposition of Hodgson's view:

> These arguments suggest that conscious decisions and actions can be rational and apposite to circumstances facing the person in question, yet not limited to just one possibility (or to mere randomness) by prior conditions and laws of nature and/or computational rules . . . because there is a contribution to the decision or action from *what the person "makes of" feature-rich gestalts* that do not engage with laws or rules, a contribution that is itself apposite so that it contributes to the rationality and appositeness of the decision or action.
>
> (2012: 156, italics added)

"What a person makes of" her experiences would seem to be her view of them or her interpretation of them. Perhaps it includes the feelings or desires she has in response to her experiences. These attitudes – interpretations, beliefs, feelings, desires – all might contribute in some way, to a greater or lesser extent, to the decision the agent makes. I think that any free will theorist would say that our decisions are made in light of these various agential states and attitudes.

Hodgson aims to show that an undetermined free choice on his theory is not capricious, arbitrary, or a matter or luck, and this non-luckiness he wants to secure by saying that the choice is "an apposite non-rule-determined response". We should keep in mind that a choice that is made in light of or in conformity with a rational rule could yet be causally determined. My conscious reasoning process may lead me to a perspective or decision that is sensible, while at the same time it was brought about in a causally necessary way by the totality of prior factors. At the same time it is true that a choice made in light of or in conformity with a rational rule could be undetermined by prior events and the natural laws. To say that a response is governed by a rule of rationality is not to say that it is causally necessitated. And a choice that is not governed by any rule at all might in fact be capricious, arbitrary, or uncontrolled.

Regarding how the apposite responses work, Hodgson himself acknowledges that his theory is not fully developed. "I accept that my account of how conscious processes that are not rule-determined can contribute to reasonable decision-making is far from complete", he writes, "and that it leaves many questions unanswered. In particular I have not gone far in explaining how and why these contributions can be apposite" (2012: 111).

Conclusion

It is remarkable that David Hodgson developed his views at length and with originality on such a wide range of philosophical topics, including consciousness, rationality, freedom, truth, and value. Despite the critiques articulated here, I find his work provocative and stimulating and view him as a kindred spirit in his defence of an event-causal indeterminist account of free will.

References

Clarke, R 2003, *Libertarian Accounts of Free Will*, Oxford University Press, Oxford.

Dennett, DC 1981, *Brainstorms: Philosophical Essays on Mind and Psychology*, MIT Press, Cambridge, MA.

Ekstrom, L 1993, 'A Coherence Theory of Autonomy', *Philosophy and Phenomenological Research* 53(3): 599–616.

Ekstrom, L 2000, *Free Will: A Philosophical Study*, Westview Press, Boulder.

Ekstrom, L 2003, 'Free Will, Chance, and Mystery', *Philosophical Studies* 113: 153–180.

Ekstrom, L 2005, 'Alienation, Autonomy, and the Self', *Midwest Studies in Philosophy* 29: 45–67.

Ekstrom, L 2011, 'Free Will Is Not a Mystery', in R Kane (ed), *The Oxford Handbook of Free Will*, 2nd edn, Oxford University Press, Oxford.

Ekstrom, L Forthcoming, 'Toward a Plausible Event-Causal Indeterminist Account of Free Will', *Synthese.*

Franklin, C 2013, 'How Should Libertarians Conceive of the Location and Role of Indeterminism?', *Philosophical Explorations* 16(1): 44–58.

Ginet, C 1990, *On Action*, Cambridge University Press, Cambridge.

Hodgson, DH 2012, *Rationality + Consciousness = Free Will*, Oxford University Press, Oxford.

Kane, R 1996, *The Significance of Free Will*, Oxford University Press, Oxford.

Kane, R 2011, 'Rethinking Free Will: New Perspectives on an Ancient Problem', in R Kane (ed), *The Oxford Handbook of Free Will*, 2nd edn, Oxford University Press, Oxford.

Mele, A 1995, *Autonomous Agents: From Self-Control to Autonomy*, Oxford University Press, Oxford.

Mele, A 2006, *Free Will and Luck*, Oxford University Press, Oxford.

Nelkin, D 2011, *Making Sense of Freedom and Responsibility*, Oxford University Press, Oxford.

Pereboom, D 2014, 'The Disappearing Agent Objection to Event-Causal Libertarianism', *Philosophical Studies* 169(1): 59–69.

Vargas, M 2013, *Building Better Beings: A Theory of Moral Responsibility*, Oxford University Press, Oxford.

4 Occam's shopper

The costs of plausible reasoning

Neil Levy

After a long period of neglect, consciousness has come to be a central preoccupation of both philosophers and, increasingly, neuroscientists. Consciousness was long neglected because it seemed so mysterious, so ineffable: Today, perhaps for the very same reason, it fascinates many. The central question in the philosophy of consciousness is the so-called hard problem: How can mere matter give rise to *experience*, with its apparently irreducibly subjective properties? This question has spawned an entire industry since David Chalmers (1996) posed it in his massively influential book.

But consciousness has continued to be neglected outside the philosophy of mind. In the free will debate, it has long been absent, or presupposed as a background condition hardly worth investigating (see Sher 2009 for discussion of this presupposition). Today, this is changing. There are two independent forces that are rescuing consciousness from its long neglect in this terrain. The first is work in neuroscience and social psychology, allegedly demonstrating that consciousness can play the role in action initiation that philosophers – again allegedly – have presupposed (Libet 1999; Wegner 2002). The other force comes from within philosophy, and consists in new models of agency and decision, according to which non-conscious decisions or actions count as authentically belonging to the agent (see Levy 2013 for discussion). These two forces together seem to promise a rethinking of the role of consciousness in action and in free will. Paradoxically, while reigniting debate on the topic they seem to lead to a view according to which consciousness is relatively insignificant.

David Hodgson was no follower of fashion. He had begun to explore consciousness-related issues well before the recent revival, in *The Mind Matters* (1991), and when he turned to consciousness in his last work (Hodgson 2012), his approach was entirely distinctive. He was impressed neither by the neuroscientific work that is alleged to show that consciousness is epiphenomenal, nor by arguments that consciousness had no significant role to play in action. For Hodgson, our capacity to make conscious decisions is central to our possession of free will.

A libertarianism centred on consciousness

Incompatibilists are philosophers who believe that free will requires the falsity of causal determinism. Either because they hold that free will requires genuine access to alternative possibilities (such that it is not settled by anything, prior to the agent's decision, how she will decide) or because they hold that a free action has its source in the agent (or both), incompatibilists maintain that freedom is incompatible with determinism. Hodgson was an incompatibilist: Moreover, he believed (on the basis of extensive reading in contemporary physics) that determinism is false and that human beings possess free will. In the jargon of the debate, he was a libertarian.

Libertarianism is confronted with a significant obstacle. While many philosophers are sympathetic to the argument that free will is incompatible with causal determinism, many are also convinced that it is also incompatible with *indeterminism*. If indeterminism is true, they argue, then though it may be the case that it is sometimes (in some sense) open to us that we decide in two or more incompatible ways, we lack control over just *which* option we choose. We might press the point home by asking what constitutes control for an agent. Presumably, I can be said to control my actions because my mental states – my beliefs and desires, my values, my principles, and so forth – play a causal role in my behaviour. But now consider the libertarian agent, deliberating which of two possible alternatives to choose. Like the determined agent, she can weigh reasons for and against the alternatives and come to a view as to which she should do. If she is to possess genuine open alternatives, though, then one of two things must be the case: Either her (motivating) reasons must not settle which option she will choose, or her reasoning must itself be indeterministic. Both options expose her to freedom-undermining luck, many philosophers believe.

Consider the first option. If we accept the account of event-causal libertarians like Robert Kane (1996), it sometimes happens that when an agent is conflicted about how she ought to act (for instance, when she is torn between doing what she judges to be the moral action and advancing her own interests), indeterministic processes are set in motion that settle whether she performs one action or the other. In that case, everything about her – her beliefs, desires, values, and so on – is held fixed, whichever option she chooses. But if all her propositional attitudes are held fixed across possible worlds in which she performs one action and others in which she performs a different, incompatible action, it is hard to see how she controls which option she selects. Though she exercises some degree of control – after all, there is an explanation of why she deliberates between those options, and not others – she does not control whether she performs one or the other. Insofar as it *matters* which she selects (insofar as one action is morally bad and the other is not, for instance), then this kind of lack of control seems to significantly reduce her freedom.

On some rival accounts of libertarian free will, the link between the agent's reasons and her action is deterministic. On these accounts, the agent has all the control over how she acts, given her settled reasons, as anyone might want. On these so-called Valerian libertarian accounts (named by Daniel Dennett 1978, after the poet Paul Valéry), she possesses libertarian free will because the inputs into her reasoning processes (what ideas occur to her and with what force, for instance) are undetermined (see Ekstrom 2000; Mele 2006). Many philosophers have found this view to be no more satisfying than the first. Though it is true that the agent may be said to control the final decision, the fact that she does not control her reasoning process seems to undermine her freedom. For a Valerian agent, a crucial input into decision-making – an input which the libertarian must suppose to be decisive (if it is to secure alternative possibilities for the agent) – is out of her control, but since the input is decisive, this lack of control entails that she is once again subject to freedom-undermining luck (see Berofsky (2018) for detailed examination of the luck argument).

Though libertarians have advanced replies to arguments like the preceding ones, there is something of a consensus in the field that the libertarian faces a very big problem: how to simultaneously secure open alternative possibilities, of the demanding sort they require, and at the same time secure control over the action selected. It is in the context of this challenge that it is helpful to situate David Hodgson.

For Hodgson, the – or at any rate, *a* – function of consciousness is to allow us to make undetermined decisions that are nevertheless controlled by us. Conscious experiences have representational contents, but at least some conscious experiences have contents that are unlike those of any other kind of representation. Each such conscious experience presents the agent with a unique set of unified qualitative features. Because each conscious experience is unique, it has features that fall under no law nor can feature in any algorithm, since laws and algorithms mention only general and shared features of the states or processes they govern. Because these conscious experiences have features that cannot be captured by laws or algorithms, they enable the agent to have access to contents that are not reducible to the kinds of contents that physical processes – which are law-governed – interact with. Instead, we have access to irreducible kinds of non-physical properties.

We make our free decisions guided by these kinds of contents. When we are so guided, we engage in what Hodgson calls plausible reasoning. Plausible reasoning is rational, because it is guided by the contents that are presented to us in our experiences, and also constrained by algorithmic physical brain processes. But plausible reasoning is also genuinely free, in the libertarian sense of the word, because it is not entirely algorithmic.

It should be noted that Hodgson's view is not vulnerable to one version of the luck argument. On standard event-causal libertarian views, our decision-making or our actions are governed by indeterministic processes. Hodgson denies that this is the case: instead, he maintains that they are not governed *at all*. There is no process which settles how we act. Instead, *we* settle how we act, by responding to our conscious experiences.

Hodgson's view is unlike any other in the free will debate. It has features of event-causal libertarian views, but also features that resemble those of non-causal views. It is deeply informed by contemporary physics and presents an entirely novel solution to the problem that, more than any other, has dogged libertarianism. I don't think it is successful, in the end, though. Like other attempts to avoid the problem of luck by invoking a power of agents to settle how we act, the account leaves too much downright mysterious to genuinely constitute a solution to the problem. It leaves a lingering suspicion that it solves the problem by stipulation: by asserting that we exercise control over our actions by exercising our free will (a little akin to the way Moliere's physician explained the soporific properties of opium as a consequence of its dormitive power (1673/1979). Without much more clarification on just what the power of free will consists in, we ought not to be moved. Moreover, Hodgson's claim that conscious experience plays a special role in enabling plausible reasoning is also somewhat mysterious. I shall elucidate these two points in turn, beginning with the second.

Plausible reasoning as non-algorithmic reasoning

Hodgson believes that there is a great deal of evidence for the existence of non-algorithmic reasoning. He finds it exemplified especially in exercises of creativity. Consider one of his favourite examples: the opening chords of *Tristan und Isolde*. Wagner's music was rule-breaking, or at least -bending, going beyond what is permitted by the long-codified rules of harmony. By the standards of the day, the opening chords are dissonant and daring. Yet, of course, this opening, though controversial at the time, has come to be accepted as a stroke of genius. For Hodgson, this kind of creativity exemplifies and provides evidence for the existence of plausible reasoning. It extends the existing algorithms, going beyond them in a manner that no one could predict antecedently. But it is the existing algorithms it extends: Wagner did not abandon tonality. Rather, by extending it in a way that was, in principle, antecedently unpredictable, he altered what was possible within the rules of harmony.

Hodgson's description of creativity, as a way of extending the limits of what is possible within a given domain, but without actually abandoning the domain, is insightful. It is less clear that this kind of creative activity requires, or is any kind of evidence for, the existence of plausible reasoning understood as Hodgson does: a kind of reasoning that is in principle non-algorithmic and which requires non-physical informational properties.

What's the alternative to Hodgson's view? If reasoning is governed by stochastic algorithms (which could, but need not, be genuinely undetermined), then novel "moves" within an existing game will be generated. Carruthers (2011) maintains that in fact this kind of view is the "emerging consensus" among researchers on creativity. Like Hodgson, these researchers accept that creativity must be constrained; for both sides, the constraints refer back to existing sets of rules and principles. Both sides also accept that genuine creativity goes beyond the existing rules and principles, but whereas Hodgson claims that this requires contents that are inexplicable computationally and processes that both are undetermined and cannot be subsumed under any law, the creativity researchers have constructed computational models showing that creativity can be generated by stochastic algorithms; moreover, reviews of the existing data on genuine creativity in the sciences seem to indicate that human creativity has exactly the features that the emerging consensus predicts (Simonton 1999, 2003). When we face a choice between a successful model, which uses only processes that are massively attested, and a highly speculative model, which postulates processes and contents that are controversial and mysterious, then we ought to prefer the first. I think the evidence clearly shows that the choice between Hodgson's model and the emerging consensus among creativity researchers is precisely such a choice.

This claim is supported by the extensive evidence that, far from allowing non-algorithmic decision-making, consciousness is preferentially the locus of logical and rule-governed processes. Manipulations which increase the extent to which information processing is driven by non-conscious mechanisms *decrease* the extent to which reasoning is algorithmic (De Neys 2006). Non-conscious processes are generally blind to the structure of formal systems, but it is this structure that is essential to rule-based reasoning. Unconscious systems can therefore process semantics but not syntax: Even two word phrases cannot be used as primes as a unit (Baumeister and Masicampo 2010). Activating concepts unconsciously has effects on subjects' attitudes, but these effects are widely held to be associative and not logical (Gawronski and Strack 2004; though see Levy 2015 for some qualifications). In contrast, rule-based reasoning often reflects "mindware" which is effortfully based and requires conscious attention for its application (Stanovich 2009).

Moreover, it is far from clear that Hodgson's argument for the existence of non-algorithmic processes succeeds. He claims that the uniqueness of conscious properties entails that they cannot be rule-governed. Uniqueness is nothing mysterious, however, nor is it at all unusual. Uniqueness is in fact the most common property in the world: *Every* event is unique. One has only to consider their relational properties to drive the point home. Events are dated particulars: The event of *this* atom decaying *now* is certainly unrepeatable. But these are the features of events that we commonly take as the relata of our causal laws. There is nothing intrinsic to uniqueness that rules out unique events entering into rule-governed relations. In fact, *only* unique events enter into rule-governed relationships.

The evidence cited by Carruthers suggests that informal reasoning is algorithmic and that creativity requires nothing more than stochastic processing. Hodgson's suggestion that true creativity requires unique properties seems unmotivated, and seems to multiply entities beyond necessity. These are high costs to pay, so high that we should be willing to pay them only if they bring us something important that cannot be had at a lower cost. In the next section, I will argue that even if we were to grant all of the claims that Hodgson makes, his model does not secure us any kind of freedom that can't be secured by existing, less demanding models.

Consciousness as securing freedom

Let's grant to Hodgson his claim that conscious experiences present us with properties that are not rule-governed, in any case. Would the suggestion solve the problem confronting the libertarian, showing that decisions may be undetermined and yet controlled by the agent? I don't think it would: This novel libertarian model is bedevilled by the same problems that beset the old ones.

We are supposing that conscious decision-making is non-algorithmic. We are thereby granting that it secures open alternatives: It is metaphysically open to the agent to settle on one of two or more conflicting courses of action. Many other libertarian views can secure this much: It is securing control by the agent that remains problematic. Suppose it is true that conscious experiences present as gestalts, in which many features are combined at once (in fact, I think something like this is likely true, though on my view neither indeterminism nor non-algorithmic processing is required; see Levy 2014 for discussion). Suppose (contrary to fact, I believe) that these feature-rich gestalts do not as wholes engage with laws or algorithms and that the person responds appositely to these gestalts. Grant all this: The problem of control – the classic luck problem for libertarians – looms as large as ever.

Hodgson's official response to the luck argument comes in his reply to Van Inwagen (2000). Van Inwagen asks us to imagine that the (putatively) free choice of an agent is replayed multiple times. He notes that given it is undetermined, on some replays the agent will make one choice and on others another. Van Inwagen's challenge to the libertarian consists in asking her to explain why the choice is not simply a matter of luck. In response, Hodgson claims that those rational choices that are the locus of free will, significant choices over which we deliberate, are not instantaneous; thus there is no instant of time at which history branches across the replays. He thus believes that he avoids the luck objection. However, even if it is true that there is a set of choices which are significant enough to serve as the loci of free will, and which have a temporal structure that prevents there being a moment at which replays can branch, it does not follow that his model is not vulnerable to a luck objection. What is needed is a positive account of decision-making, which explains how the person can "steer" (as he puts it) the process without luck intervening at crucial points. There are good reasons to think that such an account *cannot* be given.

On the picture we are granting, the agent is presented with an executive summary of the situation regarding which they deliberate, a summary that does not engage with laws or algorithms. These features present the agent with reasons for action. But we are supposing that the agent can respond to some of these reasons in ways that are metaphysically open, such that different decisions are possible for her. That is, the decision-making process is open at crucial points (the crucial points mentioned in the previous paragraph, at which the intervention of luck would be devastating). Now, the question to ask is just *how* does the agent control her response to these reasons?

Hodgson attempts to avoid the event of the agent's just happening to decide one way or another by requiring that decision-making be temporally extended. But still we have not been shown what the exercise of control consists in (if you thought that the driver of your taxi had lost control over it, would you be reassured if he insisted that driving was a process and not an instantaneous event?).

How does the agent *rationally* assess the reasons figuring in the executive summary presented to her in conscious experience? Any view which holds that indeterministic decision-making is the locus of free will faces a dilemma. Either the facts to which we respond in decision-making have a certain antecedent rational weight for us, in which case the effects of intervention would be to bring it about that a fact has more or less weight for us than it rationally ought, or (some of) the facts do not possess an antecedent rational weight for us, and we assign them a weight arbitrarily. Either horn of the dilemma entails that decision-making is subject to luck.

Let's take the second horn first. On this horn of the dilemma, when I become aware of some fact or feature of a situation, which is relevant to how I will or should act, it does not have a specific weight for me. The fact that "the money belongs to someone else" does not possess a specific weight against, or indeed in favour of, my taking it; or the fact that "waffles are on the menu" is neither a reason with a specific weight in favour of my ordering nor a reason with a specific weight in favour of my ordering something else. If this is the case, how will I go about making up my mind? Given that some of my reasons do not have an antecedent weight, my decision can't be a function of these weights (on this horn, it is this fact that ensures that how I will decide is metaphysically open). So I must decide by assigning a weight to my reasons. This assignment, note, cannot itself be settled by the weights my other reasons (antecedently) have for me; that would ensure that the reasons mentioned do after all have a settled weight for me, derivatively, and the space of libertarian freedom would thereby be closed down. So instead I must assign a weight to some of my reasons, for no reason at all. That decisively ensures that to the precise extent to which my decision is metaphysically open, it is shot through with irrationality.

It is also shot through with luck. Luck, I claim, is a function of three factors: chanciness, lack of control, and significance (Levy 2011). A decision made as described earlier satisfies all three (at least, it does when it serves as the locus of free will, thereby satisfying the significance condition). A decision is chancy if it goes one way in the actual world, but in another (or others) in a significant proportion of nearby possible worlds. A significant degree of indeterminism entails that the decision is chancy. Control consists in patterned sensitivity to reasons: An agent exercises control over a state of affairs or her own behaviour to the extent to which she is capable of detecting reasons to do so and responding appropriately (Fischer and Ravizza 1998). By ensuring that reasons lack a specific weight for the agent, a view like this ensures that control is diminished; more specifically, there is no reason to which the agent can respond in settling whether she acts one way or another.

This discussion sets the stage for the first horn of the dilemma. As we have just seen, it had better be the case that my reasons have an antecedent weight for me, on pain of my decision-making being infected with irrationality and luck. The first horn of the dilemma accepts that this is the case. But insofar as open alternatives are to be secured, it cannot allow that these antecedent weights settle how I shall act. So instead it must accept that something other than the agent varies the weight of her reasons. But clearly that's no help at all. That simply transforms Hodgson's picture into the event-causal libertarianism he aimed to avoid, on which on some replays the agent decides in one way and on others another, without her playing any role in settling which option is actual. Again, this option ensures that the resulting decision is shot through with luck.

These are perfectly general problems, which so far as I can see no libertarian theory can resolve. They entail that just to the extent to which there is difference-making indeterminism in the causal chain leading to action, there is a loss of control. By maintaining that difference-making indeterminism in the causal chain leading to action necessarily entails a diminution of control, I do not mean to subscribe to an updated version of the Hobartian view, according to which free will *requires* determinism (see Hobart 1934). Nothing in the preceding remarks entails that the control agents might possess in an indeterministic world, diminished though it is, is not sufficient for free will. Libertarians might think that the benefits of indeterminism – for instance, the fact that it entails that prior to my decision it was not settled how I would act (the so-called sourcehood condition, according to which agents must in some sense be the ultimate sources of their actions in order to be responsible for them) – are worth the cost of a slight diminution of control. What these remarks do entail is that no account can buy us genuinely open alternative possibilities, between which agents can deliberate, *and* moral responsibility. If I lack control over whether I perform one action rather than another, and those actions differ in their moral worth, I cannot be directly morally responsible for how I decided.

The remarks just ventured are conciliatory, conceding that Hodgson's picture might be able to secure a kind of free will, by simply allowing that we are subject to some degree of control-undermining luck. But a big problem lurks nearby. Were Hodgson to go this route, he would no longer need an account of plausible reasoning at all, since it is designed to explain how decision-making can be undetermined and, yet, in some sense stronger than can be secured on previous libertarian views, rational and controlled. In fact, Hodgson's view secures no more control than other libertarian accounts. Given that the metaphysics of consciousness with which he presents us is unmotivated and ontologically extravagant, he or his successors would do better to drop it. It does not buy the libertarian anything that can't be had at a cheaper cost.

Conclusion

There is no doubt that the view that David Hodgson presents is a genuinely innovative attempt to solve the central problem that besets libertarian accounts of free will. He marshals an impressive range of evidence, demonstrating that indeterministic decision-making is consistent with everything we know about contemporary science. However, while that part of his case is plausible and should prove a basis on which future libertarians can build, insofar as they care about naturalistic respectability, the case leaves untouched the central problem besetting libertarianism. Our decision-making may indeed be undetermined, but if so that fact seems to reduce our control, Hodgson's argument to the contrary. If I am right, it is impossible to secure both indeterminism and the degree of control available on determinist models; the libertarian must choose.

It is by no means obviously irrational for the libertarian to choose indeterminism: The reduction in control it brings need not be fatal to freedom (see Levy 2011 for discussion). However, if the libertarian goes this route, they will have little motivation for accepting Hodgson's account of rationality. Nothing it secures for libertarianism can't be secured more parsimoniously, postulating only processes and events that already feature in science. Hodgson's work is highly creative, but I suspect that his creativity can be explained without recourse to the mysteries of processes that are non-physical and non-rule-governed.[1]

References

Baumeister, RF and Masicampo, EJ 2010, 'Conscious Thought Is for Facilitating Social and Cultural Interactions: How Simulations Serve the Animal-Culture Interface', *Psychological Review* 117: 945–971.

Berofsky, B 2018, 'The Luck Argument Against Libertarianism', this volume.

Carruthers, P 2011, 'Creative Action in Mind', *Philosophical Psychology* 24: 437–461.

Chalmers, D 1996, *The Conscious Mind*, Oxford University Press, Oxford.

De Neys, W 2006, 'Dual Processing in Reasoning: Two Systems But One Reasoner', *Psychological Science* 17: 428–433.

Dennett, DC 1978, *Brainstorms: Philosophical Essays on Mind and Psychology*, Harvester Press, Brighton.

Ekstrom, L 2000, *Free Will: A Philosophical Study*, Westview Press, Boulder.

Fischer, JM and Ravizza, M 1998, *Responsibility and Control: An Essay on Moral Responsibility*, Cambridge University Press, Cambridge.

Gawronski, B and Strack, F 2004, 'On the Propositional Nature of Cognitive Consistency: Dissonance Changes Explicit, But Not Implicit Attitudes', *Journal of Experimental Social Psychology* 40: 535–542.

Hobart, RE 1934, 'Free Will as Involving Determination and Inconceivable Without It', *Mind* 63: 1–27.

Hodgson, DH 1991, *The Mind Matters*, Clarendon Press, Oxford.

Hodgson, DH 2012, *Rationality + Consciousness = Free Will*, Oxford University Press, Oxford.

Kane, R 1996, *The Significance of Free Will*, Oxford University Press, New York.

Levy, N 2011, *Hard Luck: How Luck Undermines Free Will and Moral Responsibility*, Oxford University Press, Oxford.

Levy, N 2013, 'The Importance of Awareness', *Australasian Journal of Philosophy* 91: 211–229.

Levy, N 2014, *Consciousness and Moral Responsibility*, Oxford University Press, Oxford.

Levy, N 2015, 'Neither fish nor fowl: Implicit attitudes as patchy endorsements', *Noûs* 49: 800–823.

1 I am grateful to an audience at the University of Sydney, and especially to Allan McCay and Michael Sevel, for comments on this chapter which have greatly improved it.

Libet, B 1999, 'Do We Have Free Will?', *Journal of Consciousness Studies* 6: 47–57.
Mele, A 2006, *Free Will and Luck*, Oxford University Press, New York.
Molière 1673/1978, 'The Imaginary Invalid', in *The Misanthrope and Other Plays*, Penguin, London.
Sher, G 2009, *Who Knew? Responsibility Without Awareness*, Oxford University Press, New York.
Simonton, D 1999, *Origins of Genius: Darwinian Perspectives on Creativity*, Oxford University Press, New York.
Simonton, D 2003, 'Scientific Creativity as Constrained Stochastic Behavior', *Psychological Bulletin* 129: 475–494.
Stanovich, K 2009, *What Intelligence Tests Miss: The Psychology of Rational Thought*, Yale University Press, New Haven.
van Inwagen, P 2000, 'Free Will Remains a Mystery', *Philosophical Perspectives* 14: 1–19.
Wegner, D 2002, *The Illusion of Conscious Will*, MIT Press, Cambridge, MA.

5 The luck argument against libertarianism

Bernard Berofsky

The luck argument

David Hume ((1977) [1748]: 107–108) famously asserted that, contrary to a widely held view, agents are held accountable for their actions *only* when the latter are *determined*, for, in order to judge a person accountable or morally responsible, we must suppose that the agent's actions are determined by or reflect her moral character. An action may be reprehensible; but if it does not issue from the agent, if it comes from nowhere, we cannot blame the agent herself. Undetermined actions – actions caused by nothing – are not caused by a moral defect in the agent. Since the moral character of the agent does not explain such an action, moral blame is inappropriate. Since that identical agent (with her character, abilities, personality, etc.) in identical circumstances in another possible world is just as likely to act completely differently, the action (in the actual world) is really just an accident, random, a matter of luck. Since, therefore, moral responsibility is incompatible with indeterminism, it must be compatible with determinism if it exists at all. (Often appealing to Hume, many philosophers have expanded his point to produce an analogous argument against those who believe that determinism is incompatible with freedom of the will.)[1]

I will use the expression "argument from luck" to refer to any argument that cites (alleged) features of indeterministic decisions or actions as grounds for concluding that the decision or action is unfree and/or the agent is not morally responsible. I will call defenders of these arguments "Humean Compatibilists".

One can, as noted, respond by conceding that the concept of moral responsibility is incoherent, meaningless, or self-contradictory. C. D. Broad (1952: 195–217) defends a view something like this. He adds that efforts to dismiss the dilemma by reverting to an agency conception of causation (libertarianism) backfire and only establish that libertarianism is impossible. But few philosophers are willing to accept Broad's drastic conclusion and, if they are of incompatibilist

1 One form or another of the argument has been advanced by many, including Alfred Mele (2013, 1999), Peter Van Inwagen (2000, 2011), Neil Levy (2011), J. J. C. Smart (1961), A. J. Ayer (1954), P. H. Nowell-Smith (1954), and R. E. Hobart (1934). Some theorists (Mele, van Inwagen, Levy) present the argument as a conundrum rather than as a basis for a defence of compatibilism.

persuasion, will attempt to save moral responsibility by rejecting the argument from luck.

David Hodgson is an example. His incompatibilist stance is stated early on: Free will is the ability to make reasonable choices that are not themselves determined by laws or rules: “real choices that are not themselves wholly determined by our genes and environment *and/or by chance*, but are in a fundamental way truly down to us” (2012: 6, italics mine).

Thus, Hodgson recognizes that randomness is inimical to, rather than supportive of, free will and is, therefore, required, as an incompatibilist unwilling to adopt Broad’s sceptical stance, to respond to the argument from luck.

This article is a defence of Hodgson’s stance. Now a defence of the view that incompatibilism can respond adequately to the worry that undetermined decisions and actions are not free because they are accidents, chance happenings, or unattributable to the agent ostensibly performing them does not establish incompatibilism. One can believe, as I do, that both determinism and indeterminism are compatible with free will and moral responsibility.

An agent displays free will, in my view, when she exercises control over her decisions and possesses the power to decide otherwise. The real enemies of free will are neither determinism nor indeterminism, but rather interferences in what are sometimes called the “compatibilist freedoms”: rationality, reflectiveness, relevant knowledge, wholehearted identification with the will, the absence of compulsion, undue coercion or manipulation, emotional stability, and moral maturity. These freedoms can all be present in deterministic *and* indeterministic circumstances.

I wish neither to defend nor to refute determinism. The issue before us is the compatibility of free will (and moral responsibility) with indeterminism, not the truth or falsity of the latter. Hodgson has much of interest to say in defence of indeterminism, especially as it pertains to our conscious lives. He argues, for example, for the indetermination of rational decision-making, especially given that much reasoning takes the form of judgements of plausibility based on inconclusive evidence. He finds further evidence in the appearance in consciousness of gestalts, experiences of unified wholes, which, he claims, cannot enter as terms of a nomic relation. There are no laws relating these conscious experiences to brain processes.

Hodgson’s elaboration of his views on freedom and responsibility is original, deeply informed, and argued with a great deal of boldness and brilliance. Yet the argument from luck has experienced a sort of rebirth in the last decade or so, and Hodgson’s defence needs to be significantly strengthened if it is to withstand these recent assaults. Hodgson devotes so much energy to a defence of indeterminism that the luck issue is barely addressed. Serious discussion begins in chapter 7 of 2012, where Hodgson observes that, although investigations in quantum mechanics undermine determinism, the indeterminism supported by quantum mechanics is random and “randomness is inimical to free will rather than supportive of it” (2012: 6). On the other hand, the refutation of determinism “supports an argument that the physical world is not closed to influences from rational conscious processes” (2012: 128). In the following chapter,

Hodgson attempts to show that the actual output among the possible outputs permitted by quantum indeterminism might be determined by conscious input. So a decision can depend on conscious reflection on reasons rather than neurological processes.

But Hodgson is committed to the view that the dependence here must be indeterministic. Yet if rational decision-making is truly indeterministic, then Humean Compatibilists would contend that the decision is arbitrary or a matter of luck. When Hodgson says in chapter 9 that the occurrence of one of the alternatives is not random, but the result of our selection between them on rational grounds, the Humean Compatibilist can easily note that the same deliberations could lead to one decision or a competing decision, with nothing determining which. If a juror, after rational reflection that does not clearly lead to a particular outcome, decides finally that the defendant is guilty, when he could have decided the opposite under identical circumstances and with exactly the same evidence, including the weighting of relevant factors, why is that not arbitrariness? I will argue, however, that an adequate response to such concerns can be made on Hodgson's behalf.

Appeal to phenomenology

The argument from luck has been with us in one form or another at least since Hume. But the argument was jolted back into the consciousness of philosophers in 1934 by R. E. Hobart. Hobart likens an undetermined action to an uncontrollable spasm. "*In proportion* as it [an act of volition] is undetermined, it is just as if his legs should suddenly spring up and carry him off where he did not prefer to go. Far from constituting freedom, that would mean . . . the loss of freedom" (7).

Many others agreed. In another well-known example, P. H. Nowell-Smith (1954: 282) describes the case of a hardened thief who is about to rob a church's poor-box and suddenly recalls the promise he made to his dying mother to live an honest life. Although he has always ignored similar visions in the past, in this case, he succumbs to his mother's wish and decides not to take the money. This sudden conversion is inexplicable and, we are told, appears to happen to the thief. It is not a genuine action, performed by a rational, deliberative agent.

It became clear to most philosophers that, as far as this phenomenological argument is concerned, there is really no reason to believe that an undetermined action *must* present itself to the agent as an involuntary spasm that is not under his or her control. The fact that there is no deterministic law governing an action or decision – there might well be a covering statistical law – tells us nothing about the phenomenology of the action. A person might decide to perform an action under circumstances that are identical to those of another person who decides differently; yet to each person, the (undetermined) decision appears completely voluntary and fully intentional.

Humean Compatibilists, then, turned away from phenomenological circumstances to concentrate on other grounds. But first, let us look more closely at the little Hodgson himself has to say to them.

Hodgson's defence

Hodgson (2012) claims that the probabilistic laws of quantum mechanics (QM) are perfectly consistent with (indeterministic) rational choice. But the fact that a rational choice does not violate QM, that QM permits non-algorithmic rational processes, does not establish that rationality alone, algorithmic or non-algorithmic, is not subject to the argument from luck. First of all, we must suppose that the reasons that confer rationality on a decision are ones that explain, at least in part, the agent's decision. I might perform a haphazard action that just happens to be the rational thing to do. I might coincidentally choose a path that luckily leads to a place at which I want to be, without at all being motivated by the recognition that my actions would have this fortuitous outcome. To render me a free and responsible agent in an indeterministic context, I must act *because* of the reason. But if I act *indeterministically* from some reason, nothing explains why I chose to act rationally; I might have chosen the irrational course. So I am apparently just lucky that I chose rationally. Or at least that is the case of the Humean Compatibilist. So Hodgson needs to do more than just note the consistency of the laws of QM with (indeterministic) rational choice.

Hodgson also appeals to evolution to argue that the capacity for rational thought must have been selected because of its conduciveness to survival. But, of course, he must show that evolution explains why rational thought is indeterministic. If rationality is valuable, would it not make more sense that evolution ensures that it is *always* invoked? How can it advance our survival to possess the power to act irrationally, to run toward the tiger rather than away?

Hodgson also contends that QM cannot anyway engage our rational dimension for this dimension, like other conscious processes (gestalt-like experiences), falls outside the domain of physical law.

In advancing a view of this sort, Hodgson is placing himself in a venerable tradition, going back at least to A. I. Melden (1961), perhaps even a lot further – to Kant – according to which human beings, in virtue of their rationality, are members of two distinct worlds. One is the world of law or cause and effect, and, in this respect, our membership places us within nature, and the other is the world of rationality, in which the agent acts on the basis of reasons in a way that cannot be reduced to the language of cause and effect. This topic is far too grand to consider in this chapter; but I can comment briefly on the argument Hodgson presents in chapter 5 for this bifurcation of the agent.

He does not actually talk there about rationality, but rather concentrates on the failure of gestalt-like experiences to fall under the domain of natural law. In any case, he notes that a gestalt is "because of its particularity, not a type with which rules can engage" (2012: 85). But I reject this argument since I do not see why two distinct agents cannot have the same gestalt experience-type. Of course, every token experience is a particular, just as every token dropping of a ball is a particular. This is not a barrier to a token's being an instance of a general law. Thus, particularity per se does not preclude gestalts from falling under general laws. Nor is the rarity of an experience a basis for its failure to be subsumable under a general law. Finally, the fact that experiences are qualitative (or composed of qualitative components) is also not a barrier to capture by a general law insofar as qualitative phenomena in general (colours, sounds) are described in quantifiable terms. And Hodgson produces no argument that establishes the unquantifiability in principle of the features of gestalt-like experiences that would preclude their nomic embrace by the natural sciences. Nor does Hodgson cite any special component of rationality that would strengthen these arguments.

If Hodgson's dismissal of the argument from luck has merit, we must seek beyond his own work for a basis for this conclusion.

Rationality

One form of the argument from luck claims that undetermined acts cannot be rational for, as undetermined, they do not emanate from the agent's reasons. In response, we may first point out that undetermined actions may be performed for reasons that are sufficient. The agent may be acting in the way she is because she has sufficient reason to do so. To see this, we must simply recognize the difference between reasons and causes. The absence of a sufficient cause or a covering deterministic law does not rule out action from sufficient reasons. The sufficient reasons might fail to move the agent to action as happens in cases of akrasia or weakness of will. I might acknowledge that I should quit smoking and may actually do so because of this reason in spite of the fact that there was a small chance I would fail. Although I overcame temptation, success was not causally guaranteed. Thus, my action was both rational and undetermined. If free will and/or moral responsibility require rationality, then indeterminism per se poses no threat. The Humean Compatibilist may reply that such an agent lacks free will because she does not exercise control over whether or not she succumbs to temptation, whether or not she behaves rationally. Nothing about her or anything else explains which outcome ensues. Whether or not this is true, the alleged deficit of indeterminism has shifted from rationality – for, after all, the agent who overcomes temptation acts rationally since she does what she has most reason to do because of that reason – to loss of control. This charge – absence of control – must anyway be addressed; but it is a different charge. Or the Humean Compatibilist may instead be complaining about the use of the term "because" when I said that the agent acted because of a sufficient reason. The absence of *causal* sufficiency, he contends, renders the term "because" inapplicable. Again, the Humean Compatibilist has shifted to yet another issue or, rather, claim, to wit, that there can be no causal relation between events unless one event is or is part of a sufficient condition of the other. This issue, too, will be addressed.

If the libertarian accepts the Humean Compatibilist's case that indetermination precludes rationality because the agent does not control the action (even if it is coincidentally rational), then she is saddled with the troubling conclusion that no free actions are rational. If control requires that rational actions be determined and determinism is incompatible with free will and moral responsibility (the latter being the fundamental postulate of incompatibilism and libertarianism), no rational actions can be performed by a free or morally responsible agent.

Libertarians can try to abandon the link between freedom and rationality by denying that free will requires rationality. This possible stance of the libertarian is not unreasonable. Clearly a free agent must be "basically rational", that is, generally responsive to reasons and their normative force. But I believe that allowance should be made for imperfectly rational agents who fulfil all other conditions of freedom. An agent confronted with the decision to quit smoking or to continue may intentionally and voluntarily choose to continue to smoke. The desire to continue smoking exerts a strong, but not overwhelming force. She is not actually addicted. Acknowledging her decision is not the overall better one, she nonetheless finds the attractiveness of the lifestyle of a smoker together with the pleasure of smoking to constitute sufficient grounds to act irrationally. That is, she realizes that she ought, in light of all considerations, to quit, and she can, with effort she can muster, do so. Her argument to justify her choice is that she possesses a deep self-image that incorporates smoking, an activity she very much enjoys. These are good reasons. (She may, but need not, be rationalizing her choice.) The choice is nonetheless still overall irrational since she acknowledges that her decision is not the better course of action (even for her).

A distinct reason to disassociate freedom from rationality is the example of tossup actions, actions for which the competing reasons have equal weight. After a thorough and impartial review, the rational agent cannot find any basis for deciding one way or the other, but must decide. The result will be in a sense arbitrary. Since one cannot accuse the agent of irrationality, one might describe the outcome as not irrational (non-irrational). So we have free will without rationality. Or, in light of the fact that the agent chooses *A* for a reason, in spite of the fact that he has no reason to prefer *A* over *B*, we may describe the outcome as rational; but, either way, there is no reason to deny free will.

The Humean Compatibilist can complain that, since nothing really determines the outcome, the agent is not in control and cannot, therefore, be counted free. So the agent controls neither rational nor non-irrational actions. Notice, however, that we are no longer worrying about the relation of free will to rationality. We are talking now about control instead.

We have seen that the opponent of Humean Compatibilism faces multiple arguments. We have dismissed two arguments, the appeal to phenomenology and the claim that undetermined actions are unfree because they must be irrational. Humean Compatibilists have appealed to four other considerations: causation, control, arbitrariness, and explanation.

Causation

Causation is, of course, intimately associated with explanation. But let us begin by addressing the case from causation as if it were a separate argument. The claim of the Humean Compatibilist is that an agent who commits an evil deed is morally responsible for that deed only if the deed is causally related to some character flaw in the agent. But that causal relation presupposes a deterministic relation between the flaw and the deed. So the underlying assumption of the Humean Compatibilist, then, is that causal relations must be or rest upon deterministic ones. Now, under indeterminism, a purported cause may fail to produce its effect for no reason whatsoever. So it is possible that the cruel man just fails to act cruelly in a context in which he could, but, for no reason, does not.

Now a "cause" that does not cause is no cause at all. Obviously, in those cases in which the cause fails, the Humean Compatibilist is right. Yet the key question is: Does the event we are disposed to count the cause in cases of *success* have the right to be so-called? So we must look at the case in which the evil man acts in an evil way.

Before we proceed, we ought to forestall any type-token confusion. "Cause" can be used in both senses. First of all, since we are trying to separate causation from explanation, let us think of causation as a relation between events rather than a relation between facts, as obtains in the case of explanation. We may then distinguish a relation between event types, as in "smoking causes cancer", from a relation between event tokens, as in "Harry's smoking [an extended event, to be sure] caused his cancer". The Humean Compatibilist's claim is that, even in those cases in which a token event, the striking of the match, is followed by ignition, the striking cannot be said to cause the ignition should the latter lack a sufficient condition. Of course, the Humean Compatibilist is not insisting that the ignition itself be sufficient, as it obviously is not. Ever since Mill, we all recognize that the term selected as the cause is hardly ever sufficient for the effect. It is selected from a group of conditions, each of which, like the presence of oxygen, is necessary to the outcome. The striking is denied causal efficacy by the Humean Compatibilist because, even if it is necessary in the circumstances, there is no sufficient condition of the effect. Since the Humean Compatibilist must also say that the ignition is uncaused in cases of success – ignition – her position is strongly counterintuitive. For example, the Humean Compatibilist must persist in this conclusion even if the lighting (type) occurs 99% of the time under relevantly identical conditions.

The Humean Compatibilist must confront not just the counterintuitive nature of his claim, but the more serious charge that almost all theories of causation do not require that causes be or presuppose the presence of sufficient conditions. This is obviously true in the case of the probability theory of causation – causes as probability raisers under the right conditions need not raise the probability to one – as well as the counterfactual theory – an event *E* might not have occurred without an event *C* having occurred even when *E* has no sufficient condition. This is also true, although less obviously so, in the case of the Woodward-Hitchcock interventionist account of causation – or causal explanation; the theory does not sharply distinguish causation from causal explanation (Woodward 2003; Woodward and Hitchcock 2003). The core idea is that a process is causal in virtue of its falling under an invariant or stable generalization (expressed as a relation between variables) such that an intervention vis-à-vis one variable would, according to the generalization, bring about an appropriate change in the other variable. Of the many details that would need to be introduced to convert this sketch into a theory, the only important one for our purposes arises from the fact that, according to the theory, these invariant generalizations do not have to be laws. They are often practical, useful generalizations that have been found to hold in a sufficient variety of circumstances. Although laws can fail in extreme circumstances, invariant generalizations are vaguer than laws and fail under an even wider variety of circumstances so that they are not entitled to be called "laws". (Thus, to say that a change in one variable *would* bring about a change in the other is not to be read as absolutely precluding counterinstances.)

It is also important to note that the Humean Compatibilist must be using "sufficient condition" in a strong sense. One cannot understand how a token event *C* can be sufficient for a token event *E* without introducing general considerations, either other tokens of the same type or general laws linking event types. For *C*'s sufficiency for *E* is constituted by what would happen in other similar cases.

But even if a general deterministic law tells us that instances of *C* are always followed by instances of *E*, the law might be *ceteris parabus*. And if things are not equal, if circumstances prevail that the law was not designed to cover, then perhaps in those cases some tokens of *C* are not followed by some token of *E* for no reason whatsoever. The Humean Compatibilist would then have to deny that, even in the cases in which tokens of *C* and *E* are covered by a "deterministic" law, since the law may be *ceteris parabus*, the causal relation does not hold. We need genuine metaphysical determinism to ground a causal world. This observation only strengthens the interpretation of the Woodward-Hitchcock theory as one that clearly does not require metaphysically sufficient conditions.

Yet another class of theories is unhelpful to the Humean Compatibilist. Some theories define causation in terms of processes that transmit or conserve quantities. [See Phil Dowe (2009) for an overview.] Simple versions of the theory fail for, like any theory, they must account for causal transactions in which quantities are *not* conserved. Another reason we will not pay attention to such theories is that they presuppose that all causation is physical and cannot, therefore, address cases of prima facie psychological causation, the sort that are of special importance to us. Moreover, there are, in the sphere of physical processes, indeterministic ones, ones where prior states are not sufficient for later ones even when we isolate the process from external influences. The decay of an atom in an excited state from level 4 to level 0 takes place only in terms of probabilistic laws. So one state is not sufficient for the next.

A theory that explicitly offers a sufficiency requirement is the J. L. Mackie INUS-condition theory (1974). A causal factor, according to Mackie, is an insufficient but nonredundant part of an unnecessary but sufficient condition for some effect. Thinking of event types and supposing the possibility of achieving the same result in several ways, we thus suppose several sufficient conditions (e.g., ways of producing ignition or killing a person), each of which is itself composed of several conditions, each of which is essential to *that* sufficient condition, although not, in light of alternative sufficient conditions, to the effect type. But

Mackie never shows why the set of conditions in each such set must be genuinely sufficient, why, for example, it is insufficient to demand that the effect follow 99% of the time.

Thus, the Humean Compatibilist view that an agent deciding to *A* in the case in which he desires *A* is not making a free decision just because there is a .0005% chance that he would not decide this way under identical conditions receives little support from theories of causation.

The failure to show decisively that a sufficient condition must be present when the agent's mental state causes her decision has enabled some libertarians to develop theories that posit indeterministic causal relations in the mental sphere. Robert Kane's event-causal libertarianism (ECL) (1996) contends that free will rests on the possibility of causal indeterminism, a situation in which an agent has the metaphysical possibility of acting in one of two ways (via the indeterminism) and chooses one because of some desire or value that led her (indeterministically) to make that choice (via the causal relation). Indeterminism provides us with counterfactual power, crucial to free will, and causation provides us with a response to charges of arbitrariness and nonrationality. (See Kane's contribution to this volume.)

Further evidence for the unimportance of the causal relation in relation to the luck argument is provided by Humean Compatibilists themselves, who often invoke either explanation or control as the keys to unlocking their case. Although not a Humean Compatibilist himself, Alfred Mele (2015, 2014, 2013, 2006, 1998), in his critique of libertarian views like those of Kane, does not object to the causal component of Kane's event-causal indeterminism. What concerned Mele in his early commentaries on Kane's book (Mele 1998) was the exclusion of a *sufficient* explanation of decisions reached indeterministically.

> If there is nothing about the agents' powers, capacities, states of mind, moral character, and the like that *explains* the differences in outcome, then the difference is just a matter of luck.
>
> (583, italics added)

If John decides to go to the meeting late and John* (John's doppelganger) decides to be on time,

> It is difficult to see why John should be thought to have exerted freedom-level control in making the decision to go to the meeting late or to be morally responsible for making that decision.
>
> (583)

In fact, Mele extended his critique of event-causal libertarianism to agent-causal libertarianism (ACL), again complaining about the absence of an explanation rather than the causal relation itself. ACL, the more familiar form of libertarianism, posits a special form of causation that relates an agent or self directly with a decision or the formation of an intention. When this form of causation is operative, there is no answer to the question "Why?" for no state or desire of the agent, no desire, value, belief, urge, or need, led to the decision. Thus, ACL appears to involve a more serious violation of an explanation requirement. In order to address this issue, the libertarian Randolph Clarke (2003) notes that the event causes of an action can provide reasons; but as Neil Levy (2011: 64–76) observes, if the mental states that function as explanatory reasons offer options whereas the agent does the real causing, it would be double counting if we tried to explain the agent's causal activity by the very same reasons that are acting as reasons on the event level. Thus, the final push by the agent is made for no reason at all. If ECL cannot explain why the agent chose one option *rather than* the other, ACL appears to offer *no* explanation of the agent's making of her decision.[2] O'Connor (2000: 61) attempts to skirt this objection by insisting that agent causation is intrinsically an exercise of control. Levy challenges this for such exercises still require reasons. O'Connor can respond if he is prepared to abandon, as I am, the requirement that free actions always be done for a reason. Recall the example of tossup cases, like the magician asking for the selection of a card, in which there is no reason at all for one option rather than the other. Yet, I do not accept agent causation, construing "I decided to *A*" as a non-causal statement that reports a mental action that can be deterministically or indeterministically caused (in the ordinary, i.e., nonagential, sense). I do nonetheless think that O'Connor is on to something in describing these actions as exercises of control, control of the sort that Clarke calls direct. We turn to that shortly.

We have examined the concept of causation in an evaluation of the Humean Compatibilist defence of the luck objection. The Humean Compatibilist correctly sees the evil act of an evil man as grounds to charge the act against the man only if a causal relation obtains between the act and the character of the agent. The difficulty arises when the Humean Compatibilist insists that that causal relation requires a deterministic connection between character and act. This insistence then entails that moral responsibility ultimately rests on determinism. But the view that a causal relation inevitably presupposes a deterministic one has been discredited. We have seen that no theory of causation except one makes this demand, and the one theory (Mackie's) that treats causation as deterministic does not offer any reasons for this assumption.

A brief review of theories of free will that accept indeterministic causation indicates that, although Humean Compatibilists find no support from reflections on causation, they also invoke other notions historically linked to free will, such as control, in order to make their case.

2 To be sure, some libertarians, faced with the absurdity of denying that the experience of hunger causes the decision to seek a restaurant, introduce other devices to account for the relevance of such states. Timothy O'Connor (2000: 97) talks of desires that "affect" structures that change agents' tendencies.

Control

The libertarian Randolph Clarke (2003) rebuts the Humean Compatibilist by arguing that indeterministic decisions are not necessarily arrived at by luck, but can be within the agent's control in a way that preserves his freedom and moral responsibility. The key is a distinction between two types of control, ensurance and direct. We all can agree that agents sometimes act so as to ensure that a certain outcome will take place in the future. So they exercise ensurance control by instituting a condition that is sufficient for this future outcome. But, if there is control over the formation of an *undetermined* intention or decision (under either event or agent causation), the form of control cannot obviously be ensurance – in the absence of a sufficient condition, the agent cannot do anything to ensure that she decides a certain way (although, obviously, the decision itself might ensure some outcome, e.g., that she acts in accordance with the decision). No one can ensure an undetermined decision other than by making the decision. One might say that the "ensurance" is direct. Instead of doing something else that ensures the decision, all the agent need do is to make the decision. Clarke contends that in these cases the agent controls the formation of the decision directly or actively rather than via some other sort of indirect agency.

Clarke's case is strengthened by the absence of control-negating features of the decision. Since the decision is undetermined, the agent is not under compulsion or constraint or whatever freedom-denying feature is supposed to be instituted under a deterministic scenario. Of course, control might be negated by forms of coercion that fall short of determination. I may surrender to a very serious threat in such a way that one might conclude that I lacked control, even though, since there was a very slim possibility that I could have defied the threat, my actual submission might have been undetermined. Even if we count this as a case of loss of control under indetermination, the important point is that there are other cases of indetermination without any of these control-undermining features. In the latter cases, the indeterminism guarantees both that the agent is not under the complete sway of antecedent circumstances and that the agent could have decided otherwise. In addition, the decision does not suddenly appear to the person as something that has happened to her à la Hobart. The decision is a genuine mental action. It is formed intentionally, deliberately, and possibly after extended reflection upon the reasons, pro and con, for that decision. The agent decides in full knowledge of the nature and consequences of her decision. Since the agent has opted for one reason over another by deciding on behalf of that reason, we can also say that the agent acted *for* that reason (even though there is a slim chance she might have decided otherwise under identical conditions). In fact, as noted earlier, the agent may even have a *sufficient* reason for deciding in the way that she did. Note that this reason is not just a justification as it plays a *causal* (but indeterministic) role in the making of the decision. Clarke rightly asks: What more do you want for a free decision? Although Mele (2006: 65) appears to concede Clarke's direct active control, and even allows assignment of freedom and responsibility to the agent, he later (2014) insists that, in virtue of indetermination (at the point of decision-making or action), and in spite of all the freedom-conferring features cited by Clarke, the problem of luck remains, presenting as the worry about whether an indeterministic agent really exercises the right sort of control (2014: 547). That is, it still remains a mystery to Mele how we are able to assign freedom and responsibility under circumstances that suggest that the agent's decision is a matter of luck.

One should distinguish arbitrariness from loss of control. Consider again tossup cases where there is no reason to choose one or the other. The magician instructs Ben to pick a card. Ben's choice is arbitrary; but beyond issues of rationality, the card is selected deliberately, intentionally, and voluntarily. Ben could have picked any card and directly controls the card he picks. Yet, says Mele, if the selection is undetermined, that is, if there is another possible world with identical history and laws, in which Ben selects a different card, we do not yet understand why actual-world Ben is free in a sense that renders him potentially morally responsible.

It should be noted that, in any deliberative process, even tossup cases, there must be some sort of causal, but not necessarily deterministic, thread that runs through the process to render it coherent and provide some explanation of later by earlier stages. Even the arbitrary selection of a card must have causal links to the brief reflection that preceded the selection. Indeed, even an undetermined decision that fulfils all the requirements of freedom must maintain some causal links to its antecedent stages. In fact, the very announcement of the decision itself, like any coherent verbalization, must possess internal causal coherence, and the agent herself must recognize that this is so. (I distinguish the announcement or unspoken verbalization of the decision from the decision itself, which, as a mental action, may last only for an instant. And even if it has some, brief duration, we can say of it what has just been said of the process as a whole. It must have internal, causal, but not necessarily deterministic, coherence and be recognized by the person as such.)

Moreover, we may suppose that Ben possesses all the compatibilist freedoms. Thus, he is generally a rational agent, even though his current choice of a card may not be counted as rational (or irrational). He is also emotionally and morally mature, even though these general traits play little role in these tossup cases.

Mele returns to the issue of control (2013), formulating the issue now as the *continuation problem*.

> Why isn't the fact that different continuations of the past are open to the agent under these conditions [that is, conditions of indetermination] incompatible with his having enough control over whether he A-s at t or does something else instead at t to be basically morally responsible for A-ing?
>
> (246)

Mele presents a variety of cases of undetermined decisions to establish that each involves a loss of agent control, and we all agree that some undetermined decisions are like that. But in the indeterministic cases that appear to present ideal conditions for attributions of freedom and assignment of moral responsibility, is there any feature that stands out that can begin to address the continuation problem? Mele's answer points to the need to consider the origins of the alleged moral responsibility possessed by such an agent in the process of the evolution of a mature sense of moral responsibility or character. Mele notes that this evolution typically incorporates a gradual transformation. We start off as children without free will or moral responsibility and acquire more as we mature. Mele's point is well-taken. In a fundamental sense, free will and moral responsibility can sensibly be understood only as matters of degree, a consideration I have also urged (2012: 49; 1995: 46–53; 1987: 82–83), but which many writers generally ignore. Hence, probabilities change and are shaped as we mature and our characters evolve. Certain tendencies eventually become ingrained and help to explain our current decision. The coherent, integrated way the past evolves into the present is crucial to moral responsibility. These considerations are key, in Mele's mind, to the solution of the continuation problem.

Mele is concerned that the probabilities associated with our acting might be "wholly independent" of our past behaviour such as obtains when these probabilities are randomly generated by a mechanism that considers only present options. Hence, moral responsibility requires an explicable evolution of probabilities of action associated with its evolution as distinct from the way a random number generator might determine probabilities.

To solve the continuation problem in this way is to suppose that the problem is genuine, that, in the absence of a solution, we remain troubled about assigning freedom or responsibility to an undetermined agent even when conditions are apparently ideal – deliberateness, absence of compulsion, etc. I claim, in contrast, that, even in a case of akrasia, where Jane decides in a way that confers greater weight on factors that incline her to act contrary to the choice she concedes to be best, so long as she decides reflectively, deliberately, intentionally, and voluntarily, and possesses all the compatibilist freedoms, there is no reason to deny Jane freedom and, possibly, moral responsibility. (I do not mean to suggest that the conferral of greater weight on certain factors is to be distinguished from the decision. In the act of announcing to oneself that *A* factors are to be given greater weight than *B* factors, one *is* deciding in favour of *A*.)

The difference between Mele and me is that I reject the demand for a sufficient explanation of a decision as a ground of free will. I see no reason to deny free will to Ben or Jane. Yet the disagreement with Mele is not as extreme as it appears. For he is interested in free will as a necessary condition of moral responsibility, and some of the components of compatibilist freedom, for example, emotional maturity and minimal rationality, are not independent of a natural development from immaturity to maturity of a sort that Mele is highlighting. A person whose emotional states fluctuate wildly over time in a way that reflects no intelligible pattern or internal stability lacks both emotional maturity as well as the coherent evolution of probabilities that Mele counts as important for moral responsibility. Thus, I agree with Mele on the importance of the development of character as a component of a fully free and morally responsible agent. But I see this requirement as a component of compatibilist freedom and, indirectly, of moral responsibility. Thus, the evolution of probabilities appears in both our stories, but in different places.

In fact, Mele is actually an ally. The very fact that he suggests a solution to the continuation problem shows that he acknowledges the possibility of libertarian free will. He ultimately rejects Humean Compatibilism as decisive against libertarianism.

More specifically, in Mele (2006), he proposes a version of libertarianism (daring soft libertarianism) that, unlike more modest versions,[3] takes on present luck. That is, the recognition that one's present indeterministic decision is a "product" of past actions and circumstances that have increased the probability that one would act in the way one does removes the sting of luck. For the decision or action that emerges, indeterministically to be sure, is not "a bolt out of the blue", but makes sense in light of the decisions of the past that have evolved in the direction of the present one. Of course, a daring soft libertarian will not be able to apply this model to those many undetermined decisions that are not appropriately related to the past – calling heads or tails on a coin toss, perhaps. But she will at least be able to identify some undetermined decisions that may rightly be called free in spite of a luck-like component.

Thus, Mele remains somewhat troubled by these arbitrary, nonhistorical cases. In contrast, I see no reason to deny freedom and, under appropriate circumstances, moral responsibility to such individuals so long as they possess all the compatibilist freedoms, which, of course, include those, like emotional and moral maturity, which themselves presuppose historical requirements.

I cannot, as a compatibilist, help noting that the historical requirements for moral responsibility – the gradual evolution of probabilities pertaining to decisions and actions that constitute the formation of moral character – posed by Mele are so much easier to understand on a compatibilist model. For the evolution of probabilities along with the maturation of a sense of responsibility are not open to the accidents and flukes that might obtain in an indeterministic world. Hence, a deterministic model offers a more coherent narrative for individual moral growth. To be sure, for a daring soft libertarian, freedom resides in such a world only if there are those occasional bursts of indeterminism once the moral setting has been established.

I agree to the extent that such "bursts" might display the control that is requisite for free will.

3 Mele (2006: 9–14) has a version of libertarianism for more modest folks, ones who concede a deterministic relation between the proximate causes of a decision and the decision itself, thereby conceding as well the need to address the problem of present luck, and are content with a kind of internal indeterminism, e.g., of the emergence in consciousness of a relevant factor in deliberation "that gives us no less proximal control than we would have on the assumption that determinism is true, while opening up alternative deliberative outcomes" (11).

We must remember that the claim being advanced here is an existential one. I am saying that *there are* instances of indeterministic decisions that fulfil the requirements, specified earlier, for free will and moral responsibility. There may also be factors in some or many indeterministic cases that incline us to *deny* free will or moral responsibility. Perhaps the agent is deliberating under conditions of undue stress, perhaps the pressures on her render the chances of her deciding one way extremely low, perhaps her upbringing was so distressing as to hinder her emotional development, or perhaps her decision did arrive like a bolt out of the blue, etc. The point again is that we can describe cases of indetermination that are *not* like these, that fulfil all reasonable requirements for free will or moral responsibility.

Neil Levy's (2011) defence of Humean Compatibilism appears as a component of a grander project, to establish that "agents are not morally responsible for their actions because luck ensures that there are no desert-entailing differences between moral agents" (10). The ubiquity of luck, not determinism, is the culprit. We can obviously not address the general case that Levy makes, but must narrow our sights to his claim that luck destroys moral responsibility by destroying even direct control. Yet given Levy's own definition of direct control, it is not clear why he denies it even in a world permeated by all forms of luck, e.g., constitutive luck (luck in the traits and dispositions that make one the kind of person one is)[4] or all sorts of chancy events, like mood shifts. For surely a person directly controls *E* "by virtue of performing some basic action which (as he knows) will bring about *E*'s occurrence" (2011: 19). But, says Levy, even in such cases, the person's action is a matter of luck. Why?

Explanation

Levy says that, in an indeterministic causal process, the chooser "does not control *which* alternative she settles for. The indeterministic causal process settles that" (51). Don't we have equal reason to say that, in a *deterministic* process, the agent does not control her selection of *A* when she *A*s because she wants to *A*? Why not say that the deterministic process rather than the agent settles that? We are supposedly puppets under either determinism or indeterminism on this account. In truth, however, the agent, not the process, selects. Moreover, in some indeterministic processes, the agent, through direct control, selects. Now, it is true that, adopting Clarke's account, as we have, what is controlled is the very action itself, not some distinct consequence of it. (So, in Levy's preceding definition of direct control, *E* is the basic action itself.) Levy rejects this, offering the familiar argument that we have rejected, to wit, that the absence of a determining factor entails luck and luck is inconsistent with moral responsibility.

4 An influential discussion of moral luck by Bernard Williams and Thomas Nagel appeared initially in *Proceedings of the Aristotelian Society Supplementary* vol. 50 (1976). Williams' account was expanded in Williams (1981), and Nagel's paper was reproduced in Nagel (1979).

The only other reason Levy gives is that, when one is deciding among a good, neutral, or evil action, one can be held (directly) morally responsible for the chosen action only if one can provide a contrastive explanation, and, under indeterminism, one cannot.

In neutral, nonmoral cases, this demand is clearly not required. We saw earlier in the magician example that arbitrariness does not preclude control or any of the other freedom-conferring properties. In other tossup cases, in which there are equally strong reasons for conflicting decisions, the agent's selection of *A* over *B* permits him to cite the reasons favouring *A* as some sort of explanation of his decision. What he cannot explain is the reason that he selected *A rather than B*.

If I have just entered a restaurant and hear you ordering the tuna and you explain your – let us suppose indeterministic – choice by telling me that you love tuna, I certainly have an explanation of your choice even if I do not know what the other options were, what you chose not to order. Also, although I may not be able to explain why you indeterministically chose tuna rather than swordfish, which you love equally, I can at least explain why you chose tuna rather than many other options that you like less than tuna.

So, to deny that the agent cannot explain his indeterministic decision in contexts of moral responsibility rests on the assumption that explanation is in *that* context always a three term relation, even when one term is suppressed. We must then explain why Jones did the evil thing rather than the neutral or good thing. Suppose that he is genuinely conflicted, eventually deciding deliberately and voluntarily to do the wrong thing in spite of the absence of any factor that explains that act rather than the good or neutral act. That choosing, by its nature, is choosing over all other alternatives does not entail that an explanation of the act of choice must be a contrastive one. If Jones non-coercively burns down a house knowing that an innocent child is inside because he enjoys hurting innocent children, does his moral blameworthiness hinge on his ability to cite an alternative action he rationally rejected? Levy offers no reason for an affirmative answer.

Another philosopher who implicitly rejects the significance of Clarke's distinction between ensurance and direct control is Peter van Inwagen (2011, 2000). Suppose I believe that, once I begin deliberating between *A* and *B*, it is up to me at each moment up to the decision (that will be made at t_2) how I will decide. Suppose as well that, at each moment prior to t_2, it is undetermined whether I will choose *A* or *B* (until the decision is made).[5] It follows, according to van Inwagen, that at no moment prior to t_2 am I either able to do *A* at t_2 or able to do *B* at t_2 (2011: 477). Before we consider van Inwagen's reasons, we should register the strangeness of the conclusion. I will choose one or the other. Suppose I choose *A*. Then at t_2 I am able to do *A*. Since my abilities have apparently not changed from the time I began my deliberating, it is odd to conclude, for whatever reason, that at any t_1 (2 > 1), I cannot do *A* at t_2. I never had the

5 As van Inwagen observes, not every libertarian requires these conditions for free will.

ability to do A at t_2 at any time prior to t_2; yet I miraculously acquire this ability only when it is exercised.

In any case, the reason offered for this inability is that, if I possess it, I should be able to promise that I will do A and, given the indeterminism, I cannot. Now, van Inwagen clearly means that I cannot prior to t_2 *sincerely* promise to do A and I cannot prior to t_2 *sincerely* promise to do B. I am not, as he says, in a position to do so. David Widerker and Ira Schnall (unpublished) challenge this claim on the grounds that people do sincerely promise when there is a small chance the promise cannot be kept. People acknowledge that special circumstances may render the possibility actual. Moreover, the existence of these cases together with the existence of actual, insincere promising has not damaged the institution of promising.

Van Inwagen does not cite familiar reasons such as the lack of control or the lack of an explanation. He just notes that, in other possible worlds with the laws of our world, some persons identical to me and in circumstances identical to mine would choose A at t_2 and some would choose B at t_2. The clear suggestion is that I lack ensurance control, although there is no reason to believe that I cannot raise the probability that I will do, say, A, to .999. But the absence of ensurance control prior to t_2, as we saw earlier, does not entail the absence of direct control at t_2. So, given (1) the possibility of qualified ensurance control, (2) the possibility of sincere, but not guaranteed promising, and (3) the actual existence of direct control, nothing of significance is left to the argument.

Hodgson on explanation and arbitrariness

One response of Kane to the Humean Compatibilist is to appeal to the teleological character of an agent's undetermined choice, to note that the freely selected alternative confers on the reason for that selection a special role denied the rejected reason, to wit, of playing a further role in influencing future action. It is not clear to some critics, including Hodgson, how that observation addresses charges of arbitrariness or inexplicability. Hodgson observes that a commitment that one set of reasons will prevail in the future does not provide an explanation or render nonarbitrary the current judgement that it will prevail.

Hodgson advances his own position to show that an undetermined choice, as he characterizes it, is not arbitrary. One feature he singles out is the operativeness of the reasons "in the selection itself by way of the agent's apposite non-rule-determined response to them" (2012: 162). Reasons, of course, are apposite and have a causal bearing on any decision, determined or undetermined. So the key to the nonarbitrariness of an undetermined choice must be the absence of a rule determining the response.

First of all, we ought to distinguish rule following from causal determination. Each move in a chess game follows the rules of chess. But since these rules determine what is permissible, each player has a variety of possible moves, and, therefore, each actual move might lack a causally sufficient condition. In any case, the absence of a rule cannot in itself establish nonarbitrariness. Yet if I abandon rules, does not anything go? Perhaps, not necessarily; but we need to see how that is so. So we look further.

Hodgson (2012: 77) says: "If plausible reasoning proceeded precisely as determined by rules of any kind, there could be no positive role for a person's conscious experiences in that reasoning". I disagree. Some rules may even require consciousness. We may demand that, when reasoning, one should attend carefully to the reasons, or one should reflect carefully on the consequences, etc. Of course, such rules do not dictate specific outcomes. So one must suppose that Hodgson has deterministic algorithmic rules in mind. Even so, it is worth pointing out that the *failure* to follow such rules cannot be *sufficient* for nonarbitrariness or explicability. The demand for consciousness in reasoning does not preclude mad, utterly arbitrary decisions.

Hodgson is concerned to establish the autonomy of the psychological or conscious level, and I am sympathetic. And even if we add the fact that reasoning is often at best plausible rather than conclusive, we do not necessarily generate indeterminacy. Again, there is a difference between the level of rules and the level of (causal) laws. I may consciously draw a conclusion that is at most plausible from the rational point of view, even though my conclusion is actually causally determined in virtue of the role of other factors, some perhaps unconscious, which, combined with the conscious reasoning, produced a sufficient condition. The reasoning is causally relevant; but other factors are involved as well, such that my decision-making is an instance of a psychological deterministic law. But we should bear in mind that the issue before us is not the truth or falsity of psychological determinism, but rather the implications of the assumption of indeterminism. Humean Compatibilists conclude that undetermined decisions are arbitrary, and the fact that some undetermined decision (1) may fail to follow a deterministic algorithm and (2) may be reached through conscious reflection does not undermine that claim. We rather need the considerations advanced in this chapter to undermine the Humean Compatibilist.

Conclusion

Incompatibilists are able to produce an account of direct control under indeterminism. The many efforts to show that they cannot account for control, rationality, explanation, causation, and arbitrariness in an indeterministic scenario all fail, and, although Hodgson's *case* against the argument from luck is not particularly strong, his *position* is thereby substantiated.

References

Berofsky, B 1987, *Freedom From Necessity*, Routledge & Kegan Paul, London.
Berofsky, B 1995, *Liberation From Self*, Cambridge University Press, Cambridge.
Berofsky, B 2012, *Nature's Challenge to Free Will*, Oxford University Press, Oxford.
Broad, CD 1952, *Ethics and the History of Philosophy*, Routledge & Kegan Paul, New York.

Clarke, R 2003, *Libertarian Accounts of Free* Will, Oxford University Press, Oxford.

Dowe, P 2009, 'Causal Process Theories', in H. Beebee, C. Hitchcock, and P. Menzies (eds), *The Oxford Handbook of Causation*, Oxford University Press, New York.

Hobart, RE 1934, 'Free Will as Involving Determination and Inconceivable Without It', *Mind* 43(169): 1–27.

Hodgson, DH 2012, *Rationality + Consciousness = Free Will*, Oxford University Press, Oxford.

Hume, D (1977) [1748], *An Enquiry Concerning Human Understanding*, Hackett Publishing, Indianapolis.

Kane, R 1996, *The Significance of Free Will*, Oxford University Press, New York.

Levy, N 2011, *Hard Luck*, Oxford University Press, Oxford.

Mackie, JL 1974, *The Cement of the Universe*, Clarendon Press, Oxford.

Melden, AI 1961, *Free Action*, Routledge & Kegan Paul, London.

Mele, A 1998, 'Review: *The Significance of Free Will* by Robert Kane', *Journal of Philosophy* 95(11): 581–584.

Mele, A 2006, *Free Will and Luck*, Oxford University Press, New York.

Mele, A 2013, 'Moral Responsibility and the Continuation Problem', *Philosophical Studies* 162: 237–255.

Mele, A 2014, 'Luck and Free Will', *Metaphilosophy* 45: 543–557.

Mele, A 2015, 'Luck, Control, and Free Will: Answering Berofsky', *Journal of Philosophy* 112(7): 337–355.

Nagel, T 1979, *Mortal Questions*, Cambridge University Press, Cambridge.

Nowell-Smith, PH 1954, *Ethics*, Penguin, Harmondsworth.

O'Connor, T 2000, *Persons and Causes: The Metaphysics of Free Will*, Oxford University Press, New York.

Smart, JCC 1961, 'Free Will, Praise, and Blame', *Mind* 70: 291–306.

van Inwagen, P 2000, 'Free Will Remains a Mystery', *Philosophical Perspectives* 14: 1–19.

van Inwagen, P 2011, 'A Promising Argument', in R. Kane (ed), *The Oxford Handbook of Free Will*, Oxford University Press, New York.

Widerker, D and Schnall, I Unpublished, 'On the Luck Objection to Libertarianism'.

Williams, B 1981, *Moral Luck*, Cambridge University Press, Cambridge.

Woodward, J 2003, *Making Things Happen: A Theory of Causal Explanation*, Oxford University Press, New York.

Woodward, J and Hitchcock, C 2003, 'Explanatory Generalizations, Part I: A Counterfactual Account', *Nous* 37: 1–24.

6 Frankfurt-style examples, impermissibility, and reasons-responsiveness

Ishtiyaque Haji

Introduction

Galen Strawson (1986, 1994) has argued that no one is ever morally responsible for anything because to be responsible, for instance, for a choice, that choice must issue from the way one is – from one's character or motives for which one is responsible. However, to be responsible, in turn, for the way one is, one must be responsible for yet prior choices that contribute to the way one is. Responding to this argument from regression, David Hodgson writes:

> Strawson ignores the possibility that the way a person is immediately prior to the choice may only pre-determine the alternatives available and the (inconclusive) reasons or motives the person has for and against each of them. The person, using his or her capacity to make a conscious choice (a capacity which all normal adults have), may then resolve the competing inconclusive reasons – such resolution being neither random nor pre-determined by the way the person is immediately prior to the decision. . . . In terms of responsibility, one may accept that nothing a person does or can do *at the time of any choice or action* can make the person responsible for what alternatives are then available, for the way those alternatives then appeal, or indeed for having the capacity to choose between them – but one may nevertheless claim that, leaving aside any question of responsibility for *these* matters, the person can still be responsible for *the way the person exercises the capacity to choose.* On this view, the way the person is, in respect of character and motivation, does not predetermine what the person does: it only predetermines what the alternatives are and how they appeal. The person is not responsible for having the capacity to choose between these alternatives, but is not predetermined in how that capacity is exercised, *even by the way the person then is in respect of character and motivation*; and so the person (and no-one and nothing else) is responsible for the way that capacity is exercised.
>
> (2000: 674, italics added)

This passage and others relevantly like it reveal that the variety of event-causal libertarianism Hodgson favours incorporates the principle of alternate possibilities

(PAP): One is morally responsible for an action only if one had alternatives – for example, one could have refrained from performing it, or, if one could not have refrained, one's action must have been appropriately related to some other action regarding which one could have done otherwise (see, e.g., Hodgson 2012: 157, 176–177). In addition, the passage and others relevantly like it in his 2012 book make clear that Hodgson's brand of libertarianism includes a principle of ultimate origination to the effect, roughly, that one is morally responsible for an action only if one is its "ultimate source" (see, e.g., in addition 2012: 166). Hodgson is also amenable to the view – the "Guidance View" – many compatibilists and libertarians share that responsibility requires that one have the ability to grasp and be guided by good reasons (see, e.g., 2005, 2012: 80–85).

In this chapter, I begin with revisiting Frankfurt-style examples that purport to show that a person can be morally responsible for doing something despite not being able to do otherwise (Frankfurt 1969). If cogent, they cast doubt on PAP. Next, I outline a first objection to these examples: They unearth a tension between the freedom requirement of blameworthiness – roughly, the requirement that if one is blameworthy for doing something, then one does it freely – and a putative moral requirement of blameworthiness, loosely, the requirement that blameworthiness entails impermissibility: If one is blameworthy for doing something, it is impermissible for one to it. Given this moral requirement, it seems that the claim that blameworthiness requires alternatives is vindicated because obligation requires alternatives. But then, too, Frankfurt examples do not undermine PAP with respect to blameworthiness – the principle that persons are blameworthy for having done something only if they could have done otherwise – *provided* that blameworthiness entails impermissibility. I propose that this first objection to Frankfurt examples is not decisive.

I then respond to a second objection: Frankfurt examples do not sit well with an attractive elaboration of the Guidance View – responsibility requires that we be appropriately responsive to reasons. The concern here is that those who retain doubts about PAP on the basis of Frankfurt examples should renounce the Guidance View, or at least a promising elucidation of this view, because these examples undermine this view. Alternatively, if one believes that this is too high a price to pay, then one should reject Frankfurt examples, and, hence, one should no longer believe that these examples compromise the view, presumably, of Hodgson and others that blameworthiness requires alternative possibilities.[1]

The broad upshot of this chapter is that although I don't side with Hodgson on his commitment to PAP, I concur with his endorsement of one promising development of the Guidance View.

1 Hodgson says little about blameworthiness and its conditions. However, he is decidedly interested in punishment, and he claims that only persons who are morally responsible for their criminal behaviour deserve punishment (2012: 210, 213, and, more generally, 206–229). It is not implausible to interpret Hodgson as proposing that only the guilty – the blameworthy – deserve punishment.

Frankfurt-style examples, blameworthiness, and impermissibility

Among other things, Frankfurt examples attempt to establish that a person can, for instance, be morally blameworthy for doing something despite not being able to do otherwise, as long as the conditions that render her unable to do otherwise play no role in bringing about her action. Think of such an example as unfolding in two stages. In Stage 1, although Augustine could have refrained from stealing some pears, he is blameworthy for stealing them. Next, in Stage 2, a "rerun" of Stage 1, something precludes Augustine from doing anything incompatible with stealing but *without* in any way interfering in Augustine's actually stealing as it turns out. A mind reader, Ernie, who can tell what Augustine is about to do, will do nothing if he detects some reliable sign Augustine displays that he, Augustine, is about to steal, but will force Augustine to steal if he discerns the reliable sign that Augustine is about to refrain from stealing. But Augustine proceeds exactly as before, so Ernie has no need to intercede. Since Augustine in the absence of Ernie's intervention is morally responsible for stealing, and since in Stage 2 Augustine does not behave any differently, he is morally blameworthy for stealing here too, even though he could not have done otherwise (see, e.g., Frankfurt 1969; Kane 1996, 2013; Fischer and Ravizza 1998; Pereboom 2003, 2014; Fischer 2006, 2010, 2013; Mele 2006). Hence, the principle of alternate possibilities is false.

One might, however, worry that whatever the merits of these examples, there are independent reasons to believe that blameworthiness presupposes our having alternatives. For, if one is blameworthy for an action, it is impermissible for one to perform it. But if it is impermissible for one to perform an action, one could have refrained from performing it. Therefore, if one is blameworthy for an action, one could have refrained from performing it. Let's begin with the second premise. Why believe that impermissibility, or more generally, obligation, calls for our having alternative possibilities?

Moral obligation, just like moral responsibility requires control. I have proposed that if no action can be obligatory for a person unless that person freely performs it – if "ought" implies "can" (*Kant's Law*) – then similar things are true regarding moral permissibility and moral impermissibility; they, too, have analogous freedom requirements. We have free will with respect to some acts if and only if we have the ability (and opportunity) both to perform and to refrain from performing them. This thesis entails that for something we did do "of our own free will" – making a decision or performing some overt action, for instance – we were at some time prior to our doing it able to refrain from doing it (van Inwagen 2008: 329). To show that impermissibility, obligation, and permissibility require that we have free will, we may argue in this way. Starting with impermissibility, if it is impermissible for one to do something, one ought not to do it. This follows from *Equivalence*, the principle that one ought not to do something if and only if it is impermissible for one to do it. If one ought not to do something, one can refrain from doing it (from *Kant's Law*). Hence, if it is impermissible for one to do something, one can refrain from doing it. But it is true, too, that if it is impermissible for one to do something, one can do it. So, impermissibility requires alternatives. Next, regarding obligation, if one ought not to do something, it is impermissible for one to do it. Exploiting the principle that "impermissibility" implies "can", we may infer that if one ought not to do something, one can do it. But given *Kant's Law*, it is also true that if one ought not to do something, one can refrain from doing it. So, obligation, just like impermissibility, requires that we have free will. If obligation and impermissibility both require that we have free will, barring cogent reason to believe otherwise, permissibility requires our having free will as well. Hence, nothing is morally obligatory, permissible, or impermissible for one unless one could have done otherwise (Haji 1998, 2002, 2011, 2012b, 2016).

Although one might not be convinced by this sequence of reasoning, one should at least grant the following. Both *Kant's Law* and *Equivalence* are widely accepted. These principles sustain the conclusion that impermissibility requires alternatives.

Here is another consideration for the view that a precondition of obligation is that one have alternatives. An enduring view in moral philosophy is that the concept of obligation is to be explained in terms of the concepts of possibility and goodness. The underlying idea is that something is obligatory if and only if it is the best of the possibilities. Call the value in terms of which possibilities or alternatives are to be ranked "deontic value". Then, for convenience, we may provisionally assume that the obligatory is the deontically best. This principle may be refined in various ways. Here is an elegant version that Fred Feldman develops and defends: If (at the time of choice) there is a complete life history – a complete way in which your life can thereafter unfold – in which you perform an action, and no better life history in which you don't perform this action, then it is obligatory for you to perform this action. More rigorously:

> (MO): A person, *S*, ought, as of time *t*, to see to the occurrence of a state of affairs, *p*, if and only if *p* occurs in some world, *w*, accessible to *S* at *t* (there is a world accessible to *S* at *t* in which *S* brings about *p*), and it is not the case that *not-p* occurs in any accessible world deontically as good as or deontically better than *w*.
>
> (Feldman 1986: 16–44)

The axiological issue of just what is deontically best need not detain us. Some may identify what is so best, for example, with what is intrinsically best, others with maximal compliance with God's commands, and so forth. MO has it that if there is a world or there are worlds accessible to you in which you do something, and there is no better world or there are no better worlds accessible to you in which you refrain from doing this thing, then you ought to do this thing.

Suppose that whenever one performs an action, mental or otherwise, one could not have done otherwise; one never has alternatives. Then, as of any time, there is a single world accessible to one, the world in which one chooses or acts as one does. The aim is to show that with only one world accessible to one (and, hence, without one's having alternatives), actions are "amoral" for one: They are not obligatory, permissible, or impermissible. The canonical form of an obligation statement (such as the statement *at t, Joe ought to keep his promise at t**) has two temporal indices. The first is the time when the obligation is acquired; the second, which may be identical to or later than the first, is the time when the obligation is to be discharged. Suppose, in a world in which one could never have done otherwise, as of *t*, Joe *A*s at *t**. Regarding the primary moral status of *A* (whether it is permissible, impermissible, or obligatory as of *t* for Joe to do *A* at *t**), there are three options. On the first, on each occasion of choice or action, the world in which Joe chooses or acts as he does is the deontically best world. But then, as of any time, if Joe does something – no matter what – at that time, it is obligatory for Joe to do it then. This follows from MO's prescription that, abridging, at *t* an act is obligatory for one if and only if it occurs in all the best worlds accessible to one at *t*. This latitudinarian view is surely implausible. There is no good reason to endorse the view that if any action of an agent is unavoidable for that agent, then it is obligatory for her to perform it (or, for any state of affairs, if it is unavoidable for an agent, then it is obligatory for her).

But isn't it possible for people to be effectively coerced into doing what they are obligated to do? If this were possible, then there could be acts that were unavoidable *and* obligatory for an agent. Suppose *S* is coerced into doing *A*. If the coercion is so strong that it rules out alternatives, then it is at least contentious whether *S* can have an obligation to do *A* because obligation requires control. If the coercion doesn't rule out alternatives – if there is a world accessible to *S* in which *S* refrains from *A*-ing – then the case is irrelevant to the issue under discussion. For this issue assumes that there is only one world accessible to *S*, the world in which *S* does *A*, in which case *S* cannot do otherwise.

On the second option, on each occasion of choice or action, the (sole) world in which Joe chooses or acts as he does is a deontically non-best world. But then, if MO is true, as of any time, if Joe does something – no matter what – at that time it is impermissible for Joe to do it then because he does it in a non-best world. This result is just as unreasonable as the first. There is no good justification for the view that it is impermissible for an agent to perform any action that she cannot refrain from performing.

On the third option, on each occasion of choice or action, whatever Joe chooses or does on this occasion in the only world accessible to him is amoral for Joe: It is, as of the relevant time, *not* obligatory, permissible, or impermissible for Joe; it lacks any of these primary moral statuses. It lacks these moral statuses because obligation requires "two-way control", the ability (and opportunity) to perform and to refrain from performing some action. This option is preferable to the other two as it avoids the unpalatable implications, previously exposed, of the other two, and it takes seriously the view that obligation requires control. We may conclude that obligation, permissibility, and impermissibility require that one could have done otherwise.[2] Briefly put, obligation calls for dual control, the ability (and opportunity) to perform and to refrain from performing an action. Thus, we have reason to amend MO in this way:

> (MO*): A person, *S*, morally ought, as of *t*, to see to the occurrence of a state of affairs, *p*, if and only if there is a world, *w*, accessible to *S* at *t* in which *S* brings about *p*, there is a world, *w**, accessible to *S* at *t* in which *S* refrains from bringing about *p*, and it is not the case that *S* refrains from bringing about *p* in any accessible world as good as or better than *w*.[3]

Imagine that in his Frankfurt situation Augustine's act is simply one in his entire life in which each act that he performs is unavoidable for him – perhaps there is a "global" counterfactual intervener who sees to it that Augustine can never refrain from doing what he does on each occasion when he does something, but as luck has it, never has to intervene. It follows straightforwardly from MO* that it is not impermissible for Augustine to steal the pears if he could not have done otherwise.

So far, I have motivated the view that obligation and impermissibility require alternatives. Perhaps libertarians, like Hodgson and others, may claim that the sorts of libertarian theories regarding responsibility they defend can accommodate this requirement because their variety of libertarianism allows for agents having genuine (or "strong") alternatives: Given exactly the same past and the laws, agents could (at least on some occasions) have done other than what they in fact did. A two-step rejection of Frankfurt examples is now inviting: (i) In Stage 2, since Augustine cannot refrain from stealing the pears, it is not impermissible for him to steal them. (ii) But if it is not impermissible for him to steal them, contrary to what "Frankfurt defenders" claim, he cannot be blameworthy for stealing them. Indeed, this proposed rejection reveals a tension between an assumed moral requirement of blameworthiness, and what we may call a "one-way account" of control – an account that does not require that agents be able to do otherwise – whatever this account precisely amounts to, that Frankfurt examples suggest is a precondition of moral responsibility.

To explain, the putative moral requirement to which (ii) appeals may be stated more carefully in this way:

> *Blameworthiness/Impermissibility*: Necessarily, one is morally blameworthy, for example, for an action, only if it is impermissible for one to do it.[4]

2 Here, I take no stance on whether the alternatives are so-called weak or strong alternatives. Weak alternatives, such as the alternative *had one desired to do otherwise, one would have done otherwise*, are alternatives one can have even if determinism is true. Strong or "genuine" alternatives are alternatives that determinism precludes. Suppose, at *t*, one does *A*. Then, at *t*, one has a strong alternative just in case, given the same past right up to *t*, and the same laws of nature, one could have done otherwise at *t*; for instance, one could have refrained from doing *A* at *t*.

3 See, e.g., Feldman (1986: 43), Zimmerman (1996: 26–27), Haji (2012a: 61, 2016: 34).

4 See, e.g., Widerker (1991: 223), Copp (1997, 2003: 286–287), Fischer (2006: 218), Campbell (2011: 33–34).

Again, if *Blameworthiness/Impermissibility* is true, it is false that Augustine is blameworthy for stealing the pears in Stage 2. So, it appears that it cannot be that both the principle of alternate possibilities concerning blameworthiness (*PAP-Blame*) – persons are morally blameworthy for what they have done only if they could have done otherwise – is false and *Blameworthiness/Impermissibility* is true. A one-way account of responsibility-level control that Frankfurt examples may induce one to uncover seemingly conflicts with *Blameworthiness/Impermissibility*.

One may, however, be convinced both that Frankfurt examples *do* impugn *PAP-Blame* and that *Blameworthiness/Impermissibility* is true. So how could one reasonably renounce the former without giving up the latter? One strategy is to jettison *Kant's Law*. It is the principle that "ought not" is equivalent to "impermissible" (*Equivalence*) together with *Kant's Law* that generates the result that impermissibility requires avoidability; if it is impermissible for one to do something, then one ought not to do it (from *Equivalence*); if one ought not to do something, one can refrain from doing it (from *Kant's Law*); so, if it is impermissible for one to do something, one can refrain from doing it. Renounce *Kant's Law* and this result is blocked. Indeed, some might propose that if Frankfurt examples undermine *PAP-Blame*, they should undermine *Kant's Law* as well. At least *intuitively*, even in Stage 2, it is impermissible for Augustine to steal the pears. As this is so, and the conjunction of *Equivalence* and *Kant's Law* entails that impermissibility requires avoidability, assuming *Equivalence* is unassailable, the culprit is *Kant's Law*.

However, it is not clear that this way of rejecting the principle that impermissibility (or obligation) requires avoidability is cogent. Notice that *Kant's Law* (if one ought to do something, one can do it), a power or control principle, is pertinently like the following highly credible control principle.

> *Blame/Control*: One is blameworthy (or, more generally, morally responsible) for performing an action only if one can perform it.

This principle simply affirms the connection between control and blameworthiness (or moral responsibility). It expresses the widely held and plausible view that one is morally responsible for an action only if one has control regarding it. Notably, Frankfurt examples do not undermine *this* principle. The principle of alternate possibilities regarding blameworthiness:

> *PAP-Blame*: One is morally blameworthy for having done something only if one could have done otherwise

is a conjunction of *Blame/Control* and

> *Action*: One can perform an action only if one can refrain from performing it. (Zimmerman 1996: 86)

It is *Action* that provides the alleged link between blameworthiness and alternative possibilities. However, Frankfurt examples undermine *Action*.

If Frankfurt examples leave unscathed the principle that blameworthiness requires control (*Blame/Control*), they should leave unscathed the principle that obligation requires control (*Kant's Law*) or that impermissibility requires control:

> *Impermissibility/Control*: It is impermissible for one to do something only if one can do it.

The link between obligation and alternative possibilities is provided not by *Action* but by *Impermissibility/Control* and *Equivalence.* Just as Frankfurt examples do not impugn the principle that impermissibility (or obligation) requires control, so they do not impugn *Equivalence.*

There is, then, this significant difference between *PAP-Blame* and the principle that obligation requires alternatives. Regarding the former, essential to the link between blameworthiness and alternative possibilities is the principle *Action*, but *Action* is false as Frankfurt examples confirm. Regarding the latter, essential to the link between obligation and alternative possibilities are *Impermissibility/Control* and *Equivalence* (and not *Action*). Frankfurt examples threaten neither of these principles. Or, minimally, if one grants that these examples leave untouched the principle that blameworthiness requires control, one should also grant that they leave untouched the principle that impermissibility (or obligation) requires control. Moreover, it is implausible to suppose that Frankfurt examples undermine *Equivalence.*

Rather than abandon *Kant's Law*, and hence, jettison the principle that impermissibility requires avoidability, a Frankfurt defender may opt for another strategy: renouncing the principle that blameworthiness requires impermissibility. The Frankfurt defender may insist that both blameworthiness does not require alternatives (as Frankfurt examples show) and Augustine is indeed blameworthy for stealing the pears in Stage 2 even though it is not true that it is impermissible for him to steal them (in this stage).

I believe that various considerations do call into question the principle that blameworthiness requires impermissibility. Here, I restrict discussion to one of them. One of its crucial components is what we may dub the *luck principle.* Provisionally, this principle says that the degree to which one is blameworthy cannot be affected by what is not in one's control. The line of reasoning against *Blameworthiness/Impermissibility* to be advanced distils to this: This principle is true only if the luck principle is false. But the luck principle isn't false. So blameworthiness does not require impermissibility.

To enthuse the luck principle, if we accept the view that one cannot be blameworthy for something that is not in one's control – and here the sense of "control" is the personal one that moral responsibility presupposes – then it is hard to see why one should not also accept the view that degree of blameworthiness is immune to what is not in one's control. Suppose that, in *Murder-1*, you are blameworthy to a certain degree for killing Sam. You take careful aim, and the bullet smatters her brain. *Murder-2* is just like *Murder-1* except that a few seconds before you fired the gun, Sam expired because of an untreated aneurism.

Although you didn't know it, you shot into the body of a dead person. You are no less blameworthy (or, if one prefers, no more blameworthy) in *Murder-2* than you are in *Murder-1*, although as Michael Zimmerman (2011: 129–130) cautions, in these sorts of circumstance you may be blameworthy for more things in the one case than in the other. For example, in *Murder-1*, you are blameworthy, among other things, for the attempt to kill and the death, whereas in *Murder-2*, you are not blameworthy for the death.

If we assume that Frankfurt examples are prima facie plausible – at least they give us reason to pause about whether a precondition of blameworthiness is that one have alternatives – then these examples also give us reason to affirm the luck principle. It is not in Augustine's power to influence any of Ernie's activities. If Ernie is not on the scene, as is so in Stage 1, we may assume that Augustine is blameworthy to some degree for stealing the pears. If Ernie is on the scene as is so in Stage 2, Augustine is just as blameworthy for stealing the pears in this stage as he is for stealing them in the former stage. Ernie's presence makes no difference to his degree of blameworthiness because Augustine has no control over Ernie's conduct.

The luck principle may be tightened up in this way:

> *Luck Principle*: If one's doing a certain sort of thing in a certain way, including doing it freely, is sufficient for being blameworthy for doing that thing in that way, then something with respect to which one had no personal control cannot affect one's degree of blameworthiness for doing the sort of thing that one did in the way (including freely) in which one did it.

Understood in this way, it should be clear why the following objection against this principle fails. Imagine that Ernie does in fact force Augustine's hand. Augustine steals only because Ernie manipulates him to steal. Surely, in this case, Augustine would not be blameworthy for stealing the pears, and so something over which Augustine has no control – the activities of Ernie – does affect his degree of blameworthiness for his deed of stealing. Presumably, in a scenario of this sort, manipulation undermines responsibility because it undermines responsibility-level control or freedom. But then in the manipulation scenario Augustine does not do the sort of thing – steal the pears – in the way, *including freely*, in which he did this sort of thing in, for instance, Stages 1 and 2 of the prior Frankfurt example.

Still, one might be reluctant to accept the luck principle because of what one may deem to be an unacceptable implication of it: If the luck principle is true, in cases of a failure to perform an obligation, *A*, when performance was made very difficult by something beyond one's control – an external impediment – that difficulty would not affect the degree to which one was blameworthy for the failure. So difficulties which resulted from factors outside one's control would have no impact on degrees of blameworthiness.

In reply, suppose that, in the absence of the external impediment, you intentionally fail to do *A* and you are blameworthy to a certain degree for this failure.

Ponder a "rerun" of this scenario where, to the extent this is possible, everything is the same as it was in the former scenario save that the external impediment now makes it harder for you to do *A* although it does not preclude you from doing *A*. If you were to do *A*, you would still be blameworthy for doing it in this rerun. Suppose, further, it is claimed that because it would be harder for you now to do *A*, you are *less* blameworthy for not doing *A* than you were for this failure in the initial scenario. It appears that, supposing all other conditions of blameworthiness with the exception of the control condition are not affected, what is assumed is that the fact that it would now be harder for you to do *A* would diminish your (responsibility-level) control in doing *A*. And in virtue of this diminishment, you would be less to blame for failing to do *A*. The problem is that the mere fact that it would be harder to do *A* seems not to moderate your responsibility-level control in doing *A* in the sort of case under consideration. Imagine that there is a degree of control, the "threshold" degree, in doing *A* that is required for you to be morally responsible to some degree for doing *A*. Suppose you do *A* with this degree – degree *tc* – of control with the upshot that you are responsible to degree *g* for doing *A*. Even if some external impediment now makes it more difficult for you to do *A*, but you *can* do *A* with the degree of control that is required for responsibility, what reason is there to believe that your degree of responsibility-level *control* that you exercise in doing *A* is attenuated, is less than *tc*? If, for a first example, this sort of control is (as some would claim) freedom to do otherwise, you can still do otherwise. If, for a second example, the control consists in expressing ill will in one's actions, one can still express ill will even if it is difficult to perform *A*. If, for a third example, the control (as we will discuss later) has essential ties to being responsive to reasons, it would be remarkable if the mere fact that it is now more challenging to do *A* were to affect reasons-responsiveness.

Against the blameworthiness-requires-impermissibility principle, we may argue in this way. Suppose (for *reductio ad absurdum*) this principle (*Blameworthiness/ Impermissibility*) is true. In Stage 1, it is impermissible for Augustine to steal the pears, and he is blameworthy to a certain degree for stealing them. In Stage 2, it is not impermissible for Augustine to steal the pears. If *Blameworthiness/ Impermissibility* is true, then although Augustine is blameworthy for stealing the pears in Stage 1, he is not blameworthy for stealing them in Stage 2. If he is not blameworthy for stealing them in Stage 2, things with respect to which he has no personal control – the presence or absence and the pertinent activities of counterfactual intervener Ernie – *do* have a bearing on his degree of blameworthiness. But this is not as it should be if the luck principle is true. It is false, then, that Augustine is not blameworthy for stealing the pears in Stage 2. As the only relevant difference between Stage 1 and Stage 2 is that in the former but not in the latter it is impermissible for Augustine to steal the pears, it is *Blameworthiness/ Impermissibility* that is at fault.

To summarize, Frankfurt examples oppose the view, which Hodgson would seemingly accept, that persons cannot be blameworthy for what they have done unless they could have done otherwise. I've considered the objection that these examples are not cogent because they violate the principle that blameworthiness requires impermissibility. However, considerations of luck cast suspicion on this principle.

Frankfurt examples still face another problem having to do with guidance control, to which I now turn.

Frankfurt examples and guidance control

Very many theorists who believe that at least some persons are morally responsible for some of their actions, who however otherwise divided on their views regarding the merits (or shortcomings) of libertarianism or compatibilism concur that the Guidance View is on sure footing, agree that responsibility requires that one have the ability to grasp and be guided by good reasons (see, e.g., Kane 1996; Fischer and Ravizza 1998; Hodgson 2012). One prominent elucidation of one component of the Guidance View appeals to the concept of responsiveness to reasons – responsibility presupposes the capacity to recognize and react to reasons.

A pair of examples helps to illustrate the underlying idea of this sort of responsiveness. The first member of the pair is simply Augustine's case minus the counterfactual intervener, Augustine's Stage-1 case. We may suppose that in this stage, a number of instantiations of the following counterfactual schema are true. If there were sufficient reason for Augustine to do otherwise, and he recognized these reasons, he would have done otherwise for these reasons. So, for instance, if his daughter had asked him to aid in an emergency involving his grandson, Augustine would have done so (instead of stealing the pears); if he had been commissioned by the emperor to appease some monks, he would have done so; and so forth. In other words, there is a relatively wide range of scenarios where Augustine would have refrained from stealing in virtue of recognizing and acting on the basis of sufficient reasons not to steal (or to do something other than steal). Or, perhaps, such recognition and response were a necessary or background condition for something else to cause the refraining – a choice or decision which may itself not be completely determined by reasons.

In the second member of the pair, as a result of complex and effective manipulation of which she is totally in the dark, Augusta steals some peaches. Her decision to steal and her subsequent stealing causally issue partly from engineered-in irresistible desires. The details of the case can be filled in to make it clear that she is not responsible for the theft. Some may be tempted to propose that in a case of this sort, responsibility is undermined precisely in virtue of Augusta's inability to have done otherwise. Given the manipulation, she could not have refrained from making the decision to steal and then stealing. A reasons-responsiveness theorist, convinced that alternative possibilities are not required for responsibility (possibly on the basis of Frankfurt examples), will offer an alternative explanation for non-responsibility. Augusta is not aptly responsive to reasons in that even if she were aware of sufficient reasons to do other than steal the peaches, she could not do otherwise on the basis of those reasons. Perhaps under certain extreme conditions – she realizes, for instance, that if she does not refrain from stealing the peaches, her son will be killed – she would act on sufficient reasons to do otherwise. But the range of scenarios where she would have recognized sufficient reasons to refrain from stealing the peaches and would have acted on those reasons is (relatively) constrained in comparison, for example, to the range of scenarios where Augustine (in Stage 1) would have recognized sufficient reasons to refrain from stealing the pears.

In sum, assuming satisfaction of all other requirements of blameworthiness, the element of the Guidance View of interest has it that because Augustine is aptly responsive to a sufficiently wide range of reasons, he is morally responsible – blameworthy – for stealing the pears, but in virtue of not being so responsive, Augusta is not responsible for stealing the peaches.[5] This element of the Guidance View has the following core.

> *Reasons-Responsiveness (The Core)*: Regarding an action (mental or otherwise) of hers, an agent is aptly responsive to reasons only if in a suitably wide range of scenarios where she would have recognized sufficient reasons to refrain from performing that action or to have done otherwise, she would have refrained from performing that action or would have done otherwise on the basis of those reasons.

The Core dovetails well with proposed lessons of Frankfurt examples – that responsibility depends on the actual sequence of events that culminates in action, and the control that responsibility requires is "one-way" control. A fully developed reasons-responsiveness account will work out pertinent details of the Core, such as the appropriate range of reasons to which one must be responsive if one is to be aptly reasons-responsive. However, these details, with the exception of one to be introduced, are of no moment to the general problem that Frankfurt examples supposedly highlight for this core.

It should be relatively straightforward to discern this problem. Revert to Augustine's Stage-2 scenario in which Ernie is on the scene. Imagine that Augustine comes to appreciate that he has sufficient reason to do other than steal the pears; he has sound reason to aid his daughter who calls on him. However, owing to Ernie's presence, Augustine cannot translate this reason into action; his reasons-responsiveness, as specified in the Core, has been hijacked. Since the condition in the Core has apparently not been met, and this condition is necessary for responsibility because its non-satisfaction would reveal that Augustine's action is not relevantly free, contrary to partisans of Frankfurt examples who also accept the Core, Augustine is not morally responsible for stealing the pears in Stage 2. In brief, the gist of the problem is that, assuming reasons-responsiveness

5 Different theorists place different constraints on reasons-responsiveness See, e.g., Fischer and Ravizza, who distinguish among weak, strong, and moderate reasons-responsiveness. I will largely ignore these constraints as they do not affect the discussion to follow. Assuming some such constraints are called for, I acknowledge appeal to these constraints by claiming that the agent is *aptly* responsive to reasons. Laura Ekstrom's and Robert Kane's contributions to this volume outline the importance of reasoning to libertarian free will.

is necessary for responsibility, Frankfurt examples are ineffective counterexamples to PAP because they undermine reasons-responsiveness.

Prima facie, there is something suspect about this putative objection. The fundamental issue it raises is whether an agent, such as Augustine in our example, is sufficiently sensitive to reasons when there is a Frankfurt-type counterfactual intervener on the scene. But if Augustine acts no differently in Stage 2 than he does in Stage 1, and there is no interference in Stage 2, why believe that he is not reasons-responsive in Stage 2 when he is so in Stage 1? We can profitably examine this issue by reminding ourselves of pertinent features of the two stages.

In Stage 1 there is no counterfactual intervener lurking in the wings. Mentally healthy Augustine decides to steal the pears and, on the basis of this decision, steals the pears. His decision is appropriately caused by apt reason states of his. Furthermore, we may duly assume that he is aptly reasons-responsive. Specifically, he is reasons-reactive in that he would have reacted to a suitable range of reasons to do otherwise. Had he had sufficient reasons to do otherwise, he would have recognized these sufficient reasons and would have acted on the basis of them. In this respect, Augustine is different from manipulated Augusta.

In Stage 2, careful not to introduce any *other* changes in Stage 1, Ernie the counterfactual intervener makes his debut. With his mind-reading capacities (or some other mechanism that enables him reliably to predict what Augustine is about to decide to do), his presence in Stage 2 ensures that Augustine could not have done otherwise, or so we are granting. Unaware of Ernie's presence, Augustine conducts himself in Stage 2 in just the way in which he does in Stage 1. We are supposing that in Stage 1 Augustine is aptly reasons-responsive (particularly, he is appropriately reactive to a pertinent range of reasons), and his choice is suitably caused. By design, Ernie does not intervene at all; he does not finagle with Augustine in any way. But then, it seems, he does not in any way affect Augustine's capacity to respond to a range of reasons. Furthermore, no additional factors affect these capacities. It isn't that Augustine's desire to steal the pears magically crystallizes into an irresistible one; Augustine acts from weakness of will; a crazy neuroscientist alters his brain; or so forth. So why believe that Augustine is no longer reasons-responsive in Stage 2?

One might object that I am simply missing a crucial fact. In Stage 2, Ernie guarantees that Augustine cannot do otherwise. Hence, there is ample reason to believe that his reasons-reactive capacity – his capacity to react to sufficient reasons to do otherwise – is detrimentally affected.

However, the vital point still remains: Ernie does *not* intervene. If one thinks non-intervention affects Augustine's capacity to react to sufficient reasons to do otherwise, one ought to provide an apt rationale. Why precisely is this so? What does Ernie do in virtue of which it is reasonable to suppose that this capacity *is* adversely affected?

One may oblige with the following story. Non-intervention from but the mere presence of Ernie makes it the case that Augustine cannot do otherwise. As this is so, non-intervention affects Augustine's capacity to do otherwise then and there in his Frankfurt situation. If this, in turn, is true, there is reason to believe that non-intervention also negatively affects his reasons-reactive capacities that he has in Stage 1. Specifically, in Stage 2 he is no longer reasons-reactive.

However, this rationale is problematic. We understand how a Frankfurt case works; we comprehend how the intervener blocks alternatives. The explanation of why Augustine cannot do otherwise in Stage 2 does not in any way appeal to the intervener's affecting any intrinsic agential properties that, presumably, are the basis or the grounds of the relevant reasons-responsive capacities. Contrary to what unfolds in Stage 2, *should* these properties be tinkered with, there may well be a problem with the capacities that are grounded in these properties.

Still not assuaged, one might press with the following. Suppose an agent is reasons-reactive. Then, in any scenario, if there were a sufficient reason for her to do otherwise, she would do otherwise for those reasons. This is what is entrenched in the Core. Augustine (by stipulation) is reasons-reactive. In Stage 2 of his Frankfurt scenario, there may well be sufficient reason for him to do otherwise. But he cannot do otherwise in this scenario. Isn't this a *big* problem for the Core?

Well, is it? The condition in the Core entails that with respect to an action, if an agent is reasons-responsive, there is a *suitably* wide range of scenarios where she recognizes sufficient reasons to do otherwise and does otherwise for those reasons. The suggestion implicit in the last few paragraphs in response to the allegedly *big* problem is that the suitably wide range of scenarios in which an agent does otherwise on the basis of apt and sufficient reasons to meet the condition that the Core demands excludes Frankfurt-type scenarios, and, moreover, that this exclusion not be arbitrary or *ad hoc*. Frankfurt scenarios may non-arbitrarily be excluded because the relevant agential properties pertinent to reasons-responsiveness – the intrinsic properties that ground the agent's capacities to recognize and react to sufficient reasons to do otherwise – remain wholly intact in Frankfurt scenarios, in contrast, for example, to scenarios (such as Augusta's) that involve responsibility-undermining manipulation.

Here is a partial but nonetheless revealing first stab to test for reasons-responsiveness. We may initially broadly differentiate scenarios in which the agent is not reasons-responsive from those in which she is. Regarding the former, with certain exceptions, if there is *no* suitably wide range of scenarios where the agent has sufficient reason to do otherwise but does not do otherwise for those reasons, she is not reasons-responsive. An exception, for example, would be global Frankfurt cases previously alluded to in which whatever an agent does, she does "on her own", but in which coincidentally she could not have done otherwise because of an ever watchful counterfactual intervener. We may, next, have a mixed bag of cases, some in which the agent has sufficient reasons to do otherwise and does otherwise for those reasons, and others in which the agent has sufficient reason to do otherwise but fails to do otherwise on their basis. Confine attention to the latter and examine why the agent cannot do otherwise in these scenarios. There are a number of possibilities, including the following. (a) Frankfurt-type scenarios or scenarios relevantly like them in that the intrinsic properties that ground the agent's reasons-responsive capacities are intact or unaffected. It is, roughly, "extraneous" factors that prevent the agent from doing otherwise in these scenarios, factors that don't have any effect on the intrinsic grounding properties of these capacities, factors that don't relevantly physically incapacitate the agent or alter her mental constitution, and so on. There is no good reason to believe that the existence of such scenarios precludes reasons-responsiveness. (b) Scenarios in which at the time of or at some time prior to action, the intrinsic properties that ground the agent's capacities to do otherwise have been finagled with so that she is unable to react to sufficient reasons to do otherwise. Manipulation scenarios (such as Augusta's) are scenarios of this sort. Presumably, the agent would not be responsible for what she does in these scenarios. (c) Scenarios in which the intrinsic properties that ground the agent's supposedly reasons-responsiveness capacities have not been finagled with, etc. Still, she is not reasons-reactive; even if there were sufficient reasons to do otherwise, she could not do otherwise for those reasons. In these scenarios, again, she is not reasons-responsive; she lacks the relevant capacities to react to apt sufficient reasons to do otherwise. There may yet be other sorts of scenario in which the agent cannot do otherwise. Some person may have (freely) made herself into the type of character who would not be reactive to reasons to do otherwise in relevant scenarios. Whether such a person would be reasons-responsive is something that need not be dealt with here.

To tie some ends together, I should note that Frankfurt examples do not undermine the condition for reasons-responsiveness laid out in the Core. The germane part of that condition entails that to be aptly reasons-responsive, the agent must be reasons-reactive in a suitably wide range of non-actual scenarios. The apparent problem for the Core under scrutiny is that the pertinent agent (like Augustine) in a Frankfurt scenario cannot react to sufficient reasons to do otherwise, and so contrary to partisans of such examples, Frankfurt examples are not effective counterexamples to PAP. They are not examples in which despite not being able to do otherwise, the agent is morally responsible for what she does. I have argued that there is no reason to deny that the pertinent agent in a Frankfurt scenario is reasons-responsive. The intrinsic properties that ground her reasons-responsive capacities remain intact, unaffected by anything in the scenario. So, such an agent does not violate the condition of reasons-responsiveness embedded in the Core.

From the fat into the fire: Frankfurt examples yet again

Appealing to intrinsic "grounding" properties to meet the objection that Frankfurt examples unseat reasons-responsiveness accounts of the Guidance View may seem to propel me from the fat into the fire. The appeal appears to threaten Frankfurt examples themselves. In Stage 1 Ernie is not on the scene, and Augustine decides to steal the pears. Assume that he could have decided to do something else instead; for example, he could have decided to refrain from stealing. Next, Ernie is introduced, but he is on the sidelines. Although he has the power to interfere, he doesn't exercise this power in Stage 2. The intrinsic properties of Augustine that ground his relevant powers (abilities or capacities), including his powers to deliberate or reason, remain unaffected. Whatever powers supervene on these intrinsic properties, both Stage-1 and Stage-2 Augustine share these very powers because in each stage they retain these properties. Call these powers "I-powers". Since Augustine in either stage has the relevant I-powers, it is false to claim that in Stage 2, he lacks the power or ability to decide to refrain from stealing (Vihvelin 2013: 102–114). Regarding Frankfurt examples, with Jones assuming the role of Augustine and Black the role of counterfactual intervener Ernie, Kadri Vihvelin explains:

> What makes someone a Preemptor is the fact that his intervention is causally triggered, *not* by the subject's beginning to act or try to act contrary to the Preemptor's plan, but by some *earlier event* that is a reliable indicator of the fact that the subject will, in the absence of intervention, perform some action (overt or mental) contrary to the Preemptor's wishes. This earlier event might be a blush, twitch, or other involuntary sign that occurs just before the subject begins to make an unwanted decision or perform an unwanted action.
>
> (2013: 98)

So, for instance, Ernie in our Frankfurt example is a Preemptor. Vihvelin explains:

> So long as a Preemptor Black [or Ernie] does not intervene, Jones is able to choose to do what he likes. It so happens, thanks to the peculiar setup of the case, that Jones is able to choose otherwise only if he chooses what Black wants him to choose. So long as Black does not interfere, Jones is able to choose otherwise, even though he doesn't. He has alternatives even though he does not take them.
>
> (2013: 105)

To be clear, Vihvelin's position is the following:

> Insofar as Black is a Preemptor, he has the *power* to make a difference to the facts about what Jones is able to choose. But since Black does not exercise his power, these facts remain unchanged and Jones remains as free to choose as he was before Black came on the scene.
>
> (2013: 106)

However, Stage-1 Augustine has a power, ability, or capacity that Stage-2 Augustine lacks. In his situation, Stage-1 Augustine can *bring it about* that he decides to do something other than steal the pears, whereas in his Frankfurt situation, Stage-2 Augustine cannot bring it about that he so decides; for example, he cannot bring it about that he decides to refrain from stealing the pears. Barring other problems with Frankfurt examples, or if there are any, assuming they are irrelevant to the objection under scrutiny, there is no scenario in which Ernie is on the scene, he is alert, and Augustine decides to do something other than steal the pears. There is no power whose manifestation is impossible. Should this be disputed, the onus is on one to describe, in relevant detail, such a scenario.

Call the additional power that Stage-1 Augustine has (to bring it about that he decides to do something other than steal) but which Stage-2 Augustine lacks the "bringing about" power. What we should conclude is that the presence of Ernie (and his mind-reading machinery, if he makes use of such machinery) affects Augustine's bringing about powers. Lest this still appear mysterious, maybe we should say that in Stage 2, Augustine cannot exercise his relevant I-powers owing to the presence of Ernie and his mind-reading equipment.

When they insist that responsibility requires freedom to do otherwise, partisans of the principle of alternate possibilities have something like the following in mind. Robert Kane calls choices or actions by which we may form and reform our existing wills (our characters, motives, and purposes) "self-forming actions". He writes:

> They are the actions, I argue, that are required at *some* times in their lifetimes, if agents are to have libertarian free will; and they are the actions that cause the Core Problem for FSEs [Frankfurt-style examples]. For it can be shown that if vicious regresses are to be avoided, two conditions must be satisfied by such will-setting or self-forming actions (SFAs): They must be undetermined by the agent's pre-existing will and the agents must have what I call *plural voluntary control* (PVC) over them. That is, agents must have the power to voluntarily and purposefully perform them and the power to voluntarily and purposefully do otherwise (where "voluntarily" here means that actions are not coerced or compelled and "purposefully" that they are not done merely by accident or mistake, inadvertently or unintentionally). . . . It would not suffice, for example – if these actions are to be "will-setting" and not already "will-settled" – that the agents could voluntarily and purposefully perform them, but could only do otherwise by accident or mistake, inadvertently, involuntarily or unintentionally. If that were the case, agents could never form or *reform* their own wills, for they would always be acting *from a will already formed* and set one way. And having the power to form and reform one's own will is a precondition on my view for having freedom of *will* of the kind required for moral responsibility in a genuine libertarian sense, rather than merely freedom of *action*.
>
> (2013: 61, notes omitted)[6]

Taking our cue from this passage, defenders of PAP should concur that, minimally, if one is to have the control that responsibility requires in performing a certain bodily action or making a choice, *A*, in one's circumstances, in those circumstances one can *bring about* both *A* and some alternative (including the alternative that one refrains from doing *A*). Such a defender would insist that if

6 Also, see Kane's chapter in this volume.

Augustine is responsible for his decision to steal, assuming all other conditions of responsibility are satisfied, it is not merely because he has the I-powers to decide to do otherwise; he must also have the relevant bringing about powers. Or, if one wants, Augustine must also be able to exercise his I-powers in "both directions": He must be able to so act that he brings about his decision to steal (if he brings about this decision) and he brings about some alternative decision (if he brings about this alternative). I doubt, then, whether PAP is to be understood as entailing that an agent is morally responsible for doing *A* (or making decision *A*) only if she can bring about *A* and she has the I-powers to refrain from *A*-ing, when it is borne in mind that one's having the I-powers to refrain from *A*-ing does not entail that (in my terminology) one can bring it about that one refrains from *A*-ing. Vihvelin says that so "long as Black does not interfere, Jones is able to choose otherwise, even though he doesn't. He has alternatives even though he does not take them" (2013: 105). However, again, it is not simply that Augustine does not "take" the alternatives that he has in his Frankfurt situation; it is also true that he cannot bring it about that he makes some decision other than the decision that Ernie wants him to make. PAP presumably is not to be taken as a principle that entails that an agent is morally responsible for making some decision only if she voluntarily and intentionally makes that decision, and she has "alternatives" to this decision, albeit ones she cannot bring about.

In Stage 2 it is false that Augustine can bring it about that he decides to do something other than steal the pears even though he retains the I-powers that he has in Stage 1. But it looks as though he is still responsible for making the decision that he does in Stage 2. If this is indeed so, then PAP is in trouble.

There is an additional concern with Vihvelin's strategy to undermine Frankfurt examples. Some Frankfurt examples have no Preemptors. Here is one such example. Pemba decides on his own to squeeze the trigger at time t_1, and squeezes the trigger at t_1, thereby bringing it about that Rubens is killed by t_2. Assume that his decision to squeeze the trigger is indeterministically caused. In this case, *Murder-1*, a libertarian would presumably agree that, provided all other conditions of moral responsibility are met, Pemba would be morally responsible for his decision and for the state of affairs *Rubens' being killed by* t_2.[7]

Modifying *Murder-1*, imagine that Black implants a mechanism in Pemba that initiates a certain deterministic process – process *p* – in Pemba's brain. Process *p* causes Pemba to arrive at the very decision that he does to squeeze the trigger at the precise time t_1 when he indeterministically decides on his own to squeeze the trigger. So there are two independent causal routes, one indeterministic (Pemba's ordinary practical reasoning) and the other deterministic (the sequence of events triggered by the fancy mechanism), neither influencing the other, but each causally producing the very same event – Pemba's deciding at t_1 to squeeze

7 Here, I set aside concerns of luck. In his chapter in this volume, Neil Levy explains this problem of luck, especially as it arises for Hodgson.

the trigger – in *Murder-2*.[8] The mechanism works in lockstep with Pemba's indeterministic deliberative process – process *d* – between the time at which Pemba starts to deliberate about killing Rubens and time t_1 at which he arrives at his deadly decision. As *p* unfolds, it "neutralizes" neural pathways whose activation is required to allow Pemba to deliberate, at each stage in his deliberations, in ways different from the way in which he does and that would culminate in a decision not to kill Rubens, without affecting what goes on in *d*. For instance, imagine that having reflected on his reasons, at time *t*, Pemba forms the all-things-considered best judgement that he ought to murder Rubens. By *t*, *p* has neutralized neural pathways that would allow Pemba to form a best judgement contrary to the one he forms at *t* without affecting *d*. Borrowing a card from Alfred Mele and David Robb's Frankfurt case (1998: 104–105), by t_1, *p* has neutralized all of the "nodes" in Pemba for decisions that are contrary to a decision at t_1 to kill Rubens but without influencing what goes on in process *d*. If this still allows for "divergences" in the two processes in that Pemba's reasoning favours the decision not to kill Rubens, process *p* prevails; *p* trumps indeterministic process *d*.[9] In addition, I see no reason why *Murder-2* cannot be aptly adjusted to reproduce Hodgson's picture of plausible reasoning in which apt responses to conscious gestalts indeterministically influence decision.[10] Simply suppose, first, that Pemba does so respond to such gestalts in *Murder-1*, and, second, in *Murder-2*, Pemba again responds to these gestalts "on his own" in exactly the way in which he does in *Murder-1*. It's just that, in *Murder-2*, process *p* blocks alternative responses without interfering in the responses that Pemba actually makes.

Determinism's (or process *p*'s) elimination of Pemba's alternative possibilities does not in any way influence how Pemba's decision is caused by the indeterministic causal pathway. As this is so, determinism's elimination of Pemba's alternative possibilities cannot, it seems, bear on the issue of Pemba's moral responsibility.[11]

In conclusion, while I disagree with Hodgson about PAP – I don't think responsibility requires that we have alternatives – I join him in accepting the Guidance View. Frankfurt examples motivate rejection of PAP without standing in opposition to a proposed central element of the Guidance View that responsibility requires our being suitably responsive to reasons.[12]

8 Compare this case with Mele and Robb's (1998, 2003). In Mele and Robb's case, process *p* will cause the relevant agent to make the germane decision unless the agent makes this decision on her own.

9 Fischer (2010) has also developed Frankfurt examples that feature determinism.

10 Hodgson suggests that, in making decisions, "persons respond appositely to gestalt experiences that are too feature-rich to engage as wholes with laws of nature and generally do not engage with computational rules, so that the response is not determined by laws or rules of any kind" (2012: 153. See, also 2012: 79–85).

11 Mele and Robb (1998, 2003) also develop a dual pathway example in which deterministic process *p* will cause the relevant agent (like Pemba) to make the apt decision under all conditions save the one in which Pemba makes this decision on his own. This sort of example that involves "trumping" is also free of Preemptors.

12 Many thanks, indeed, to Allan McCay and Michael Sevel for their very kind invitation to contribute to this volume and for their comments and suggestions.

References

Campbell, JK 2011, *Free Will*, Polity Press, Oxford.

Copp, D 1997, 'Defending the Principle of Alternate Possibilities: Blameworthiness and Moral Responsibility', *Nous* 31: 441–456.

Copp, D 2003, '"Ought" Implies "Can", Blameworthiness, and the Principle of Alternative Possibilities', in D Widerker and M McKenna (eds), *Moral Responsibility and Alternative Possibilities: Essays on the Importance of Alternative Possibilities*, Ashgate Press, Aldershot.

Feldman, F 1986, *Doing The Best We Can*, D. Reidel Publishing, Dordrecht.

Fischer, JM 2006, *My Way: Essays on Moral Responsibility*, Oxford University Press, New York.

Fischer, JM 2010, 'The Frankfurt Cases: The Moral of the Stories', *The Philosophical Review* 119: 315–336.

Fischer, JM 2013, 'The Frankfurt-Style Cases: Philosophical Lightning Rods', in I Haji and J Caouette (eds), *Free Will and Moral Responsibility*, Cambridge Scholars Publishing, Newcastle upon Tyne.

Fischer, JM and Ravizza, M 1998, *Responsibility and Control: A Theory of Moral Responsibility*, Cambridge University Press, Cambridge.

Frankfurt, H 1969, 'Alternate Possibilities and Moral Responsibility', *The Journal of Philosophy* 66: 829–839.

Haji, I 1998, *Moral Appraisability: Puzzles, Proposals, and Perplexities*, Oxford University Press, New York.

Haji, I 2002, *Deontic Morality and Control*, Cambridge University Press, Cambridge.

Haji, I 2011, 'Obligation, Reason, and Frankfurt Examples', in R Kane (ed), *The Oxford Handbook of Free Will*, 2nd edn, Oxford University Press, New York.

Haji, I 2012a, *Reason's Debt to Freedom*, Oxford University Press, New York.

Haji, I 2012b, 'Modest Libertarianism and Practical Reason', *Philosophical Issues* 22: 201–216.

Haji, I 2016, *Luck's Mischief: Blameworthiness and obligation on a Thread*, Oxford University Press, New York.

Hodgson, DH 2000, 'Guilty Mind or Guilty Brain? Criminal Responsibility in the Age of Neuroscience', *The Australian Law Journal* 74: 661–680.

Hodgson, DH 2005, 'Responsibility and Good Reasons', *Ohio State Journal of Criminal Law* 2.2: 471–483.

Hodgson, DH 2012, *Rationality + Consciousness = Free Will*, Oxford University Press, Oxford.

Kane, R 1996, *The Significance of Free Will*, Oxford University Press, New York.

Kane, R 2013, 'Frankfurt-style Examples and Self-forming Actions', in I Haji and J Caouette (eds), *Free Will and Moral Responsibility*, Cambridge Scholars Publishing, Newcastle upon Tyne.

Mele, A 2006, *Free Will and Luck*, Oxford University Press, New York.

Mele, A and Robb, D 1998, 'Rescuing Frankfurt-Style Cases', *Philosophical Review* 107: 97–112.

Pereboom, D 2003, 'Source Incompatibilism and Alternative Possibilities', in M McKenna and D Widerker (eds), *Freedom, Responsibility, and Agency: Essays on the Importance of Alternative Possibilities*, Ashgate Press, Aldershot.

Pereboom, D 2014, *Free Will, Agency, and Meaning in Life*, Oxford University Press, New York.

Strawson, G 1986, *Freedom and Belief*, Oxford University Press, Oxford.
Strawson, G 1994, 'The Impossibility of Moral Responsibility', *Philosophical Studies* 75: 5–24.
van Inwagen, P 2008, 'How to Think About the Problem of Free Will', *The Journal of Ethics* 12: 327–341.
Vihvelin, K 2013, *Causes, Laws, and Free Will*, Oxford University Press, New York.
Widerker, D 1991, 'Frankfurt on "Ought Implies Can" and Alternative Possibilities', *Analysis* 51: 222–224.
Zimmerman, MJ 1996, *The Concept of Moral Obligation*, Cambridge University Press, Cambridge.
Zimmerman, MJ 2011, *The Immorality of Punishment*, Broadview Press, Peterborough.

Part II

Libertarian free will and the law

7 How judges are free to decide cases

Michael Sevel

Most philosophers of law since Plato have speculated in some way about the nature of free will, and its consequences for the administration of law, indeed for the very possibility of legal governance (Bourke 1964). But they have commonly approached these issues through a rather narrow lens: from the point of view of an individual citizen, and as they bear on the law's regulation of their conduct, and for whom, it is supposed, the law establishes an array of rights, permissions, and obligations. The focus is often narrower still. Philosophers have for the most part been preoccupied with questions about the freedom of persons who must live under a body of *penal* law, that is, law which is meant to guide conduct by the establishment of a range of offences, and which includes standards for the imposition of punishment, such that those who commit those offences will be subject to sanction according to those standards. One familiar line of thought related to free will is this. If persons rarely make free choices or, worse, if free will itself is an illusion and all actions are but the inevitable consequences of antecedent events, then the practice of judging persons morally responsible for their actions, which presumes the freedom to do otherwise, would lack adequate foundation. Consequently, attributions of legal guilt or innocence, which are at least partly based on such practices and judgements, would also no longer make sense under a body of criminal law, and any system of punishment which coerces citizens on the grounds of such attributions would be unjust, or at the very least pointless. This recurring preoccupation with questions of free will for the purpose of developing theories of criminal responsibility and punishment is not merely a matter of history; it remains the dominant approach in discussions among writers working at the intersection of free will and legal philosophy.[1]

While there may be sound historical and pragmatic reasons for the persistent focus on only the free will of citizens subject to a regime of criminal law, a moment's reflection suggests that this choice is theoretically arbitrary. Whether and how humans are capable of free choice bears equally on how to understand

1 Examples of this trend can be found in these recent collections of essays: Freeman (2011), Pardo and Patterson (2013), Vincent (2013), and Nadlehoffer (2013). An illuminating history of this trend in Anglophone legal philosophy over the last century can be found in Green (2014).

and evaluate both the governance of law that is not punitive, as well as the freedom and responsibility of other participants in a legal system besides would-be offenders, such as various officials whose conduct and decisions are essential to the functioning of primary legal institutions. And so, for example, little attention has been paid to the question of whether *judges* are free, and therefore responsible, both in imposing punishments on offenders and in acting across the standard range of other rule-governed, adjudicative contexts. Nor have the consequences of the possible answers to those questions been considered for general theories (both conceptual and normative) of law and adjudication.

The neglect is unfortunate, since questions about the freedom and responsibility of judges are at least as significant as ones about that of criminal defendants. After all, if in fact judges are not free, and so fully determined, to reason and decide as they do – from ordering injunctions, to imposing sentences on criminal defendants, to deciding "hard cases" – then the issue of whether a person facing punishment for committing an offence was free or not to commit it would be, at best, of secondary significance. In that case, too, it would make little sense to attempt to hold judges to account for their decisions, since they would be unable to decide other than they do. By contrast, if judicial decision was not determined at all by antecedent events, such that their decisions occur at random, we would be faced with a different problem. If one purpose of law is, as is often said, the administration of justice, and insofar as justice involves a sort of regularity, perhaps in the form of judges "treating like cases alike" (Rawls 1999: 206–213; Hart 2012: 155–167), then in an indeterministic universe, judging in the pursuit of justice would be impossible or, at least, a matter of chance.

My primary concern here will therefore be with the question of judicial freedom, and to examine several prominent views which address, implicitly or explicitly, whether (and how) judges are free to decide cases.[2] A selective survey of some of the major movements in the theory of adjudication over the last century in Anglophone legal philosophy shows an equivocal, undisciplined, and perhaps at times unwitting engagement with the issue. For example, scholarly discussions of the legal formalism of the late nineteenth and early twentieth century standardly integrate the language of compulsion and necessity to express its core idea: that legal rules fully "determine" judicial decision, and function in the minds of judges as so many "chains" or "fetters", that judges must apply such rules "mechanically", and so on. Such claims seem to suggest that judges can*not* decide otherwise than they do in particular cases; the legal sources somehow render judges unfree. The American legal realists famously responded that law does not compel judges, at least not to that extent, and that the actual causes of judicial decisions lie mostly outside the law. Most of the realists, nonetheless, maintain that a full and complete causal explanation of the decisions of judges

2 I will follow many writers in legal philosophy by focusing on rendering final judgements in cases as paradigm judicial acts, though the discussion easily extends to other examples, e.g., granting or denying a motion during a court proceeding, or, in courts with discretionary review, deciding whether to accept a case on appeal.

in particular cases is in principle attainable, and, further, that knowledge of the factors referenced in that explanation would help interested observers of judges better predict those decisions.

While these claims may appear to require substantial assumptions about the free will of judges, I will conclude, in the next two sections, that most realists, as well as the many writers on formalism, have largely left open the question of whether and how judges are free. Despite their rhetoric, these writers have been inattentive to even the most basic distinctions often made by theorists of free will. This brief survey will, however, serve as a useful propaedeutic for examining the theory of free will recently developed by David Hodgson (2012, 1991: 379–464). Hodgson's theory is especially interesting in the context of formalism and realism, and of judicial freedom more generally, for a number of reasons. First, from a historical perspective, the context in which his views were developed is novel. Like several of the American legal realists, Hodgson was a lifelong legal practitioner. And like two notable realists, Jerome Frank and William O. Douglas, Hodgson was also an appellate judge, having served as a judge on the Supreme Court of New South Wales, Australia, for nearly thirty years. Unlike his realist judicial counterparts, however, he was a trained philosopher as well, having completed a DPhil at Oxford supervised by H. L. A. Hart alongside other students, such as John Finnis and Joseph Raz, who would themselves become influential philosophers of law.[3] Second, like Frank (Leiter 2005: 51), Hodgson never held an academic appointment, yet over the course of his career on the bench produced a substantial corpus of theoretical writings.[4] Finally, Hodgson's relevant published writings (approaching a thousand pages) also constitute a very rare case in the history of philosophy, in which a sitting judge has developed systematic, philosophically sophisticated views about the nature of free will. In fact, Hodgson's theory is the first such discussion of free will from the bench since that of Henry Home, Lord Kames, a judge on the Court of Session (Scotland's supreme civil court) and an important figure in the Scottish Enlightenment, who published his *Essays on the Principles of Morality and Natural Religion* in 1751 (Haakonssen 2005).[5] And just as with Kames (Harris 2005: 103–106), Hodgson's philosophical views are also informed by his experiences of deliberating in the course of resolving disputes brought before him in his capacity as judge.

In addition to this novel context, Hodgson's substantive views are also distinctive. Hodgson argues for a kind of libertarianism about free will, according to which practical choices are controlled by the chooser yet not completely determined by the operation of the laws of nature.[6] These undetermined choices he

3 See the Introduction to this volume for discussion of Hodgson's legal career.

4 Douglas, before being appointed to the United States Supreme Court in 1939, was for a brief period a professor at Yale Law School (Kalman 1986).

5 While Kames took up his judicial appointment a year after publishing the *Essays*, he made substantial revisions in its subsequent editions while serving on the Court (Haakonssen 2005: xiv–xvii).

6 See Robert Kane, "Making sense of libertarian free will: consciousness, science, and laws of nature", Chapter 2 of this volume, for further discussion.

contextualizes within a theory of what he calls "plausible reasoning". He did not, however, fully draw out the consequences of his views for an account of how judges decide cases, though some of his remarks, as well as his occasional use of judicial examples, are suggestive. The view of judicial freedom that emerges from Hodgson's libertarianism, which I sketch out in the fourth section, suggests interesting contrasts and comparisons with certain realist and formalist themes. After drawing out those points of comparison, I conclude that, because he clearly develops his general theory of free will with many features of judicial reasoning in mind, that theory can be usefully adapted and understood as not only a novel view in the history of legal philosophy of judicial freedom, but also, and to that extent, a theory of judicial reasoning and adjudication. The view prompts us to ask new questions of old theories, which I now consider.

Legal forms and judicial freedom

I begin with legal formalism, an allegedly popular view among lawyers and legal academics throughout the common law world in the nineteenth and early twentieth century, and which was influential for even longer in Continental Europe (Tamanaha 2010; Schauer 1988). Formalism is often said to be a set of mutually supportive claims about the nature of both law and adjudication. Law, on this view, is an autonomous, rationally ordered system of principles, structured as an axiomatic system with a small number of foundational abstract concepts and principles, such that the principles and rules applying to concrete cases are derivable deductively from the more general and abstract ones. The contents of a legal system are constructed by logical inference out of these strictly legal materials and so without reference to, say, moral considerations, or the social or political contexts in which the legal materials were made or given legal effect. The law is accordingly comprehensive and complete, and thus sufficient to yield unique and determinate results in each and every case brought before a court. This determinacy and uniqueness is partly explained and reinforced by how judges decide cases according to law thus understood. It is judges who derive the unique and determinate answers to cases before them by way of formal and deductive methods of reasoning from abstract principle to particularized legal decisions.

Notice that on this view, because their decisions are logically derivable from strictly legal materials, judges do not, and in fact cannot, exercise *discretion* in any meaningful sense. Legal reasoning appears akin to mathematical reasoning, in that its steps are explicit and each is strictly governed by an *a priori* principle of inference. As a result, the decisions of judges, insofar as those judges are generally competent, rational, and conscientious, are perfectly predictable; that is, if one could know all the contents of the legal materials relevant to a case, as well as what deductively followed from those materials given the facts of the case, then how a judge is to decide the case could be reliably, indeed infallibly, predicted. Formalism is referred to, often disparagingly, as "mechanical jurisprudence" (Pound 1908), because, if true, it would leave no room for any recognizable form of *judging* at all. Deciding a case would be a matter of identifying logical relations between the more or less abstract legal rules and principles, and the relations between those materials as applied to facts, all of which invariably yields a unique, and uniquely correct, disposition of the case.

This picture of adjudication invites the question of whether it requires any assumptions about the metaphysical freedom of judges: for example, the assumption that they lack it, or have it only in some limited sense. The issue becomes more urgent given that, in addition to the familiar label of "mechanical jurisprudence", the language which scholars have often used to express the basic tenets of formalism seems to suggest a strong form of determinism in regard to the free will of judges in deciding cases. That is, discussions of formalism appear to imply that, invariably, the judges cannot, in a metaphysically significant sense, do otherwise than they do in deciding cases; their decisions are fully determined by antecedent, and specifically legal, causes. And so formalism casts judges as "calculating machine[s]" (Posner 1993: 21), as "will-less" (Sebok 1998: 53), as "tied down on every side by rules of law" (Pound 1913: 710), and as "simple automata" (Gilmore 1977: 77). A central premise of formalism is the "ascription of responsibility [for decisions] elsewhere" than to the judge (Sebok 1998: 50); formalism, it is said, "reduce[s] adjudication to a mechanical task, thereby . . . fully eliminating freedom in judicial decision" (Lind 1993: 166). Now, one could easily imagine a *philosopher* using just such phrases to express a view, sometimes called "hard determinism", according to which free will simply does not exist: that it is an illusion or a myth (Smilansky 2000). But is formalism necessarily committed to such a view in regard to the freedom of judges, i.e., that they lack, in a strong, metaphysical sense, free will to decide as they do?

If the matter is properly understood, and despite appearances, it is doubtful that formalists so claim. More philosophically sensitive discussions of formalism present it as committed to either the *descriptive* claim that judges respond primarily to the rational demands of applicable legal rules, or the *normative* claim that judges *ought* to decide cases only in accordance with strictly legal sources, that is, that judges ought to appeal only to legal reasons to justify their decisions. Sometimes both claims are included in traditional versions of formalism (Schauer 1988; Leiter 2007: 23–25). Even so, most views about the nature of free will are compatible with each of them. The descriptive claim could be true whether or not judges have free will. And in regard to the normative claim, despite the hyperbole of judges being "automata" when constrained by law, formalists seem to make just the opposite assumption. That is, they seem committed to the view that judges *are* genuinely free to choose how to decide cases; however *if* they wish to decide a case properly, then they will choose to engage in, and thereby be constrained by, formal, deductive forms of reasoning using the reasons only the law provides. The normative view is thus more plausibly construed as the claim that judges *ought* to decide cases formalistically, and, since "ought" (generally) implies "can", then formalists assume that judges *can* do otherwise than they do in deciding cases. And all but deeply sceptical theories of free will can make sense of the idea that judges are free to do otherwise than they do in this sense. The language of compulsion and necessity often used to express formalism references at most *logical*, and so not metaphysical, necessity; that is, that judges are bound to adhere to the valid principles of logical inference in deciding cases, insofar as they are rational. Legal formalism, therefore, is not committed to any view of the nature of judicial freedom, at least in the sense that interests philosophers of free will.

Legal realism[7]

I turn now to consider the multifaceted twentieth century movement of American legal realism. Much has been written in recent years attempting to identify and evaluating its central claims and themes.[8] Luckily, we can sidestep these lively interpretive debates, for the most part, by focusing on a limited set of realist ideas. In its critical aspects, the central task of legal realism is usually taken as the refutation of formalism, as a descriptive account of how judges decide cases. For this very reason, and given the conclusion of the previous section, one might think from the outset that, just as the core claims of formalism do not require any particular assumptions about the free will of judges, realism is likewise agnostic about whether judges are free and, if so, in what sense and to what extent. It may be thought, that is, that formalism and realism are equally compatible with virtually any position one might take in the free will debates.

However, in their more constructive mode, there is a persistent, and more than superficial, concern among realist writers with aspects of judicial decisions – their causes, predictability, and efficacy – which more directly prompts questions about what view (or views) of judicial freedom, if any, they require in making claims about how and why judges decide cases. The various claims of the realists who suggested that the (deterministic) methodology of the then-nascent social sciences should be extended to jurisprudence, the so-called sociological wing of legal realism (Leiter 2007: 28–29), are of particular interest, given the traditional concern among theorists of free will about the significance of adopting the modern scientific worldview for the very possibility of free choice (Kane 2005). Despite the recent explosion of scholarly interest in American legal realism, the relations between its core claims and substantive positions about the free will of judges have not been explored, and are potentially more illuminating and suggestive for the future development of realist ideas than in the case of formalism.

The relevant concerns are evident from the very beginning of the realist tradition. Oliver Wendell Holmes, an inspiration for the realists in both their critical and positive modes, famously advised law students (1897) that the key to a successful career in the law is to always view the law from the perspective of their client. By this, he did not mean the point of view of their actual future clients, nor

7 I thank David Frydrych, Brian Leiter, and Kevin Walton for discussion of the issues in this section.

8 Helpful recent studies of American legal realism can be found in Schauer (2013), Postema (2011: 79–140), Leiter (2007), Duxbury (1995).

did he mean the ideal client as good citizen, but rather the *bad person*, "who cares only for the material consequences of his actions and who wishes 'to avoid an encounter with the public force'" (Holmes 1897: 457). From this (he thought) theoretically privileged point of view, Holmes claims that the law is nothing more than a matter of "predictions of the incidence of the public force through the instrumentality of the courts" (1897: 457). Holmes then remarks, almost in passing, that "the prophecies of what the courts will do in fact, and nothing more pretentious, are what I mean by the law" (1897: 461). We can set aside the many ambiguities in and obvious objections to these claims, and ask instead whether Holmes is committed to any view about whether judges are free to do what they do when deciding causes, or whether, on his view, ascertaining reliable predictions of judicial behaviour implies that judges are fully determined to decide as they do. In other contexts, he seems to accept the common sense view that people (presumably including judges) do indeed have free will. For example, he speaks freely of the policy "to give a man a fair chance to avoid" liability in tort (1881: 144) and whether someone acts as "a free person and himself responsible" (1921: 51). He even writes of the central importance in the law of "freedom of the will" in the sense used by Kant and Hegel (Holmes 1881: 206–207). Such remarks may imply a kind of compatibilism about free will, one which would become the default position in legal theory in the twentieth century. Holmes, however, was generally disinterested in substantive philosophical theories and how they may apply in the context of the law or legal philosophy (Postema 2011: 47), and was otherwise circumspect about how any view on free will related to the "prophecies of what the courts will do in fact".[9]

Following Holmes, many of the writers most associated with realism became more focused in regard to both their objections to formalism and their proposals to enhance jurisprudential enquiries about judicial behaviour with methods from the social sciences. Many of these theorists thought that when one takes a hard look at what judges actually do when they decide cases, it was quite clear they were not deductively and demonstratively applying a complete and comprehensive set of legal rules and principles – even if on occasion judges claimed and took themselves to be doing just that. Instead, realists were united in the idea that, as the realist Hermann Oliphant succinctly puts it, "courts respond to the stimulus of the facts in the concrete cases before them rather than to the stimulus of over-general and outworn abstractions in opinions and treatises" (1928: 75). A complementary view among the realists was that the ostensible justifications given for decisions in particular cases – for example, the lines of reasoning we find in the judicial opinions that make up the common law – are not only invariably *ad hoc*, but also *post hoc*, essentially rationalizations constructed in support of the initial "response to the stimulus of the facts". A judge has a response to the facts and then sets about to find acceptable legal or political arguments to acceptably justify it. Judicial reasoning was argument *from* the conclusion, not *to* it (Radin

9 See, however, Green (2014: 39 n14), who argues that Holmes was a sceptic about free will.

1925: 359). The purported *ratio* of a case was, the realists said, nothing more than "judicial window dressing" (Postema 2011: 118). The whole foundation of the workings of the courts is, as realists put it, judicial "hunches" (Hutcheson 1929; Cohen 1935) or a "situation sense", developed and conditioned by legal training, of the proper resolution of cases (Llewellyn 1951). Argument from precedent might be the vehicle, but these hunches are the engine, of what the courts do in fact.

Many realists thought that these "hunches" that judges have about how to resolve a dispute conformed to certain patterns, and that these patterns were discoverable and in fact useful to ordinary citizens, and particularly to the lawyers arguing in their courts. The core of the realists' positive research programme, which many of them thought should proceed according to the empirical methodologies of the social sciences and behaviourist psychology, was to develop explanations of judicial decisions by identifying the sets of sufficient causal factors which determine those decisions, what Jerome Frank called the "hunch-producers" (1930 112–113). For present purposes, we can distinguish two sorts of accounts that realists gave of such factors. First, those who gave an "externalist" account identified the causally efficacious factors that lie *outside* the mind of the judge, usually norms or practices that are not, or not a part of, strictly legal rules or principles.[10] Felix Cohen, for example, claimed that a judicial decision is "a product of social determinants and an index of social consequences. A judicial decision is a social event" and that "only by probing behind the decision to the forces which it reflects, or projecting beyond the decision the lines of its force upon the future, do we come to an understanding of the meaning of the decision itself" (1935: 843). Discovering such forces would involve investigating "human psychology, economics and politics" (1935: 844). So, for example, prevailing political norms of deregulation or protection of traditional marital rights might be essential parts of an explanation of a decision. Realists such as Llewellyn (1960) and Oliphant (1928) adduced examples of judicial decisions which, they claimed, showed that the efficacious causal factors which explain those decisions were really certain "background facts, those of mercantile practice" (Llewellyn 1960: 126). That is, norms practiced and accepted by a sufficient number of commercial actors in the industry in which a particular dispute arose often could be shown to have had a determinative effect on a judge's "hunches" and subsequent reasoning in a given case. Similarly, norms of conventional or individual morality may have a similar effect on the judge's reasoning, and the hunch on which it based (Radin 1925).[11]

The second, "internalist" sort of proposed account of the causes of judicial decision makes essential reference to causal factors *within* the mind of the

10 Some realists, like Frank (1930: 290), concede that legal rules are in many cases explanatorily relevant to understanding particular judicial decisions, though incomplete in and of themselves.

11 See Frank (1930: 113 n5) for an even longer list of realist speculations about the causal antecedents of judicial hunches.

judge. Edward Levi (1949), for example, recommends that decisions are best explained by reference to a judge's adoption of a set of professional norms governing the structure, relevance, and disciplined construction of legal arguments. Oliphant suggests (1928: 160–161) that the intuitions of judges shaped by their experience of "social reality", rather than (aspects of) the reality itself, should serve as the primary explanans: "Individual temperament and our self-interest cause us, in the most subjective fashion, to select from the totality of our experience that which satisfies our temperament, and fortifies our interests" (1928: 161).

One proponent of this second kind of account deserves special mention. Jerome Frank, an American federal appellate judge, diverged from his realist colleagues by focusing attention primarily on the idiosyncrasies of judges' personality to explain the outcomes of cases. It was the "peculiar traits, dispositions, biases, and habits of the particular judge" (1930: 119) that were more often the underlying causes of decision, independently of legal rules, political affiliations, commercial norms, or moral conventions. Frank's view has often been expressed by the crude idea that how a judge decides a case is a function of what the judge had for breakfast that morning (Dworkin 1986: 36). However, the view is more sophisticated than that. Frank started writing in the late 1920s when Freud's theory of the mind was all the rage, which famously emphasizes the role of unconscious drives in both thought and action. Frank, inspired by this theory, thought that what best explained judicial decisions were the hidden, unconscious drives within a judge's mind, as shaped by that judge's childhood experiences and developmental history. To know the hunch-producers of any particular judge we would therefore need to know intimate details of her personality and psychological profile as borne out by extensive psychoanalytic investigation.

But on Frank's view, even knowing a judge's complex psychology is not enough to make reliable predictions as to how that judge will decide a case. One must also know the facts of the case, sets of facts that are always unique. Ex ante claims about a judicial outcome are then really about how a judge with such a psychology will engage with such facts to produce the all-important "hunch". But if the daunting complexity of the personalities of individual judges is then multiplied by the radical uniqueness of sets of facts which they are asked to assess, we are lead, Frank argued, to the conclusion that judicial behaviour is after all *not* predictable. The complexities and idiosyncrasies of a particular judge's psychology, combined with the infinitely variable sets of facts that make up a particular case, make it impossible to know precisely how a judge will decide a case, much less how the judge will justify the decision. What a judge will do when presented with a unique set of facts governed by a particular legal regime is thus necessarily shrouded in mystery, except perhaps to a virtuoso and omniscient psychoanalyst. In this way Frank ran counter to the realist tradition: He agreed that the law mostly does not determine cases, but nor do social, political, moral, or other extra-legal factors amenable to study by the social sciences. Reliable predictions of judicial decision *would* be based on the idiosyncrasies of the judge's personality combined with the facts of the case, but the inherent complexity of it all makes these predictions ultimately out of our cognitive reach (Frank 1930: 113–125).[12]

What, if anything, do these views imply about the nature and extent of the free will of judges? Unlike the case with discussions of formalism, realists do not routinely invoke hyperbolic metaphors of judicial freedom or constraint, at least when pursuing their positive research programme. Their views, however, are not as easily dismissed as ones entirely unrelated to positions within the free will debates. These otherwise diverse views are unified in a general purpose, indeed the very purpose inherited from Holmes, at once theoretical and practical: to develop a framework sufficient to ground accurate, or at least reliable, predictions about how judges will decide cases. These writers therefore assume that judicial behaviour is predictable, and it may be thought that on that basis realists assume that such behaviour is to be understood deterministically and is therefore unfree. That is, predictability requires the assumption that the causal factors which explain judicial decisions, whether external or internal to the judge's mind, completely determine particular decisions in a way that is not subject to the control of the judge.

However, it has long been recognized that the mere fact of reliable predictability of the behaviour of a person does not entail that that person does not act freely. For example, we may know intimately the motivations and dispositions of a close friend, such that we may be able to accurately predict things such as what meal she will have or who she will marry, and yet it be the case that the friend chooses freely (Flew 1969). Thus, insofar as realists assume a connection between their causal explanations and improvements in the predictability of judicial decisions, then it remains that no particular position in the free will debates follows.

One substantive, albeit negative, connection between realism and commitments about judicial freedom is, perhaps, the following. If the "externalist" causal explanations of judicial decisions – citing factors independent of the judge's mind such as social, political, and commercial norms – are put forth as in themselves complete and sufficient, then that would seem to rule out giving certain other kinds of explanation of the freedom of the judge. For example, certain incompatibilist accounts of free will, which require that the efficacious factors producing the action be within the agent, seem incompatible with such purely "external" explanations of the judicial decisions. More precisely, agent-causal libertarian explanations (O'Connor 2011; Palmer 2014) appear to be strictly incompatible with such realist accounts. But as is often the case, the realists' stated positions are not sufficiently precise to pass such categorical judgements on the issue.

12 For example, Frank notes that the relevant aspects of a judge's personality are "innumerable" (1930: 119) and that "no one can know in advance what a judge will believe to be the 'facts' of a case" (1930: 125). In addition to these claims, Frank advocated for judicial discipline to *bring about* uniformity in how judges decide cases, so that they would be more predictable (1930: 35–41). This would seem to suggest that a judge has *control* over her responses to the facts, and so control over the ultimate disposition of the case. Judges would then seem to have free will in some non-trivial sense. Frank, however, never explained how this view is consistent with those described earlier.

There is a related lack of clarity in regard to "internalist" accounts such as those of Frank and Levi. While both can be interpreted as consistent with indeterminist, agent-causal theories of freedom, Frank often oscillates between implying determinist and implying indeterminist positions. At times, he maintains that study of the psychological profiles of particular judges will yield more reliable predictions about what those judges will do, because the relevant psychological factors fully determine their actions (e.g., Frank 1963: 281–282). At others, he seems to suggest that such factors exhibit a complexity and elusiveness that render their efficacy mysterious, and perhaps for that reason not fully determinative of action.[13] We will return to Frank's views in a moment, after consideration of David Hodgson's theory of free will and how it may explain the freedom of judges.

Hodgson on libertarian free will

While David Hodgson was, like Frank, an appeals court judge for many years, his philosophical interests were, unlike those of Frank and the realists, not primarily in the nature of adjudication or the reliable prediction of judicial decisions, but rather in traditional questions of free will. Indeed, in interpreting Hodgson's views, we confront the opposite problem as encountered earlier in understanding the realists; that is, we must speculate about how his developed libertarian theory of free will may imply or suggest a view about the free will of judges and judicial reasoning that can fruitfully be compared with the formalist and realist views already discussed.

Hodgson was well aware of recent advances in neuroscience over the last couple of decades (2012: 133–142), but was sceptical that those advances show, or could show, that human choice was wholly determined by "highly complex brain activity" (2012: 133). He thought that those advances, though important and illuminating, left room for an incompatibilist, libertarian kind of free will. As he was a practicing judge, it is perhaps surprising that he never extends his theory of free will to an account of how judges are free to decide cases, though his occasional use of the example of judicial reasoning to explain and illustrate the theory (e.g., 2012: 34–35, 38, 71) is suggestive of the contours of such an account. After briefly explaining his general libertarian theory, I will apply it in the context of judicial decision-making, and then make some observations about how the theory can be understood as a novel contribution to the theory of adjudication.

There are two interrelated claims that form the foundation of Hodgson's libertarian theory of free will. One is that we have conscious experiences, which he takes, in a Cartesian spirit, as virtually undeniable (2012: 10–14). The other is that minds with the capacity for conscious experiences characteristically engage in what he calls "plausible reasoning" to make decisions about what to believe and do (2012: 37–40). Every type of formalized and deductive reasoning depends on such reasoning, though it is itself not completely formalizable (2012: 45–47). His

13 Cf. Robert Kane's application of chaos theory to explain indeterministic neural processes (1999: 128–130).

account of plausible reasoning is intended as an explanation of the role of consciousness in the occurrence of such reasoning, and at the same time an account of how both conscious reasoning and its outputs – choices or decisions – are not completely determined by antecedent events, and for that reason are done or made freely.

The relevant features of conscious, plausible reasoning for our purposes are that such reasoning is *rational*, *non-random*, and yet *indeterministic* (2012: 69–75) Plausible reasoning is *rational* in that it involves the recognition and response to reasons, in the sense familiar to moral philosophers (Skorupski 2010: 35–56). There are features of the world (including ourselves, our character, dispositions, and so on) which we can and do recognize as normatively significant, as considerations counting in favour of or counting against doing and believing things, such that we can appreciate that significance in our reasoning and reflect that appreciation in our actions and attitudes. Plausible reasoning is *non-random* in the sense that the alternative courses of action, constituted and structured by those reasons, open to us in a given circumstance of practical choice are themselves determined by a set of natural laws operating to cause the physical and psychological circumstances in which we reason and act. Thus, which career options are open to a person at a given moment of her life, whether to buy a banana or pear at the market, or whether to go to New York by car or train, and so on are all menus of practical options which themselves can be explained deterministically by reference to physical (and psycho-physical) laws. Nonetheless, Hodgson argues that *how* we respond to such options so constituted, that is, how we reach the particular outcomes of plausible reasoning (beliefs, decisions, and the actions that execute them), is *not* determined by such laws.

Hodgson argues that the (indeterministic) freedom exhibited in our responses to rational options in plausible reasoning is explained by the (again, indeterministic) role of a specific type of experience, what he calls "feature-rich gestalts of conscious experiences" (2012: 97), unique counterfactual combinations of factual circumstances and the reasons arising out of them, which support one alternative over another. As gestalts, they are grasped as complex unities of such facts and reasons, held in the imagination in deliberation as an object of choice. For example, in regard to whether to travel to New York by car or train, iterations of the price and time of the journey, the differing aesthetic qualities of travel, the efficiency and direction of the route, and so on all form a variety of gestalts in deliberation which are candidate objects of choice. Hodgson suggests that the *uniqueness* of these gestalts makes them undetermined by the otherwise applicable laws of nature; their singular composition, he thinks, renders them resistant to nomological explanation (2012: 104). Because we can synthesize the complex set of facts and reasons before us in a particular choice situation in robustly unique ways, and respond to those combinations "appositely" (i.e., according to their rational significance), what we end up doing or believing is, while constrained in terms of the spectra of alternatives we start with, ultimately not determined by the physical laws which determine those spectra, but is chosen freely yet indeterministically.

He illustrates the point with examples of practical reasoning involving artistic creativity. So when we assess a painting by Picasso, we grasp the unique combinations of qualities of the painting ("the look of particular faces . . . the painting's overall appearance"), the experience of which, Hodgson claims, "generally does not engage with computational rules" (2012: 105). While these qualities are subject to explanation in terms of such rules, our engagement with them is reflected in and is productive of our (freely made) appraisal of the painting, an essential part of which is the grasping of just these feature-rich gestalts of our experience of the painting. Another example is Wagner's composition of *Tristan und Isolde* (2012: 106–107). When Wagner considered what the opening bars of its Prelude should be, he considered unique and unprecedented possible concatenations of notes, rests, and tempos. These combinations admit of causally deterministic explanations, referencing the history of the development of music, the nature of composition, and so on. But just as with Picasso, Wagner's responses to these, Hodgson claims, could not be sufficiently explained by computational rules. The uniqueness of the combination of features prevents such rules from governing Wagner's apposite responses to the gestalt to which he actually did respond and which appears in the finished work. Hodgson thinks such aesthetic examples exhibit the same libertarian, free choice as in more mundane ones.

Hodgson holds that these features of plausible reasoning are not displayed in every decision to act or adopt a belief. Some actions, for example, we do unconsciously, out of habit, on the basis of "snap" judgements, and so on,[14] but many practical contexts, he thinks, require employing it. The law is just such a context that calls for discursive reasoning: "The superiority of careful conscious reflection over intuitive snap decisions in the type of reasoning with which I am most familiar, namely judicial decision-making, is I believe well established" (2012: 71).

Hodgson, realism, and how judges are free to decide cases

A *judge* therefore is a paradigm case of a plausible reasoner. In deciding a case, a judge has to carefully and deliberately examine the often complex facts of a case, study the relevant statutory provisions and case law as to their meaning and application, perhaps consider extensive expert and non-expert testimony from witnesses, and patiently and attentively consider arguments from lawyers about what, in their view, the proper outcome of the case should be and why. If serving on an appellate panel, then the judge must confer with her colleagues about their views about many of these matters. And more generally, the judge must assess the rational significance of all these things, including the reliability of the factual record, the credibility of the assertions of witnesses and experts, the merits of legal arguments, their coherence with other legal rules and principles, and so on.

14 Cf. Joseph Raz's notion (1999: 71 and 232) of acting for and conforming to a reason "automatically" and without conscious thought. Hart (2012: 139–140) makes a similar point in regard to acting on a rule.

According to Hodgson, the most general possible practical alternatives that the judge is presented with (e.g., finding a defendant innocent or guilty, given that certain facts are established or have failed to have been established, or granting or denying a motion to dismiss the case) are determined and circumscribed by natural and physical law-governed processes. The facts which determine these alternatives for the judge include not just the judge's particular psychology but also the state of the legal system, the factual history of the case, the credibility of witnesses, and much more. But beyond these alternatives so presented, in order to reach a decision, judges as plausible reasoners make use of what we might call conscious *gestalts of justice*. That is, the judge imagines complex scenarios comprising various combinations of all the factors just mentioned to constitute a menu of practical options. Just as Wagner, when he composed the opening bars of the Prelude to *Tristan und Isolde* (2012: 106), considered various "unique" and "unprecedented" aesthetic wholes of that passage of music, and responded appositely to the one which now forms part of that composition, so too judges consider unique and unprecedented wholes composed of complex combinations of facts, legal materials, and ways in which those materials might apply to those facts, as well as estimations of the credibility of witnesses, of the probabilities of unknown facts being the case (or not), and so on, in order to decide the case in a way that is inexplicable by psycho-physical laws. The ultimate judicial decision is, then, not completely determined by the (direct and indirect) operation of physical laws shaping the judge's deliberations, and is genuinely free, as the result of the judge's role in producing an undetermined, apposite (and efficacious) response to the gestalts of justice so constituted by those laws, specifically the gestalt that represents the decision so taken.

So given this outline of a libertarian explanation of judicial freedom, as a direct extension of Hodgson's theory, how might it relate to the views already canvassed? While, as we have seen, the various versions of realism and formalism do not themselves necessarily imply any particular view about free will, we may ask, if Hodgson's view of free will is true, whether that would cast doubt on the plausibility of any of these theories of adjudication. Would he be sympathetic to Holmes' recommendation to attend to what the courts actually do as a guide to advising clients? Does he share the realists' optimism that we can discern the causes of judicial decisions, whether it be in the extra-legal social forces influencing judges, the particular psychology of the judge, or even perhaps, as the formalist maintained, the legal sources themselves?

There are no definitive answers to these questions, but I think that considering Hodgson's view alongside those of the formalist and realist allows us to see that his is a novel addition to these views, and so a novel contribution to the theory of adjudication. For it seems to me the picture of judicial reasoning as libertarian, plausible reasoning finds truth in each of these theories, though departs from them in interesting ways.

Recall the view of formalism that legal sources completely determine the outcome of cases by mechanically and deductively applying them to a given set of facts. Hodgson would, of course, deny this, for the simple reason that on his view judicial decisions are not completely determined by *anything*, including the applicable legal sources. That is not to say, however, that the law is inert and plays no role in those decisions, as the realists tend to claim. What the law is in a given case will obviously constrain the spectra of alternative courses of action open to a judge when disposing of a case, but it does so in non-obvious and dynamic ways not recognized by the formalist. For example, the applicable law will shape (in part) the ongoing strategies of the litigants, and its history will constrain the possible interpretations of its meaning, and will constrain generally how the lawyers argue the case, particularly in an appellate context. This will in turn constrain the gestalts of justice the judge may consider in reasoning out what seems to her the proper outcome. So while the law does not completely determine decisions, it will be one salient factor in determining the range of possibilities of decision.

What about the (what I have called "external") realists' insistence that social, political, and commercial norms are the real causes of the outcomes of cases? The theory of plausible reasoning can concede some truth in this suggestion as well. For these extra-legal causal determinants, just as much as the legal ones, play a role in constraining the alternative courses of official action available to a judge in a particular case. Hodgson clearly recognizes that the reasons that bear on a particular decision often may be multifarious and in fact incommensurable. However, Hodgson would disagree with Frank when he claims that the "peculiar traits, dispositions, biases and habits of the particular judge will, then, often determine what he decides to be the law" (Frank 1930: 119) and, of course, deny that even these factors do not fully or completely determine the outcome. As to whether judicial behaviour can reliably be predicted, as was the realists' aspiration, Hodgson again presents a more complex view. Realists assumed that there were factors that could be identified which, taken together at least, could offer an adequate explanation and basis for predicting decisions. Hodgson agrees that given the set of laws of nature, combined with the facts of a judge's psychology, probabilities could be reasonably assigned to each alternative a judge is faced with in a given case. But it seems to me he would clearly deny that those probabilities will ever approach one. The indeterministic role of gestalts of justice in the reasoning of the judge ensures that.

For Frank, the appellate judge, was the only one of the realists who thought that judicial decisions were ultimately unpredictable. Recall that Frank thought that the unpredictability of judges was due to their own complex set of psychological idiosyncrasies in responding to the facts of a case, as well as the infinite variability of the facts themselves. Hodgson, I think, would clearly agree with Frank that judicial decision-making is at bottom an unpredictable matter. But it's interesting that Hodgson and Frank give different explanations for the unpredictability. Frank attributes it to the unknowable depths of the Freudian mind and the infinite variations in fact patterns, whereas Hodgson attributes it to the role of indeterminate gestalts in promoting and facilitating rationality.

Conclusion

Hodgson's libertarian theory of free will, developed in part on the basis of experiences of the kind of discursive, practical deliberation required of judges, suggests a novel account of how judges are free to decide cases. It also raises previously unexplored questions regarding the commitments of earlier views of adjudication in the twentieth century, in particular formalism and American legal realism. These views are ultimately unclear about such commitments, but as I have tried to show, they provide useful comparisons to illuminate key features of Hodgson's views. Given the dominance of compatibilism about free will in legal theory over the last several decades, the theory of judicial reasoning which I have only outlined here, based on Hodgson's libertarianism, is a long overdue addition to discussions of free will and the law. While the theory leaves many issues unaddressed, it should carve out a distinctive set of possible views in debates across a range of topics, in the theory of both punishment and adjudication.

References

Bourke, VJ 1964, *Will in Western Thought: An Historico-Critical Survey*, Sheed and Ward, New York.

Cohen, F 1935, 'Transcendental Nonsense and the Functional Approach', *Columbia Law Review* 25(6): 809–849.

Duxbury, N 1995, *Patterns of American Jurisprudence*, Oxford University Press, Oxford.

Dworkin, R 1986, *Law's Empire*, Belknap Press, Cambridge.

Flew, A 1969, 'Divine Omnipotence and Human Freedom', in A Flew and A MacIntyre (eds), *New Essays in Philosophical Theology*, SCM Press, London.

Frank, J 1930, *Law and the Modern Mind*, Anchor Books, New York.

Freeman, M (ed) 2011, *Law and Neuroscience*, Oxford University Press, Oxford.

Gilmore, G 1977, *The Ages of American Law*, Yale University Press, New Haven.

Green, TA 2014, *Freedom and Criminal Responsibility in American Legal Thought*, Oxford University Press, Oxford.

Haakonssen, K (ed) 2005, *Henry Home, Lord Kames, Essays on the Principles of Morality and Natural Religion*, Liberty Fund, Indianapolis.

Harris, JA 2005, *Of Liberty and Necessity: The Free Will Debate in Eighteenth-Century British Philosophy*, Oxford University Press, Oxford.

Hart, HLA 2012, *The Concept of Law*, 3rd edn, Clarendon Press, Oxford.

Hodgson, DH 1991, *The Mind Matters: Consciousness and Choice in a Quantum World*, Clarendon Press, Oxford.

Hodgson, DH 2012, *Rationality + Consciousness = Free Will*, Oxford University Press, New York.

Holmes, OW 1881, *The Common Law*, Little, Brown and Company, Boston.

Holmes, OW 1897, 'The Path of the Law', *Harvard Law Review* 10: 457–474.

Holmes, OW 1921, *Collected Legal Writings*, Harcourt, Brace, and Company, New York.

Hutcheson, JC 1929, 'The Judgment Intuitive: The Function of the "Hunch" in Judicial Decision', *Cornell Law Quarterly* 274–288.

Kalman, L 1986, *Legal Realism at Yale 1927–1960*, The University of North Carolina Press, Chapel Hill.

Kane, R 2005, 'Introduction: The Contours of Contemporary Free Will Debates', *The Oxford Handbook of Free Will*, 1st edn, Oxford University Press, New York.

Leiter, B 2005, 'American Legal Realism', in M. P. Golding and W. A. Edmundson (eds), *The Blackwell Guide to the Philosophy of Law and Legal Theory*, Blackwell, Oxford.

Leiter, B 2007, *Naturalizing Jurisprudence: Essays on American Legal Realism and Naturalism in Legal Philosophy*, Oxford University Press, New York.

Levi, E 1949, *An Introduction to Legal Reasoning*, University of Chicago Press, Chicago.

Lind, D 1993, 'Free Legal Decision and the Interpretive Return in Modern Legal Theory', *American Journal of Jurisprudence* 38: 159–188.

Llewellyn, K 1951, *The Bramble Bush*, Oceana, New York.

Llewellyn, K 1960, *The Common Law Tradition: Deciding Appeals*, Little, Brown, Boston.

Nadelhoffer, TA (ed) 2013, *The Future of Punishment*, Oxford University Press, Oxford.

O'Connor, T 2011, 'Agent-Causal Theories of Freedom', in R Kane (ed), *The Oxford Handbook of Free Will*, 2nd edn, Oxford University Press, New York.

Oliphant, H 1928, 'A Return to Stare Decisis', *American Bar Association Journal* 14: 71–76.

Palmer, D 2014, 'Free Will, Libertarianism, and Kane', in D Palmer (ed), *Libertarian Free Will*, Oxford University Press, New York.

Pardo, M and Patterson, D 2013, *Minds, Brains and Law: The Conceptual Foundations of Law and Neuroscience*, Oxford University Press, Oxford.

Posner, R 1993, *Cardozo: A Study in Reputation*, University of Chicago Press, Chicago.

Postema, G 2011, *Legal Philosophy in the Twentieth Century: The Common Law World*, Springer, Dordrecht.

Pound, R 1908, 'Mechanical Jurisprudence', *Columbia Law Review* 8: 605–623.

Pound, R 1913, 'Justice According to Law', *Columbia Law Review* 13: 696–713.

Radin, M 1925, 'The Theory of Judicial Decision: Or How Judges Think', *American Bar Association Journal* 11: 357–362.

Rawls, J 1999, *A Theory of Justice*, rev. edn, Belknap Press, Cambridge.

Raz, J 1999, *Engaging Reason*, Oxford University Press, Oxford.

Schauer, F 1988, 'Formalism', *Yale Law Journal* 97(4): 509–548.

Schauer, F 2013, 'Legal Realism Untamed', *Texas Law Review* 91: 749–780.

Sebok, A 1998, *Legal Positivism and American Jurisprudence*, Cambridge University Press, Cambridge.

Skorupski, J 2010, *The Domain of Reasons*, Oxford University Press, Oxford.

Smilansky, S 2000, *Free Will and Illusion*, Clarendon Press, Oxford.

Tamanaha, B 2010, *Beyond the Formalist-Realist Divide: The Role of Politics in Judging*, Princeton University Press, Princeton.

Vincent, NA (ed) 2013, *Neuroscience and Legal Responsibility*, Oxford University Press, Oxford.

8 Responsible agency in the criminal process

RA Duff[1]

Introduction

I did not meet David Hodgson until 2003, at a legal and social philosophy congress in Sweden; but I had first come across his work when, as a postgraduate student, I read his first book in the 1960s (Hodgson 1967). The book offered a characteristically meticulous critique of utilitarianism (in both its "act" and its "rule" versions) as a decision procedure: We cannot efficiently serve utility, Hodgson argued, by thinking and acting either as act utilitarians or as rule utilitarians. That kind of critique has, of course, become familiar, as have various utilitarian responses to it; but Hodgson did much to show its significance, and to work out in detail just how it could be best articulated.

However, my focus in this chapter will not be on that aspect of his work, but on the work that dominated his later philosophical career, and for which he rightly became better known: his development of a distinctively libertarian account of free will, and his discussion of its importance for the criminal law. More precisely, I will focus on his argument that if we are to justify criminal punishment (as we should) in partly retributivist terms, we must be able to suppose that those who are punished "have free will in a robust and indeterministic sense" (Hodgson 2012). In his last book, he neatly summarizes the central claim for which he argues, and which I want to critique:

> The capacity to grasp and be guided by good reasons is a reasonable basis for retribution and justice, but this capacity depends on conscious decision-making not readily explicable by compatibilist views.
>
> (Hodgson 2012: 224)

I will argue, first, that he is right to emphasize this capacity, and that he understates its importance for the criminal law and the criminal process: The capacity matters not only as a precondition of just punishment (which is his focus), but as a necessary precondition of the whole criminal process. However, I will then suggest that he is wrong to argue that the kind of capacity required by the criminal

1 Thanks are due to the editors for helpful comments on an earlier version of this chapter.

process cannot be understood in compatibilist terms, but depends on a "robust and indeterministic" free will. By attending, as I will argue we should attend, to the criminal process as a whole, we can provide a better account of the idea of just retribution as an aspect of this social practice of holding wrongdoers responsible, answerable, for their deeds; we will then be able to see that the capacities that just retribution must presuppose are the capacities for practical reasoning necessary for participation in such a social practice, and that those capacities can be adequately explained without appealing to an indeterministic notion of free will.

My argument therefore appears, at first glance, to be quite different from, and opposed to, Michael Corrado's argument in his chapter in this volume.[2] Corrado agrees with Hodgson that "the notions of retribution and desert are inextricably tied up with punishment . . . that to have punishment you must have desert [and that] to say that a person deserves punishment for certain behavior entails that he is morally responsible for that behavior" (145). He also believes, unlike Hodgson, that "no one is morally responsible for anything, so that no one deserves punishment" (153); but, he argues, while we should therefore abandon punishment, we can avoid the morally worrying implications that Hodgson thought would follow for our treatment of those who commit crimes by introducing a system of "correction", involving "the imposition of limited, proportional harsh treatment . . . upon individuals who are capable of reasoning more or less soundly, and capable of implementing their reasoning more or less accurately in action" (156). Now I agree with Corrado (if not for his reasons) that if punishment is understood in crude retributivist terms as a matter of inflicting pain or suffering on those who deserve it for their culpable wrongdoing, we should abandon it. But whereas he would therefore abandon punishment in favour of "correction", I would rather rethink punishment, and the associated ideas of retribution and desert, and argue that what responsible criminal offenders deserve, as a suitable response to (retribution for) their crimes is to be required to undertake or undergo an intentionally burdensome process not altogether unlike what Corrado calls "correction"; and that what responsibility requires is the kind of capacity for practically effective reasoning that is on his account a condition for the imposition of correction (see further Duff 2001, 2012). Corrado and I are thus not perhaps quite as far apart in substance as we appear to be.

It is by now something of a commonplace to say that in disciplines like philosophy, we show our respect and admiration for another's work by engaging critically with it; it is in that spirit that I offer this brief critique of one central aspect of David Hodgson's work, and thus also hope to help celebrate his remarkable career as jurist and as philosopher.

Criminal trials and criminal punishment

Hodgson's argument for the importance of a "robust" idea of responsibility and free will in relation to criminal law (the argument comes in chapter 11 of

2 Michael Louis Corrado, "Hodgson on retribution", in this volume; see also his further articles cited there.

Rationality + Consciousness = Free Will) focuses on criminal punishment. He rejects the suggestion that retribution could by itself constitute an adequate justification for, or purpose of, punishment, partly because we cannot make the kinds of "reliable and accurate" determinations of responsibility that would be needed if we were to "*accurately* align" retribution with "ultimate desert": But he argues that we can make sufficiently confident "broad approximate assessments of responsibility and desert" to enable us to judge "what is fair and permissible in pursuit of consequentialist goals" (Hodgson 2012: 222). This suggests a familiar kind of "mixed" account of punishment, according to which the offender's penal desert makes it permissible to subject him to hard treatment (treatment of a kind that is normally impermissible) for the sake of some consequential benefit; retribution thus provides "a restriction on state compulsion" (2012: 216), by allowing us to punish only those who deserve it (and forbidding us to punish them more harshly than they deserve).[3] I will not discuss this account of punishment here, though I'll say more about retribution and its proper meaning in the next section; the key point that I want to bring out here is that the defendant's responsibility has a far wider significance than this for his treatment in the criminal process.

The question of the defendant's penal desert, and thus of his responsibility as a criterion of that desert, focuses on his condition at the time of the alleged offence: He now deserves to be convicted and punished only if he was at that time a responsible agent with "[t]he capacity to grasp and be guided by good reasons"; and the severity of his sentence should be limited to the extent that his responsibility was impaired or diminished. Hodgson is surely right that we should understand responsibility for a past crime in this way – as a matter of the capacity to grasp and to be guided by reasons. However, the defendant's condition at the time of his trial and punishment also matters: If he is to be legitimately tried and punished, he must now be a responsible agent who is capable of grasping and being guided by reasons of the appropriate kind; he must be fit to be tried, and fit to be punished. The significance of this point is often overlooked, because we too often see the defendant as a purely passive figure in the criminal process of trial and punishment: We see the trial as a process of which he is the object, and an often uncomprehending observer, and punishment as something that is simply done to him, or imposed on him. That might well be empirically accurate as a picture of what often actually goes on in our courts and our penal institutions; but it is lacking as a normative conception of what trials and punishments should be, and cannot do justice to some important features of our actual practices.

The most salient of those features for present purposes is that defendants must be fit to be tried, or competent to stand trial; and that convicted offenders must likewise be fit, competent, to be punished. A defendant who is found to be "unfit to plead", for instance, due to a mental disorder that he is suffering at the time of his trial, cannot be tried: not because it would then be impossible to prove his guilt, which might be conclusively established; but because he is then unable to

3 See, most famously, Hart (2008). For a sophisticated Hartian account, see Scheid (1997).

play his proper part in the trial, as an active participant. So too, I will suggest, a convicted offender might be "unfit to be punished", if he lacks the rational capacities needed to play his proper part in his punishment – to undertake punishment rather than merely suffer it.

Under current English law, for instance, the defendant may be found "unfit to plead", or "under a disability [that] constitute[s] a bar to his being tried".[4] The test of fitness dates back to the nineteenth century: The fit defendant must "be able to: plead to the indictment, understand the course of the proceedings, instruct a lawyer, challenge a juror and understand the evidence".[5] The English Law Commission has argued that this test should now be replaced by one that focuses more clearly on the capacities that are needed not just to understand the trial, but to participate in it: The test should be whether the defendant has the "decision-making capacity" necessary for such participation.[6] Evidence that the reason to make incapacity a bar to trial is not that it might be hard to prove the guilt of an incapacitated defendant is provided by the fact that when a defendant is found to be unfit for trial, the court must still conduct an enquiry into the facts. The jury must consider the evidence offered by the prosecution or by someone "appointed by the court . . . to put the case for the defence"; if the jurors "are satisfied . . . that [the defendant] did the act or made the omission charged against him", they "make a finding" to that effect; if they are not thus satisfied, they must acquit him.[7] The Law Commission now suggests a procedure that is even more like that of a trial, as far as proof of guilt is concerned: The prosecution should "be required to prove all elements of the offence", both *actus reus* and *mens rea*, at the enquiry; if the offence is thus proved, the result should be not a conviction, but a "finding that the allegation is proved"; if it is not proved, the defendant is to be acquitted (unless, the Commission suggests, it is proved that he would have been entitled to a defence of insanity at trial, in which case a special verdict of "not guilty by reason of insanity" should be returned, to enable an appropriate kind of legal disposal).[8]

I cannot discuss the Commission's account of the necessary "decision-making capacity" here; my concern is rather with the underlying claim that what matters is the defendant's capacity to participate in the trial – a capacity that might plausibly be described as a "capacity to grasp and be guided by good reasons" (Hodgson 2012: 224). A defendant who is to participate in his trial must be

4 See *Criminal Procedure (Insanity) Act 1964* (as amended), ss 4–5.

5 Law Commission, *Unfitness to Plead* (vol. 1 Report; Law Com. No. 364; London: Stationery Office, 2016), para. 3.5; drawing on *Pritchard* (1836) 7 C&P 303, *Davies* (1853) Car & Kir 328.

6 *Unfitness to Plead* (note 5), ch. 3. The European Court of Human Rights has also emphasized participation: The right to a fair trial under article 6 of the European Convention on Human Rights "guarantees the right of an accused to participate effectively in a criminal trial" (*Stanford v United Kingdom* App No 16757/90, at [22]; quoted in *Unfitness to Plead*, para. 3.19, n. 27).

7 *Criminal Procedure (Insanity) Act 1964*, s. 4A.

8 *Unfitness to Plead*, paras 1.70–75, ch. 5.

able to understand the charge that he faces, not merely as a factual claim that he did certain things, but precisely as a charge of criminal wrongdoing; he must be able to decide whether to plead "guilty" or "not guilty" – which requires an understanding of the meaning of each plea and of the reasons for pleading one way or the other; he must be able to follow the evidence given in the trial, and to decide whether to give evidence himself; if he is to give evidence, he must be able to understand and respond to the questions put to him. The trial is concerned with two kinds of reason: There are, most obviously, the reasons that are given in the course of the trial for and against the conclusion that the defendant is guilty (reasons that will often involve a normative dimension, for instance, as to whether his conduct should be judged as "reasonable"); but there are also the reasons why what he is alleged to have done is defined as a criminal offence, since if he is to understand the charge as a criminal charge, he must be able to have some grasp of how and why such conduct is defined as a public wrong.[9]

The European Court of Human Rights talked of a "right . . . to participate effectively in a criminal trial", which might suggest that there need be no expectation that the defendant will, or should, participate – only that he should be allowed and enabled to do so if he wishes. But that right is in fact also seen, if not as a legal duty, at least as a civic duty: The defendant is expected to participate. He is indeed required to attend his trial,[10] and can be arrested and brought to court if he fails to do so; he is expected to enter a plea, although that expectation is no longer enforced, as a stringent legal duty, by the "*peine forte et dure*" (Mckenzie 2005); there is also a normal expectation that, if the prosecution leads plausible evidence of his guilt, he will give evidence in his own defence – though the right of silence, which serves to protect defendants against the potentially oppressive power of the state, precludes turning that expectation into a legal duty. That is also why a defendant's refusal to enter a plea or to take part in the trial (for instance, because he denies the court's standing to try him) can have such rhetorical force; he is not simply refraining from exercising a right that is his to exercise or not as he sees fit; he is refusing to play the part assigned to him in this formal, indeed ritual, legal procedure. (The defendant's participation is, of course, often through his counsel, rather than direct, and there are important questions to be asked about the role of defence counsel and its relationship to the defendant; but they cannot be asked here.)

One way to explain this expectation (an expectation that could even be seen as a matter of civic duty) of participation is to characterize the criminal trial not simply as an enquiry into the defendant's guilt or innocence, but as a process in which an alleged wrongdoer is called to account, or called to answer: The defendant is

9 He must thus be capable of grasping and engaging with reasons for belief as well as reasons for action. See Hodgson (2012: 155ff).

10 For the English provisions, see *Bail Act 1976*, s. 7. For summary trials, the defendant can plead guilty by post, and the trial can proceed even in his absence (*Magistrates' Courts Act 1980*, ss. 11–13).

called to answer *to* the charge of wrongdoing by entering a plea of "guilty" or "not guilty"; and if the prosecution proves the commission of the offence, he is called to answer *for* that commission, either by offering a defence or by accepting his conviction. He is called to answer by and in the criminal court, but is called to answer through the court to his fellow citizens, for his alleged violation of what is claimed to be their shared or common law. Such a view of the criminal trial can be grounded in a larger conception of the criminal law as part of the political structure of a democratic republic, as a polity that treats its citizens as responsible agents who are involved together in the enterprise of living under the law – a law that is their law (Duff et al. 2007; Duff 2007).

If such a conception of the criminal trial is plausible (not as a description of what actually happens in our courts, but as a normative ideal of what criminal trials ought to be) we can see why it matters not only whether the defendant *was* a responsible agent, capable of "grasp[ing] and be[ing] guided by good reasons" at the time of the alleged commission of the offence, but also whether he *is* such a responsible agent at the time of his trial: Only then is he capable of playing his proper part in the trial, as someone who is called to answer. This also reminds us of two important features of the idea of responsibility: that it is a matter of answerability, and that it is therefore essentially relational.

To be responsible for *X* is to be answerable for it: If *X* is an action (or omission), to say that I am responsible for *X* is to say that I can properly be held responsible for its commission (or omission); and to be held responsible for *X* is to be called to answer for it. But if I am to be legitimately called to answer for *X*, I must be capable of answering: I must have whatever rational capacities are needed to recognize *X* as my action or omission, to grasp and explain the reasons why I did it, and to assess those (motivating or explanatory) reasons in the light of the normative or guiding reasons by which I should have been motivated.[11] If I now lack such capacities (and even if I did not lack them at the time of the action in question), I cannot now be held responsible for *X*: You might be able to judge that, for instance, I committed a culpable wrong, and my present incapacity to answer for myself might not undermine the epistemic status of that judgement; but what you cannot do is engage with me in the enterprise of calling me to account for it.

However, second, to be answerable is to be answerable *to* someone – to some person or body who has the standing to call me to account. This is the sense in which responsibility is a relational matter: I am responsible not merely *for X*, but *to S*, who has the standing to hold me responsible – to call me to account.[12] Thus when it is said that *A* is responsible for *X*, we can always ask to whom *A* is responsible; and although the answer might sometimes be "only to herself" (or "only to God"), it cannot be "to no one". I suggested earlier that in a criminal trial, in a democratic polity, the defendant is answerable to her fellow citizens: It is they

11 On "guiding" as against "explanatory" reasons, see Raz (1990); on "normative" as against "motivating" reasons, see Alvarez (2016: s. 3).

12 See further Duff (2007: 19–36).

who have (or claim) the standing to call her to account for her alleged violation of their common law. This point will be important in what follows.

I have talked so far of a defendant's role in the criminal trial; but what of the punishment that typically follows on a conviction? Some normative accounts of punishment might imply that at that stage the defendant's current condition – as responsible or non-responsible – is no longer important. If, for instance, the point of punishment is to incapacitate the dangerous, or to deter others, the fact that the convicted offender is no longer a responsible agent need not bar her punishment.[13] If the aim is to inflict an appropriate quantum of suffering or hardship on her as retribution for her crime, it might (depending on how the relevant idea of suffering or hardship is understood, and in particular on what subjective dimension it involves) matter that she is capable of suffering, but does not seem to matter that she is a responsible agent with the capacity to grasp and be guided by good reasons. However, our own legal systems show a striking reluctance to inflict punishment on those who are now rationally incapacitated, even if they were demonstrably sane and responsible at the time of their crimes – a reluctance that we should surely share. This point is illustrated most dramatically in the context of capital punishment: The United States Supreme Court repeatedly declared it to be unconstitutional to execute someone who was insane at the time scheduled for his execution;[14] and it was taken as obvious in Britain that it would be cruel and inhumane to execute a person who had become insane since his commission of a capital offence (Walker 1968: 194–218; Duff 1986: 15–22). The point also holds good, however, for other modes of punishment. Under s. 37 of the Mental Health Act 1983, for instance, English courts can make a Hospital Order on a defendant who has been convicted of an imprisonable offence, but who is at the time of sentencing suffering from a mental disorder; this reflects, I think, not the consequentialist idea that a Hospital Order is likely to be a more cost-effective disposal than imprisonment, but the non-consequentialist conviction that there is something inherently inappropriate or grotesque about punishing a person who is now insane.[15]

Why should it be inappropriate or grotesque – and what kinds of mental disorder, having what kinds of effect, should preclude punishment? One answer to these questions emphasizes understanding: Although we must, of course, sometimes subject people to coercive treatment that they cannot understand (especially when we detain someone who is seriously disordered, for his own protection or that of others), it seems wrong to *punish* those who are incapable of understanding what is being done to them as a punishment. An obvious way to explain this thought is by appealing to the by now familiar idea that punishment

13 Matters are, of course, more complicated if part of the purpose is to deter *her*.

14 See *Ford v Wainwright* 477 U.S. 399 (1986); *Panetti v Quarterman* 127 S. Ct. 2842 (2007): It is far from clear, however, that mentally ill defendants are in fact adequately protected from execution – apart from the horrific possibility that they might be medicated to make them fit for execution; for a concise critique of the way that different states have dealt with the issue, see American Civil Liberties Union (2009).

15 See further Duff (1986: 22–28).

serves a communicative function: If an, or the, immediate purpose of punishment is to communicate to the offender an appropriate kind of censure for his criminal wrongdoing, it is essential to the legitimacy of the punishment that the offender be able to understand it as punishment – as something that is imposed on him for his crime.[16] If understanding were all that mattered, the offender would, of course, need to have the rational capacities that such understanding requires, in particular a capacity to *grasp* the good reasons that supposedly justify and make sense of his punishment: He must be able to understand the claim that the burdens imposed on him are being imposed as a deserved punishment for the wrong he committed. But he would not need the capacities for practical deliberation, the capacity to guide his conduct by good reasons, that are required for responsible, rational agency: It would be enough that he could understand what was being done to him as the passive recipient of that punishment.

Now it is true that punishment is often portrayed and discussed as a one-way enterprise in which only one party is active: The punisher is active, imposing or inflicting punishment; the punishee is simply the passive recipient who suffers punishment. But that is not the reality of most punishments, in which the person being punished has an active role to play. This is most obvious in the case of such punishments as probation, or "community payback". The offender is required to undertake certain – often quite demanding – courses of action: to report to her probation officer regularly, and discuss her progress; to undertake any programmes that are a condition of her probation; to undertake the work that is specified as her community payback. If she is fined, it is (initially) up to her to pay the fine – although there might be provision for the money to be extracted from her bank account or her wages if she refuses to pay. Indeed, in some countries imprisonment is also something that offenders must undertake, rather than simply undergo: They might be, for instance, sentenced to a specified term of imprisonment, and instructed to report to the prison on a specified date to begin serving that term; if they are in an open prison, remaining within the prison (or returning to it from day release or work) is required of them as something they must do, not something simply imposed on them. Indeed, even in a closed prison to which the convicted offender is taken, willy-nilly, from the court that sentenced her she is still, qua prisoner, an agent: She is subject to a disciplinary regime of rules that she is expected to obey, and is required to engage in a range of activities. One of the reasons why the most extreme kinds of "super-max" prison are so inhumane lies in the extent to which they seek to negate the prisoners' agency, by making them no more than the passive recipients of their incarceration, from whom nothing is normatively expected or required: In any minimally decent prison system, the prisoners are treated as responsible agents.

16 See, classically, Feinberg (1970) (although to talk of "expression" does not bring out the crucial point, as "communication" does, that punishment seeks a response), and more recently von Hirsch (1993) and Duff (2001). I am not making here the ambitious claim for which I argued in that book, that punishment's primary justification lies in the attempt to communicate to and with the offender; I need only the more modest claim that punishment is a communicative enterprise.

One could portray this requirement – that prisoners be treated as responsible agents – as a side-constraint on punishment: That is, one could claim that it is not integral to the meaning or justification of punishment qua punishment that it treats the person punished as a responsible agent, but that the imposition of punishment, like other kinds of state coercion, is subject to a general demand that wherever possible the state should treat us as responsible agents. But one could – and I would – go further than that, and argue that it is integral to punishment itself, as a communicative enterprise, that it addresses the offender as a responsible agent who should undertake his punishment for himself (rather than simply undergoing it passively). On this view, the offender's sentence tells him that this is what he must do, must undertake, in order to make appropriate moral reparation for his crime; this is how he can communicate to his victim (if there was one) and to his fellow citizens his recognition of what he has done; this is how he must "pay for" his crime – this is the reparative debt that he owes. That debt will, of course, be extracted from him if he refuses to pay it: I do not suggest that punishment should be or become a purely voluntary matter, or a matter of obligations that cannot in the end be coercively enforced.[17] But if we think we are justified in punishing a person, we must also think that the punishment is something that he ought to accept for himself – since he ought to recognize and accept the good reasons that, we believe, justify it; and we should then also, I suggest, think that it is something that he ought to undertake for himself, as a responsible agent who can guide his own conduct by the good reasons that he grasps. This applies even to imprisonment – even when the offender is taken to prison rather than being instructed to take himself, and even when the prison is closed rather than open: I can make imprisonment something that I undertake for myself as my own penitential project.[18]

The upshot of this discussion should be that responsibility, understood as requiring "[t]he capacity to grasp and be guided by good reasons", is even more important to the criminal law than Hodgson suggested. Not only must the person who is to be punished for his crime have been a responsible agent at the time of his crime; he must also now, at the time of his trial and punishment, be a responsible agent who can be expected to play his appropriate, active role in the criminal process – one who can be called to account for what he has done, and expected to undertake (rather than merely to undergo) his punishment. He might, of course, refuse to do so, for any of a variety of good and bad reasons, and there are further questions to be asked about how we should respond to such refusals; but the crucial point for our present purposes is that our treatment of alleged criminal wrongdoers should address them as people who are still responsible agents. This is, of course, not a criticism of Hodgson: It is to say only

17 Though we should think more seriously about what we should do with those who refuse to undertake their punishments, and in particular about whether imprisonment should always be the ultimate breach sanction.

18 This is one way in which "alternate possibilities" (compare Frankfurt (1969)) are not necessary for free and responsible agency: Even if I know that I can do nothing else, I can make what I do my own as its responsible agent.

that his account of responsibility as grounded in this kind of rational capacity has application beyond the specific context in which he discussed it. However, a significant aspect of that application is that what matters when we attend to the defendant's responsibility as a participant in the criminal process, what displays or constitutes his responsibility, is his capacity to participate in this distinctive kind of social practice – his capacity to engage with others in this practice of criminal accountability. I will argue in what follows that such a practice-based conception of responsibility will enable us to resist, or undercut, Hodgson's claim that the responsibility-constituting capacity to grasp and be guided by good reasons "is not readily explicable by compatibilist views" (2012: 224), and must therefore be understood in his incompatibilist terms.

"Robust" responsibility

Hodgson talks often of what is required for free will or responsibility "in a robust sense"; of actions being "in a fundamental way our own free choices and our own responsibility"; of having responsibility "in a substantial sense" (2012: 206); of being "truly responsible" for one's criminal conduct (2012: 210); and of "ultimate responsibility" (2012: 216, 222).[19] Such "robust" responsibility and free will are, he argues, necessary for penal desert, and thus for the justice of retributive punishment; but compatibilist accounts of free will do not give us anything that is robust enough. In this argument he is in good company: Galen Strawson, for instance, argues that punishment can be fair (as opposed to merely being an efficient means to some consequentialist end) only if those who are punished can be said to be "truly or ultimately morally responsible for [their] actions"; and compatibilist accounts of free will do not give us the right kind of "true" or "ultimate" responsibility.[20] The difference between Hodgson and Strawson is that Hodgson asserts, while Strawson denies, that we do have such true, ultimate, robust, fundamental, substantial free will and responsibility. What interests me here, however, is what they agree on – that without this, retributive punishment cannot be justified.

The use of such terms as "true", "ultimate", "robust", "fundamental", and "substantial" in this kind of context should arouse our suspicion. We are to contrast "true" or "ultimate" *X* with a (purported) *X* that is false, superficial, weak, or insubstantial. We might think of real diamonds as contrasted with paste diamonds; or of true love as contrasted with superficial, passing infatuation: While the latter may suffice for some purposes and in some contexts, for the important things in life we need the true, the ultimate, the substantial. Now the institution of criminal law is certainly an important feature of our socio-political life – one that can have dramatic effects on the lives of those who come into contact with it; the judgements of guilt (or innocence) that our courts pass, the sentences of

19 For "ultimate responsibility", see also Kane 2002, cited by Hodgson (2012: 159).

20 Strawson (2011); see also Strawson (1986) and (1994). See Hodgson's comments on Strawson's "luck swallows everything" argument at Hodgson (2012: 173–177).

punishment that they impose, are serious matters – and might seem to have an especially or more deeply serious significance if what they reflect is not merely a consequentialist calculus of costs and benefits, but a judgement that the person who is convicted deserves censure and punishment. But should this line of thought lead us to conclude that retributive punishment, and the kind of desert on which it depends, require the metaphysically ambitious species of responsibility and free will that Hodgson and Strawson claim that it needs; that the more mundane, (supposedly) superficial or non-ultimate kind of responsibility that is possible in a deterministic world, which might suffice were our concerns merely pragmatic, cannot suffice for just retribution?

This conclusion might seem more plausible if we understand retribution in the way that Strawson seems (with others) to understand it. "True" or "ultimate" responsibility is, he argues:

> responsibility of such a kind that, if we have it, then it *makes sense* to suppose that it could be just to punish some of us with (eternal) torment in hell and reward others with (eternal) bliss in heaven. . . . [Such] responsibility exists if punishment and reward can be fair without having any sort of pragmatic justification whatever.
>
> (Strawson 2011: 128)

Now this is indeed one way to understand the idea of punishment as retribution; we imagine the criminal court as engaged in a human version of the Final Judgement, assessing the "true" or "ultimate" deserts of the wrongdoer appearing before it, and inflicting a punitive burden that is supposed in some sense to match those deserts.[21] If we understand retribution in this way, we might be led to think that it requires a radical kind of free will, an "ultimate" kind of responsibility, for which there is no room in a deterministic or materialist world. However, I will not pursue here the question of whether to be led in that direction would be to be misled (whether divine punishment on the day of judgement would require a robustly indeterministic type of free will). My argument will rather be that that is not how we should understand the idea of retribution in criminal law; and that once we get a better understanding of what it can plausibly mean as a feature of a human practice of criminal law, we will also see that it does not require the kind of "ultimate" responsibility that Hodgson asserts and Strawson denies.

I argued, in the previous section, that we should understand responsibility as a matter of answerability, and therefore also as relational: To be responsible for *X* is to be answerable for *X* to some person or body who has the standing to call me to answer – to hold me responsible. Often, and especially in relation to the criminal law, I am called to answer only after (indeed, sometimes long after) the

21 See too Murphy (2012: 22) on "character retributivism" and the "cognitive obstacles" to it. One can also discern this understanding of retribution in Moore's defence of it (Moore 1997: 104–188), though Moore thinks that a compatibilist account of free will and responsibility gives us all that we need to justify retribution.

event: I am held responsible, called to account, for the *X* that I did some time ago; and we need to ask what capacities I must then have if I am to be answerable. It might then seem that responsibility as understood in this way, as consisting essentially in a capacity to answer for my past conduct, is not what matters for penal desert: What matters for desert is not whether I can now answer, but whether I was responsible for my actions at the time I committed them; and that kind of responsibility is a matter not of being able to answer, but of having "[t]he capacity to grasp and be guided by good reasons". That much is true, but the two kinds (or, I would rather say, dimensions) of responsibility are intimately linked.

We can begin to bring out that linkage by noting that the answering that constitutes being held responsible can be simultaneous with, rather than (long) after, the action for which I am to answer. As I act, I might be challenged to explain myself, to account for what I am doing; and if I am a responsible agent, I will be able to answer that challenge with an account of the reasons for which I am acting (which will also be an account of what I am doing). I will also be able to grasp, and respond to, claims that I should not be doing what I am doing – that the reasons for which I am acting are not good reasons, or that there are stronger reasons against acting thus; and even if I (stubbornly or rationally) remain unpersuaded that I should alter my course of conduct, or anyway fail to alter it, to see and treat me as a responsible agent is to assume that in a relevant sense I "could" do so. Answerability is thus the public dimension of responsibility as involving a capacity for rational action: The dialogue in which I engage with those who call me to account is a public version of the deliberation that I undertake, or that I should undertake, in deciding whether and how to act.[22] This point still applies if I am called to answer some time after the event: When I answer, I answer still in the first person, as the agent who then deliberated and acted, not in the third person, as someone now reporting on that past agent; I reconstruct, from within, the practical reasoning that informed my action.[23]

That dialogue, whether it is with others who call me to account or with myself as I decide what to do, certainly presupposes that I have (and had at the time of the action in question, if it is in the past) "[t]he capacity to grasp and be guided by good reasons": If I am accused of not guiding my actions by the good reasons that bore on them, it must be assumed that I "could" have done so – that I could have grasped what I failed to grasp, or could have been guided (or could have guided myself) by reasons that did not in fact guide my conduct; likewise, if I am told that I ought now to answer for what I did, or be criticized for refusing or failing to do so, it must be assumed that I "could" do so. So we must, it seems,

22 Or, we might say in more Wittgensteinian tones, that the deliberations I undertake silently with myself are the private dimension of the conversations I might have with one who calls me to account.

23 That is why amnesia should bar a defendant's trial, even if she is now rationally competent, and even if she could work out, as it were in the third person, why she did what she did; her amnesia bars her from the first person engagement in her own past agency that is required.

embroil ourselves in the long debate about how that "could" is to be analyzed,[24] in particular whether it must be analyzed as involving the kind of unconditional or categorical ability to do otherwise that incompatibilists claim is necessary for ("true") responsibility. I cannot engage in that complex debate here, but suggest that if we think about the context of the criminal trial as I have sketched it here, we can see that the truth of "she could (have) respond(ed)" in the sense that is relevant to this context does not depend on her possession of the kind of "ultimate" or "robust" responsibility that Hodgson asserts and that Strawson denies.

We might be confident in advance, and with good reason, that a particular agent will not respond in the way that we seek: that he will, given the chance, commit a particular kind of crime; that he will not, when summoned to trial, admit his guilt, or answer for what he has done in the way that he should; that he will not be persuaded, by the trial or by punishment, to reform his ways. Analogously, we might be confident in advance, with good reason, that a moral wrongdoer will not be persuaded by anything we say to recognize his wrongdoing for what it is, to repent it, or to change his ways. If asked why we think he will be unmoved, we might talk about the entrenched aspects of his character that underpin his wrongful conduct and his resistance to our persuasive endeavours. If then asked whether we suppose that he is or was responsible for those aspects, for being the kind of person he is, we might (if asked outside the peculiar context of philosophical discussion) be puzzled by the question,[25] but ask in reply whether his upbringing was such as to deprive him of exposure to the kinds of moral influence that contribute to moral education, or whether he suffered a congenital incapacity that rendered him wholly insusceptible to such influences. If he did suffer some such radical malformation in upbringing or heredity, so that he was and is cut off from any understanding of the values to which we would appeal in judging his actions or in calling him to account for them, we must, of course, agree that he was not, and is not, a responsible agent whom we can hold to account. But neither a well-grounded certainty that he will not respond appropriately, nor a Strawsonian denial of his "ultimate" responsibility, implies that he suffers such a radical, responsibility-negating malformation; they do not imply that he is not in the relevant sense reasons-responsive – capable of grasping and responding to good reasons.

To say that he is reasons-responsive is to say, roughly, that there is an intelligible route from where he is now, in terms of his conceptions of value and of the reasons that bear on his actions, to where we think he should be and where we are trying to persuade him to be: for instance, from his willing or enthusiastic commission of the crime, to a repentant recognition of the wrong that he has done. To make the idea of "an intelligible route" slightly clearer, we could say that there is such a route if we could tell a coherent narrative of his persuasion: a narrative that might well be fictional, if he remains unpersuaded, but that we could imagine

24 For a helpful survey, see McKenna and Coates (2015).

25 But see Hodgson (2012: 177) for his view of how we can "become partly responsible for the way we are".

being true. If the person concerned is so seriously disordered as to be beyond the reach of reason, or if he is a psychopath, no such narrative is possible – no such narrative could make sense; for to be thus disordered, or psychopathic, is precisely not to be within the imaginable reach of rational moral persuasion.[26] But absent such disorder or incapacity, we can treat the person as in principle persuadable, which is what matters for responsibility; he is in principle persuadable even if we are certain that he will not in fact be persuaded.

But why should we try to persuade him, if we are sure that the attempt is doomed? Can we even be said to be *trying* to persuade him if we are sure of failure? Even if we can, won't our reasons for the attempt now have to do not with him, but with our desire to send some message to others, or to express our own feelings, in which case we may be accused of using him merely as a means to our own ends (a charge disturbing for retributivists who argue that purely consequentialist conceptions of punishment illegitimately treat those punished "merely as means" to the social goods that punishment can bring) (Murphy 1973: 219–220; Duff 2001: 7–8)? We do have reasons independent of the offender for trying to call him to account: We owe it, we might say, to the victim of his wrongdoing, and to the values he has flouted, to take that wrongdoing seriously – and calling him to account is at least a way of taking it seriously. But we also owe this to him – and that is why this is not just *an* appropriate way to respond to his wrongdoing, but presumptively *the* appropriate way to respond to serious public wrongdoing. We owe it to him because we owe it to him to treat him, as far as possible, as a fellow member of the normative community in which he lives (and commits his wrongs), and not to treat him as someone beyond moral and social redemption. It is an important aspect of our conception of ourselves and of each other as moral and social agents that we are redeemable – that we are not wholly beyond the reach of moral reason, however firmly or stubbornly we might be committed to wrongdoing. This is what makes sense of a continued effort to persuade the wrongdoer, even when we have good reason to be empirically confident that the attempt will fail. We can see why this is important if we ask what the alternative is. It is not to ignore the wrongs that people commit, since that would be neither practically prudent nor morally appropriate: It is rather to see those who commit them not as fellow members of a normative community with whom we must engage as responsible agents, but as dangerous objects whom we must control, incapacitate, or seek to modify.[27]

The key point to note here is that a denial of "ultimate" responsibility does not undermine this conception of ourselves and others, or of what we owe to the

26 I am assuming here something that admittedly requires detailed argument: that we can identify a kind of responsibility-negating disorder that can usefully be called "psychopathy". See Malatesti and McMillan (2010).

27 It's true that much contemporary penal policy and rhetoric, at least or especially in Britain and the United States, precisely portray offenders (or those who commit certain kinds of offence) as excluded from the political community of the law-abiding (an exclusion symbolized by the loss of the right to vote); but that is an expression of the uncivilized character of our existing penal system.

wrongdoer: What matters is that it is possible to treat him, without deception or denials of what we know, as a participant in our moral and social practices; and that possibility depends on the way he now is, not on whether he was in some sense responsible for being that way.

However, it might be replied, that possibility also and crucially depends upon our ignorance. For given the truth of some form of determinism, if we possessed the omniscience of Laplace's imagined "intelligence" to whom "nothing would be uncertain", and to whose eyes "the future as well as the past would be present",[28] we would be able to know with complete certainty whether or not a person would in fact be persuaded through the criminal process to answer for or repent what he had done; and if we knew that he would not in fact be moved by the reasons that we, or the law, could offer, the "attempt" to persuade him would surely be empty. It is, therefore, only because we lack such omniscience that we can believe the attempt to be other than futile, which is hardly a sound basis on which to construct a system of criminal responsibility. Now there are some puzzles about the idea of such omniscient foresight: about what it would be to have it, and about just what would be foreseen; in particular about the relationship between the movements of bodies and atoms that Laplace's intelligence would be able to foresee, and the human actions and responses that interest us. But the lack of such foresight is not merely a contingent feature of human life, as other kinds of even massive ignorance are ("If only we knew more about *X*, we could improve our lives"): It is a basic presupposition of a whole range of practices, attitudes, and relationships. If human beings were immortal, or wholly immune to physical injury, human life and ethics would be transformed (though one might wonder whether these would still be *human* lives and ethics); but that does not undermine the categorical status of existing moral views about how we should treat each other. Likewise, the radical and perhaps unimaginable difference that such Laplacian foresight would make to human practices does not undermine the legitimacy of those human practices as practices in which we, as fallible and very far from omniscient beings, can live.

But, it might now be objected, even if it can plausibly be argued that our practices of holding ourselves and each other responsible, of calling each other to account for the wrongs that we do, of blaming and censuring each other for those wrongs, do not depend for their intelligibility or legitimacy on the kind of "ultimate" responsibility that Hodgson asserts and Strawson denies, this does not yet justify the practice of punishment, if we understand it in retributive terms as the imposition of a burden that the wrongdoer deserves. Punishment, as thus understood, surely aspires to be a human form of the "(eternal) torment in hell"

28 "Given for one instant an intelligence which could comprehend all the forces by which nature is animated and the respective situation of the beings who compose it, an intelligence sufficiently vast to submit these data to analysis, it would embrace in the same formula the movements of the greatest bodies of the universe and those of the lightest atom; for it, nothing would be uncertain, and the future, as the past, would be present to its eyes" (de Laplace 1902: 4).

to which a vengeful Christian God was supposed to condemn sinners,[29] and surely such penal burdens are unjust and unfair if the offender was not ultimately responsible for being or becoming the person who would commit such a wrong. Now retributive punishment is indeed sometimes portrayed, both by its advocates and by its critics, in this way: The court is to pass a definitive judgement on the defendant and her moral character – a judgement of the same kind, albeit less infallible and all-encompassing, as will be passed by God; thus insofar as, for whatever reason, we cannot be confident of the accuracy or justice of that judgement, we cannot be confident of the legitimacy of the punishment to which it leads.[30] But that is not the only, or the most plausible, way to understand punishment as retribution.

We could instead explain punishment as a forceful continuation of the communicative process that, I have argued, the criminal trial involves: The central aim of punishment is to bring the offender to recognize the wrong she has done, to repent it, and to make appropriate moral reparation for it, by undergoing the burden that punishment imposes. I cannot discuss the details of such an account here, and do not pretend that it is free of problems or open to no objections.[31] The point to note here, however, is that this is one way in which we can understand punishment as retribution (as a deserved response to the offender's wrongdoing, which is appropriate to the character and implications of that wrongdoing), without requiring the punisher to claim a God-like power of judgement on the wrongdoer's "ultimate", "robust" responsibility for her character. Punishment is part (admittedly a forceful, coercive, and potentially oppressive part) of our social and political dealings with each other as agents who are responsible in the modest sense sketched previously. It matters that it be "fair" independently of "any sort of pragmatic justification",[32] in that we can legitimately punish someone only if and because she deserves the censure that punishment communicates, in virtue of her culpably responsible commission of a wrong: But for it to be thus fair, for her to be thus responsible, she need not have or have had that "ultimate responsibility" that Hodgson asserts and Strawson denies; it is enough that she is, and that she was at the time of her crime, responsible in the sense of being reasons-responsive.

Our practices of criminal law and punishment do indeed depend on the assumption that those engaged in them or subjected to them are responsible agents who can justly be called to account for their actions and condemned and punished for their crimes; but they do not, I have argued, depend on the assumption of any metaphysically puzzling kind of "ultimate" responsibility.

It might now be objected that the argument I have sketched here sidesteps, rather than engaging with, Hodgson's central argument for a "robust" conception of responsibility: His argument that the requisite "capacity to grasp and be

29 Strawson (2011: 128); see p. 136 above.

30 Compare Murphy (2012) on "character retributivism" and its implications; and see Hodgson (2012: 216) on our lack of "capacity to accurately assess ultimate responsibility".

31 See citations in note 16 earlier in the chapter; also Bennett (2008).

32 Strawson (2011: 128); see text at note 20 above.

guided by good reasons . . . depends on conscious decision-making [that is] not readily explicable by compatibilist views" (2012: 224), but that can be plausibly explained by his distinctive, incompatibilist account of deliberation and decision-making.[33] That argument is rich and provocative, and is the focus of several of the other chapters in this volume;[34] but it is not an argument with which I need to engage for my purposes in this chapter. For I have argued that once we understand responsibility, at least as it properly concerns the criminal law, as a matter of being able to participate, and being a person who can be treated as a participant, in this distinctive social practice of accountability, we can see that it need not be the kind of "robust", or "fundamental", "substantial", or "ultimate" responsibility that Hodgson takes to be required; nor, as a capacity for this kind of participation in a social practice, does it require a kind of capacity whose reality is threatened by a deterministic world.

References

Alvarez, M 2016, 'Reasons for Action: Justification, Motivation, Explanation', *Stanford Encyclopedia of Philosophy*, https://plato.stanford.edu/archives/sum2016/entries/reasons-just-vs-expl/.

American Civil Liberties Union 2009, *Mental Illness and the Death Penalty*, www.aclu.org/files/pdfs/capital/mental_illness_may2009.pdf.

Bennett, C 2008, *The Apology Ritual: A Philosophical Theory of Punishment*, Cambridge University Press, Cambridge.

de Laplace, PSM 1902, *A Philosophical Essay on Probabilities*, trans. FW Truscott and FL Emory, Wiley, New York.

Duff, RA 2012, 'Responsibility, Restoration and Retribution', in M Tonry (eds) *Retributivism Has a Past: Has It a Future?*, Oxford University Press, Oxford.

Duff, RA 2007, *Answering for Crime: Responsibility and Liability in the Criminal Law*, Hart Publishing, Oxford.

Duff, RA 2001, *Punishment, Communication, and Community*, Oxford University Press, New York.

Duff, RA 1986, *Trials and Punishments*, Cambridge University Press, Cambridge.

Duff, RA, Farmer, L, Marshall, SE, and Tadros, V 2007, *The Trial on Trial: Volume 3: Towards a Normative Theory of the Criminal Trial*, Hart Publishing, Oxford.

Feinberg, J 1970, *Doing and Deserving*, Princeton University Press, Princeton.

Frankfurt, H 1969, 'Alternate Possibilities and Moral Responsibility', *Journal of Philosophy* 66: 829–839.

Hart, HLA 2008, *Punishment and Responsibility*, 2nd edn, Oxford University Press, Oxford.

Hodgson, DH 1967, *Consequences of Utilitarianism*, Clarendon Press, Oxford.

Hodgson, DH 2012, *Rationality + Consciousness = Free Will*, Oxford University Press, New York.

33 See especially Hodgson (2012: 37–113); also Hodgson (1993: 114–156).

34 See especially the chapters in this volume by Robert Kane, Neil Levy, and Nicole A Vincent.

Kane, R 2002, 'Some Neglected Pathways in the Free Will Labyrinth', in R Kane (ed), *The Oxford Handbook of Free Will*, 1st edn, Oxford University Press, New York.
Law Commission (England and Wales) 2016, LCN364, *Unfitness to Plead*, Volume 1, viewed 21 August 2017, ww.lawcom.gov.uk/project/unfitness-to-plead/.
Malatesti, L and McMillan, J (eds) 2010, *Responsibility and Psychopathy*, Oxford University Press, Oxford.
McKenna, M and Coates, J 2015, 'Compatibilism', *Stanford Encyclopedia of Philosophy*, https://plato.stanford.edu/entries/compatibilism/.
Mckenzie, A 2005, '"This Death Some Strong and Stout Hearted Man Doth Choose": The Practice of Peine Fort et Dure in Seventeenth- and Eighteenth-Century England', *Law & History Review* 23: 279–313.
Moore, MS 1997, *Placing Blame: A General Theory of the Criminal Law*, Oxford University Press, Oxford.
Murphy, JG 1973, 'Marxism and Retribution', *Philosophy and Public Affairs* 2: 217–243.
Murphy, JG 2012, *Punishment and the Moral Emotions*, Oxford University Press, Oxford.
Raz, J 1990, *Practical Reason and Norms*, 2nd edn, Oxford University Press, Oxford.
Scheid, DE 1997, 'Constructing a Theory of Punishment, Desert, and the Distribution of Punishments', *Canadian Journal of Law and Jurisprudence* 10: 441–506.
Strawson, G 1986, *Freedom and Belief*, Oxford University Press, Oxford.
Strawson, G 1994, 'The Impossibility of Moral Responsibility', *Philosophical Studies* 75: 5–24.
Strawson, G 2011, 'The Impossibility of Ultimate Responsibility', in R Swinburne (ed), *Free Will and Modern Science*, British Academy, London.
von Hirsch, A 1993, *Censure and Sanctions*, Oxford University Press, Oxford.
Walker, N 1968, *Crime and Insanity in England*, Volume 1, Edinburgh University Press, Edinburgh.

Legislation

Bail Act 1976
Criminal Procedure (Insanity) Act 1964
Magistrates' Courts Act 1980

Cases

Ford v Wainwright 477 U.S. 399 (1986)
Panetti v Quarterman 127 S. Ct 2842 (2007)
R v Davies (1853) Car & Kir 328
R v Pritchard (1836) 7 C. & P. 303
Stanford v United Kingdom, App No 16757/90

9 Hodgson on retribution

Michael Louis Corrado

In Hodgson's view, the notions of desert and responsibility are bulwarks against inhumane treatment of human beings. In *Rationality + Consciousness = Free Will* (2012: 210, 213), he says:

> [Retributive] purposes are based on the idea that a person who has acted criminally *deserves* to be punished for this conduct, and that it is *just* that appropriate detriment be inflicted on that person. And the idea that a person deserves punishment for criminal conduct presupposes that the person is truly responsible for it. . . . To have regard only to the consequences of whatever is done to citizens, without regard to whether they deserve it, is to deal with them not as responsible persons but as vehicles for treatment to be manipulated for the general good. That is not appropriate in relation to people who are capable of acting rationally; and it does not encourage people to take responsibility for their conduct.

There are a number of separate claims here:

a Punishment may be inflicted, and may only be inflicted, on persons who deserve it.
b Only persons who are morally responsible for criminal behaviour deserve punishment.
c To take only the general good as justification for doing something to someone is to treat them not as responsible actors but as "vehicles . . . to be manipulated for the general good".
d Treating people who are capable of acting rationally as mere vehicles to be manipulated for the general good is not appropriate.

These four propositions are premises for Hodgson's conclusion that "there are good reasons for retaining retribution as a guiding purpose of the criminal law" (2012: 212). I take it that retaining retribution here means the criminal justice system holding people responsible for what they do, and administering punishment in accord with what each person who is responsible for a crime deserves.

The argument is of special interest to me because I reject the conclusion – I don't believe that human beings are morally responsible for what they do, and I don't believe that anyone deserves to be punished by the state for their wrongdoing – and yet I agree with all four propositions. I believe that the notions of retribution and desert are inextricably tied up with punishment, and that to have punishment you must have desert. I believe that to say that a person deserves punishment for certain behaviour entails that he is morally responsible for that behaviour. I believe that taking only the consequences of our actions as a guide in our treatment of human beings, without side constraints, means treating them as pawns in the pursuit of some good, and I believe that that is inappropriate. What I hope to be able to explain here is how I can accept all four of those propositions and yet insist that we cannot and should not retain retribution as a "guiding purpose" in the criminal law.

Let me first set out Hodgson's reasons for concern about treating rational persons as vehicles for the common good, a concern that I and most (but not all) other writers on criminal law share. When I have done that, I will explain why I think that reliance on retribution, desert, and responsibility to allay that concern is wrong-headed, and I will offer another way of thinking about these things.

I

One of the things that worries Hodgson, if I understand him correctly, is the belief that in the absence of desert we cannot maintain the line between malice and madness upon which our criminal law seems to be founded. Australia and the United States share a common tradition in criminal justice, a tradition based upon two institutions: punishment on one side (the retributive side) and therapy and indefinite detention on the other (the preventive side). There are a number of theories about the ways in which these two institutions should be distributed, and intuitions about this (as I will try to show) are beginning to crumble. But the most prevalent theory, I believe, is one shared by Hodgson: Punishment should be reserved for those who are rational and in control of their behaviour (the *malicious*); therapy and preventive detention should be reserved for those who are dangerous and are not rational or not in control of their behaviour (the *mad*).

The fear is that if we eliminate the marker "desert" we will lose the line between these two institutions (2012: 214–215). The reasoning goes like this – a humane system of punishment is justified in two complementary ways: We punish to promote the general good; and we punish because those who have done wrong deserve it.[1] If we eliminate desert from the calculation, then all that is left is promotion of good consequences. Whatever the most efficient way for the criminal justice system to promote good consequences may be, the final test will always be the maximization of the good outcome. But, as we know, to look solely to the

1 On the mixed theory, see Kaufman (2012: 73–92). Alan Goldman (1979) has shown that the mixed theory described here has inherent conceptual difficulties. Nevertheless, it remains one of the leading theories, and it is the one Hodgson accepts (2012: 210–211).

greatest possible total (or average) of the good is to ignore the rights and needs of individuals, and leads to atrocities like the punishment of the innocent for the good consequences that follow, where "the innocent" would include both the scapegoat, the bystander plucked off the street and punished solely for the general good, and the dangerous or violent person who has not yet committed a crime. Moreover, even if only those who committed crimes were used in the pursuit of good consequences there would be no limit on what could be done with them, short of upsetting the balance of good consequences over evil ones. They could be subjected to coercive treatment, and they could be detained indefinitely (or worse).[2]

Hodgson makes these points in his discussion of the work of the philosopher Derk Pereboom, who denies that human beings are responsible for what they do, and who argues for a preventive therapy/detention approach to crime. According to Hodgson:

> Pereboom contends that we do not have free will of the kind required for moral responsibility, and that accordingly criminal punishment cannot be justified as retribution for wrongdoing. . . . [He] concludes that the appropriate response to crime is similar to that accorded to carriers of dangerous diseases. Just as we have the right to quarantine carriers of severe communicable disease to protect society, we also have the right to quarantine a person whose criminal activity has shown that he or she is a comparable danger to society. . . .
>
> I suggest that a society with that system would be a nightmare of insecurity and uncertainty, as well as injustice. . . . [T]he imposition of quarantining or monitoring . . . would not even be conditioned on a person's having actually done anything, so that people could not order their lives in such a way as to be assured of freedom from this kind of intervention. In the absence of any requirement for intervention other than established danger . . . there would be no principled or transparent basis on which the State officials could determine what was to be done, and on which the appropriateness of their decisions could be reviewed. . . .
>
> I suggest it would be grossly unjust for the law to authorize the subjection to coercive treatment of a person (having the capacity for reasonable decision-making and control of conduct) otherwise than through application of due process.[3]

There is plenty of precedent for Pereboom's reasoning, and many of those who deny that human beings are responsible for what they do in fact tend to

2 For example, Jeffrey Murphy says that when a person persistently ignores the rights of others, "his 'rights' may be suspended and he may be subjected to involuntary preventive detention and therapy and perhaps even (if his case is hopeless) to painless extermination" (1972: 296). He has subsequently renounced that position (Murphy 2007).

3 *R + C = FW*, pp. 219–220.

argue like this:[4] Wrongdoing is the result of a character flaw, one that should be treated with therapy, compulsory if necessary, and if therapy doesn't work the only alternative left for a humane criminal justice system is indefinite detention. Hodgson's concern is that if we abandon desert and cease treating human beings as responsible, this terrible choice between therapy and detention is inevitable.

To make one more point, one that might seem to go without saying but does not: Free will is a key player in all this. Hodgson believes that moral responsibility requires free will, and the relationship between moral responsibility and free will is one of the reasons he is committed to establishing the possibility of free will. "For my part", he says, "I don't think that retribution could be justified if there is no free will or responsibility for conduct".[5] As we wend our way through this we will see that some writers believe that responsibility requires free will and some don't, and that some believe that free will is inconsistent with causation of action by things outside our control and some don't. Most writers, though, both those who believe there is responsibility and those who don't, agree with Hodgson that without responsibility and desert the line between malice and madness disappears, and we are left only with the alternative of therapy or detention.

I think that Hodgson's goal is a worthy one; like him I think it is essential to keep madness and malice separate. Nevertheless, I think he is mistaken in two ways. He is mistaken, first, in believing that desert, responsibility, and retribution can do the job, in particular that they can do anything at all to protect us from a system in which the rational, competent criminal may be subjected to coercive treatment and indefinite detention. And he is mistaken in thinking that if desert, responsibility, and retribution are not available (for whatever reason) to do the job, we are compelled to treat all criminality much as we treat illness.

II

How exactly is desert supposed to constrain conduct that is not properly described as punishment? To be more specific, how does the requirement of desert keep the state from imposing treatment and indefinite detention on rational and competent wrongdoers when it is imposed (as we will see) as a form of *regulation* and not of punishment?

4 We find well-developed examples of what Pereboom calls the Quarantine theory going back to the work of the positive criminologist Enrico Ferri and the sociological criminologist Franz von Liszt at the end of the nineteenth century. See Enrico Ferri, *The Positive School of Criminology* (tr. Ernest Untermann) (Charles H. Kerr & Company, Chicago, 1908); Hermann Mannheim, "The German Prevention of Crime Act 1933", *26 J. Crim. L. and Criminology* 517 (1935); Werner Landecker, "Criminology in Germany", 31 *J. Crim. L. and Criminology* 551 (1941).

5 *R + C = FW*, p. 223.

A

Desert, if it ever did actually attach to a human being, would mark the limits of justification in the imposition of punishment on that human being. But it would say absolutely nothing about a host of other things, including whatever the state does outside the imposition of punishment.

But, you may say, that restricts the concept of desert too much. Someone who has paid the price for his crime does not deserve to be detained further, and someone who has committed no crime at all does not deserve to be detained just because he is dangerous. That's surely true (and *a fortiori* true if you believe as I do that no one deserves anything in this deep, moralistic sense of desert). But so what? The person who asks about detaining the dangerous or about forcibly treating the dangerous is not asking whether they deserve it. He is asking whether there is another justification for detaining and treating, and desert or the lack of desert doesn't enter into that calculation at all. This point is so important that to ignore it leaves us more or less vulnerable to pernicious changes that are taking place in the world of criminal justice.

B

To begin with the system I know best, the due process line between the mad and the malicious in the United States appears to be disintegrating. The disintegration in the courts began, I would say, with the decision in *United States v Salerno*,[6] a case testing the constitutionality of the Bail Reform Act of 1984. To the traditional grounds for the denial of bail – protecting the judicial process and preventing flight – the 1984 Act added dangerousness:

> If . . . the judicial officer finds that no condition or combination of conditions will reasonably assure the appearance of the person as required and the safety of any other person and the community, such judicial officer shall order the detention of the person before trial.[7]

For many crimes the prosecutor must establish dangerousness on a case by case basis, but in the case of certain specified crimes there is a presumption under the statute that the safety of others could not be ensured, and that pretrial detention is appropriate.

In the *Salerno* case, the petitioner had been denied bail in trial court on these grounds, and the Second Circuit Federal Court of Appeals had reversed the trial court's decision. According to the Second Circuit, due process "prohibits the total deprivation of liberty simply as a means of preventing future crimes".

> The system of criminal justice contemplated by the Due Process Clause – indeed, by all of the criminal justice guarantees of the Bill of Rights – is a

6 481 U.S. 739 (1987).

7 Bail Reform Act of 1984, Pub.L No. 98–473, §§202–10, 98 Stat. 1837, 1976–87 (codified as amended at 18 U.S.C. §§3141–50 (2000)).

> system of announcing in statutes of adequate clarity what conduct is prohibited and then invoking the penalties of the law against those who have committed crimes. The liberty protected under that system is premised on the accountability of free men and women for what they have done, not for what they may do. The Due Process Clause reflects the constitutional imperative that incarceration to protect society from criminals may be accomplished only as punishment of those convicted for past crimes and not as regulation of those feared likely to commit future crimes.[8]

The government petitioned for certiorari, and the Supreme Court took the case. The defence (now the respondent) argued, as it had in the lower court, that denial of bail on grounds of dangerousness was impermissible punishment before trial. In a decision written by Chief Justice Rehnquist, the Court responded that because this was not intended as punishment, and because it served a legitimate state purpose – regulation – it was not punishment and therefore did not run afoul of the constitutional limits on punishment.

> Unless Congress expressly intended to impose punitive restrictions, the punitive/regulatory distinction turns on "whether an alternative purpose to which [the restriction] may rationally be connected is assignable for it, and whether it appears excessive in relation to the alternative purpose assigned [to it]".[9]

The Court found that there *was* an alternative purpose, namely, "preventing danger to the community", and that Salerno's detention was not punishment. It was preventive detention, and so it was not necessary that he have been convicted first. The test was a balancing one, Salerno's liberty interest against the state's interest in security.

Now I think that an argument can be made against preventive detention before trial. But it also seems to me that the Court was right to reject an argument based upon the constitutional limits on punishment, and would have been right to reject one based upon desert. And what I think this illustrates is that in the effort to keep the state within bounds a device that operates only upon punishment is no help at all. We do allow the state to deprive people of freedom in cases in which it is not meant as punishment; and when it is not meant as punishment we do not insist on the safeguards that punishment requires. Taxation restricts freedom; enforced military service restricts freedom; quarantine of those with contagious diseases restricts freedom. Whatever we think of those impositions, it would be foolish to insist that they could be imposed only on people who had committed crimes. The law restricts our freedom when it permits zoning ordinances. We think such restrictions are justified when they are called for by the general welfare. We may believe that compensation is required

8 *United States v Salerno*, 794 F.2d 64, 71–72 (2d Cir. 1986) (reversed in the Supreme Court decision in the same case, cited earlier).

9 481 U.S. at 747.

when property rights are limited, but it would seem odd to suppose that only the property of convicted criminals could be zoned (Corrado 2013c: 14). It is important for me to repeat that I am not defending preventive detention for competent persons, even before trial. I am arguing that to insist upon desert as a way to avoid it is to miss the point.[10]

Of course, *Salerno* was not the end of the story. Had the Court's reasoning been limited to pretrial detention, it would not have been so alarming. Although pretrial detention can be abused, it has a natural ending point with either acquittal or conviction, and is not indefinite. Unfortunately in later cases the Court did approve of indefinite detention of persons who were at least competent enough to justify punishment. One example is sex offender legislation, which Hodgson mentions as being part of Australian law as well.[11]

In the American cases,[12] the Court approved of post-sentence detention of sex offenders who remained dangerous. It is true that the Court imposed a limitation on such detention: Offenders could be detained indefinitely, but only if it could be shown that they had difficulty controlling their behaviour. But here's the thing: It wasn't the notion of desert that set that limit. The individuals involved had been adjudged to deserve punishment, and by the time they were committed for preventive detention they would have satisfied their retribution-debt, if I may call it that. They did not *deserve* anything more. Nor could they be said to be beyond desert because of mental incompetence; had that been so, they would not have been punished at all. Instead, they were to be both punished in proportion to their desert, and then detained as regulation limited only by the fundamental right to freedom from restraint. That right, the Court said, prevents the state from detaining everyone who is judged to be dangerous, and limits it to those who have difficulty controlling their behaviour.

To repeat once more, the point is that desert played no role in any limitation upon their detention. It limited the amount of punishment that could properly be imposed, at least in theory. But when punishment came to an end, so did the useful role of desert. The Court looked elsewhere for a reason to limit the detention of mentally competent offenders, and it settled, in a very controversial decision, on the desire to avoid permitting the wholesale detention of dangerous actors. Notice, however, that there is nothing in the theory carved out by the Court that would prevent the state from detaining individuals who had not committed a crime and who were not sufficiently incompetent to justify civil commitment, on the ground that they were dangerous because they would find it difficult to avoid criminal behaviour. Any argument to the contrary based upon constitutional limitations upon punishment, or upon the moral notion of desert, would only betray confusion.

10 The notion of competency that I employ here does not depend upon freedom of the will (see Corrado 2017).

11 *R + C = FW*, pp. 217–218.

12 *Kansas v Hendricks*, 521 U.S. 346 (1997); *Kansas v Crane*, 534 U.S. 407 (2002); *United States v Comstock*, 560 U.S. 126 (2010).

There are other examples in addition to the sex offender legislation: the indefinite detention after sentence imposed in some states under a "guilty but mentally ill" verdict authorized every time a defendant dares to raise an insanity defence; the current treatment of suspected terrorists, which does not require any showing of difficulty in avoiding criminal acts. I have reviewed the progression toward preventive criminal justice in the United States elsewhere.[13] Desert, retribution, and responsibility have played no role in obstructing or slowing that progress. They could not have played any role; they are beside the point.

C

I think it's fair to say that because of our naïve faith that limitations upon punishment were enough we were caught off guard by the advance of preventive justice. It seems to grate against the Anglo-American conscience to permit both punishment and detention for the same individual, based on the same sort of evidence; and yet the old safeguards appeared to have nothing to say against it. The patch created by the Supreme Court to block wholesale detention of dangerous individuals – the requirement that the offenders in question have difficulty avoiding criminal behaviour – is a makeshift solution, one that cries out for a theoretical justification, and such justifications have begun to appear. Needless to say, they do not rely on desert.

The attitude in Europe, or at least in many European countries, is very different. Just to take two leading examples, Germany and Italy have had "double track" systems, providing for both punishment and subsequent detention, since before the Second World War. Granted, those systems were developed under fascist regimes, but they have become part of standard thinking about criminal justice, and legal commentators do not seem to be discomfited by them. Furthermore, the only limitation upon detention is demonstrated dangerousness.[14]

And it is worth pointing out that the origin of such systems is not in fact fascist, but is found, surprisingly, in the twentieth century history of British law. Under the Prevention of Crimes Act of 1908, which was designed in part to deal with "persistent offenders", a judge might sentence a convict to penal servitude followed by a period of preventive detention. According to the Act:

> Where a person is convicted . . . of a crime, and subsequently admits or is found to be a *habitual criminal*, and the court passes a sentence of penal servitude . . . the court, if . . . it is expedient for the protection of the public . . . may pass a further sentence ordering that on [the termination of his penal sentence] he be detained for a period not exceeding ten nor less than

13 *Presumed Dangerous*, *supra*.

14 On the double track in Europe, see the discussion in my "Chapter Two: Retribution and the Limits of Criminal Justice", from *After Responsibility* (in progress), available at SSRN: http://ssrn.com/abstract=2771325, pp. 10–11.

> five years . . . and such detention is hereinafter referred to as preventive detention.[15]

To many this seemed shocking in the British system, upon which the American and Australian systems are founded. Winston Churchill, not generally regarded as a bleeding heart liberal, thought so, but he voiced the wrong objection. He is reported to have said: "There is a great danger of using smooth words for ugly things. Preventive detention is penal servitude in all its aspects".[16] Preventive detention may have been wrong in the circumstances, but not because it was punishment. It was precisely *not* punishment, and that is why those due process limits that reflect the requirement of desert were ineffective against it.

One conclusion to be drawn from this survey of existing criminal justice systems in the United States, Germany, Italy, and Britain might be that these are all evil systems, at least in regard to preventive detention and coerced treatment. I would argue that that is a not very helpful conclusion to draw. A more helpful conclusion would be that the notion of desert does not have the cash value we once thought it had. As attitudes toward preventive methods have changed, our intuitions about justice have begun to change, and the change is reflected in evolving philosophical theories. We find prominent scholars arguing that there is a place for preventive detention of the competent,[17] and there is no refuge from this advancing wave in the notion of desert.

What is necessary is a comprehensive theory of criminal justice that tells us what the limits of state action are, regardless of whether that action is characterized as punishment. Since my intuitions about these things – I don't mean theoretical principles but intuitions about what the state is actually entitled to do, regardless of how it is labelled – are very close to those of Hodgson, what I would like to see is a theory that explains why preventive detention and coerced treatment of the mentally competent should be impermissible in most, though perhaps not all, cases.

D

In summary, the rights we are concerned with are not protected by a principle that says:

> D. Punish only when deserved, and only to the extent deserved.

15 Prevention of Crimes Act (1908) (emphasis added). See Cicely Craven, "UK Report of the Department Committee on Persistent Offenders", 3 *Howard Journal of Criminal Justice* 69 (1932); Leon Radzinowicz and Roger Hood, "Judicial Discretion and Sentencing Standards: Victorian Attempts to Solve a Perennial Problem", 127 *U.Pa.L. Rev.* 1288 (1979).

16 Leon Radzinowicz and Roger Hood, *supra*, at 1347.

17 Alec Walen, "A Unified Theory of Detention, with Application to Preventive Detention for Suspected Terrorists", 70 *Md. L. Rev.* 871 (2011); Kimberly Kessler Ferzan, "Beyond Crime and Commitment: Justifying Liberty Deprivations of the Dangerous and Responsible", 96 *Minn. L. Rev.* 141 (2011).

It is true that we might argue for a more expansive principle that said something like this:

> UD. When dealing with the rational and competent, punishment to the extent deserved is the only justification for limiting freedom.

But in addition to the fact that that principle is generally false – think of the preceding discussion of such things as military service, compulsory education, and limitation of freedom through zoning ordinances – such a principle would require justification that goes beyond desert itself; for desert itself says nothing at all about what should happen outside punishment.

Consider this concrete example: In New Zealand there is some concern about the proposed new "post-sentence detention orders", which permit judges to impose detention after completion of a prison sentence if the person under consideration poses "a very high risk of imminent and serious sexual or violent reoffending". The New Zealand Law Foundation published a criticism of the proposal, suggesting that it would violate various rights of detainees, including double jeopardy.[18]

That question has been answered in the United States: Post-conviction detention of individuals who have difficulty controlling their violent actions is not punishment but regulation, and therefore such due process protections as double jeopardy don't apply. (One difficulty, remember, is that the fact that the detention follows conviction entails that the detainee is responsible for what he has done.) I am opposed to the use of post-sentence detention in most cases, but I find it hard to disagree with this particular answer: It *isn't* punishment, and so the safeguards that surround punishment don't apply. That doesn't mean that it is acceptable; far from it. It means that a better foundation for prohibiting it has to be found.

My conclusion is that Hodgson is wrong in thinking that the notions of desert, retribution, and responsibility are helpful in avoiding a world in which the same methods are applied to the mad and the malicious. What they do in fact do is to lull us into a comfortable sense of security – as long as we insist on desert and retribution as a prerequisite for punishment we can avoid those horrific consequences – when the horrific consequences are already piling up outside the greenhouse in which philosophers have cultivated and pruned their ideas of punishment.[19]

III

Where does that leave us? It is one thing to believe, as I do, that no one is morally responsible for anything, so that no one deserves punishment. It is another

18 See Lynda Hagen, New Zealand Law Foundation, "Government Rethinks Post-Sentence Treatment of High Risk Offenders", 11 April 2014, online at www.lawsociety.org.nz/lawtalk/lawtalk-archives/issue-839/government-rethinks-post-sentence-treatment-of-high-risk-offenders.

19 For explanation of the "greenhouse" metaphor, see Corrado (1996: 813–814).

thing to argue, as I have just done, that even if the notion of desert were to find application it would not serve the purposes Hodgson means for it to serve. That argument does not depend upon any metaphysical claims about human freedom or any moral claims about responsibility.

If the notion of desert does not protect us from the world of *A Clockwork Orange*, does it follow that we have no choice but to make our peace with such a world, a world in which those who come to the attention of the criminal justice system are treated (to use Hodgson's mild word) inappropriately? Once it is put so bluntly, the oddity of the question becomes apparent. What a strange thing it would be if in rejecting one justification for appropriate behaviour we somehow found ourselves condemned to behave inappropriately! What has to be done instead is to dismiss the easy but faulty explanation and to look for a better justification, one that jibes with our considered judgements about appropriate behaviour.

A

Let's start with the following three propositions:

ED. The notion of desert is not available to patrol the line between madness and malice.

NA. If the notion of desert is not available to patrol the line between malice and madness, it is morally appropriate to treat the malicious in the same way we treat the mad, that is, with therapy (rational or pharmaceutical) and preventive detention.

IT. To treat the malicious in the same way we treat the mad is morally inappropriate.

The first proposition expresses what I would call "the Emptiness of Desert". You should accept ED if you do not believe the notion of desert has any application in the real world. But you should also accept it if you accept my argument of the last section, that is, that even if some individuals do on some occasions deserve praise or blame, reward or punishment, that in no way protects them against what Hodgson calls inappropriate treatment. The second proposition, "No Alternative", expresses the belief that there is no alternative to desert if we want to avoid subjecting competent individuals to compelled therapy and preventive detention. The third proposition expresses the view that such treatment (therapy and preventive detention) is inappropriate for competent individuals; we can call it "the Inappropriateness Thesis".

You know how this goes: The three propositions are inconsistent, and we are compelled in reason to reject one of them. Libertarians, compatibilists, and semi-compatibilists all agree that desert makes sense, and if they are not persuaded by my argument of the last section, they will reject ED. That means that NA and IT present no problem for them; they can insist on the truth of each of them. Indeed, I suspect that much of the support for libertarianism, compatibilism, and semi-compatibilism, and for the reliance on the notion of desert, comes from the conviction that to believe otherwise would require us to deny proposition IT: We would have no alternative but to accept the inappropriate world of *A Clockwork Orange*.

What the structure of the inconsistent triad makes clear, however, is that in fact the rejection of IT does not follow from the acceptance of ED. There is an implicit middle step, NA, that is rarely acknowledged and to my knowledge never defended. The person who accepts ED is committed to rejecting IT only if she also accepts NA. Almost everyone *does* accept NA, of course, not only those who, like Hodgson, accept the applicability of desert in the world, but also sceptics like Derk Pereboom and Gregg Caruso, who do not.[20] I agree with Hodgson and others that we should not reject proposition IT, and that to subject competent human beings to preventive measures in response to crime is inappropriate. But what I would like to argue here is that the proper move to make is to reject NA, No Alternative, rather than ED, the Emptiness of Desert.[21]

Although nearly everyone accepts NA, it is hard to see what it has in its favour. I have never seen an explicit argument in support of it, but I believe the implicit reasoning must be something like this: The basis of the difference between legal competence and criminal insanity, and the justification for the difference in treatment, is the presence of responsibility in one case and the absence of it in the other. If you reject the possibility of responsibility, or if you think that responsibility cannot do the job, then you are left without a distinction: The two must be treated the same. But, of course, we are not left without a distinction; we *can* tell the difference, even if we deny metaphysical freedom and moral responsibility. What is missing is a justification for treating them differently, and we should not be quick to conclude that there cannot be one. What is wanted here is a theory that rests a justification for different treatment for the two groups upon a genuine distinction between the two, one that has nothing to do with retribution and desert.

B

Why do we feel the need to accept the Inappropriateness Thesis? What is it we want to avoid? I suggest that what we are afraid of is a world in which harsh treatment of offenders is avoided in favour of the attempt to "fix" them. Enforced therapy and preventive detention (which, together, I will call "the therapeutic approach") are, of course, harsh, but that is not the point. If they could be made less harsh, if the danger could be eliminated without any harshness at all, that would be preferable in such a world. And a world in which harsh treatment is inflicted as an end in itself, as it necessarily is in a system that retributively punishes in response to crime, is seen as inhumane.

20 Caruso and Pereboom (2017) explicitly argue for this conclusion.

21 Jeanette Kennett and Cordelia Fine (2004) also reject NA. I am grateful to the editors for this citation.

There are many sorts of objections to this "humane", therapeutic approach, and I will not try to canvas them all here (see Bosanquet 1919: 200–202; Lewis 1953; Morris 1968). Hodgson has summed them up eloquently: Such an approach treats human beings as "vehicles to be manipulated for the general good". There is no insurance that a dangerous but innocent person will not be plucked from the street to be repaired or simply detained. A system of punishment, on the other hand, is based upon trust and a desire for order in our lives: It requires trust that human beings are capable of responding to the threat of punishment, and it sacrifices some of the certainty that might come with warehousing and treating everyone who shows signs of being dangerous in order to preserve the control each of us has over our future. It imposes the threat of harsh treatment in limited and proportional measure as the most appropriate way to exercise some control over the amount of crime that society is willing to bear without at the same time depriving people of a say in how they respond to that control.

But it is too much to suppose that punishment, harsh treatment imposed in part because the offender *deserves* it, is the only alternative to the inappropriate "humane" approach. What is called for, I believe, is an alternative justification for the imposition of limited, proportional harsh treatment imposed upon individuals who are capable of reasoning more or less soundly, and capable of implementing their reasoning more or less accurately in action. I have sketched out a justification of that sort in another paper, a justification that is intended to support a system of *correction* rather than punishment.

Correction is like punishment in consisting in the imposition of harsh treatment intended to be harsh, but the justification for it lies not in desert and the benefit to society but in the benefit to the individual corrected. It is a benefit in two different senses: First of all, it is a limitation upon the state's regulatory power to keep the peace; the acceptance of the applicability of correction in a given case insulates the recipient against enforced treatment and detention based upon dangerousness. The individual who qualifies for correction but has not committed a crime may not be seized on grounds of dangerousness alone, and he may not be subjected to coerced treatment and indefinite detention if he does commit a crime.

But there is also a benefit in giving the offender the opportunity (once within the system) to convert harsh treatment into more appropriate calculations, leading to socially more acceptable behaviour. For this reason, correction is limited to those who have the capacity to comprehend what is happening to them, to draw more or less sound conclusions from that comprehension, and to act upon those conclusions.

As I intend the theory, the benefit to the offender is not the resulting correction in his thinking, which would instead be a benefit to society. The theory is not meant to be consequential in that sense. The benefit, rather, lies in the *opportunity* to change. The theory is a kind of character theory, aimed at giving the offender a chance to correct faults that interfere with his proper functioning in society, and it depends, therefore, upon the offender's ability to convert harsh treatment into better reasoning patterns, and, trusting to that ability, guaranteeing that the offender will not be subject to the therapeutic approach.

A prerequisite, therefore, for allocating an offender to the correction system rather than to the preventive system is that the offender in question be able to carry out this processing of harsh treatment. The offender who is incapable of sound reasoning, or incapable of conforming his behaviour to his reasoning, would not be a candidate for correction, but would be consigned to therapy and prevention. The ability to convert harsh treatment into socially acceptable behaviour is what distinguishes the two groups that we want to distinguish, the competent from the incompetent. Competence of this sort has nothing to do with moral responsibility or metaphysical freedom.

How is correction different from punishment? You might be tempted to think of correction as non-retributive punishment. I think that is a mistake, and is based upon a confusion. The notion of punishment is tied to the notion of retribution; I have argued elsewhere that you can't have one without the other.[22] But whether you think of it as correction or as non-retributive punishment, two things must be kept in mind. The first is that correction is based upon benefit, discussed earlier. The second is that the notion of desert is alien to it. The offender is not to be treated as someone who "has it coming to him", because he doesn't.

To suppose that a person deserves harsh treatment is to suppose that the harsh treatment is a good thing in itself, and that it is not something to be regretted. Michael Moore (1984: 242–243) has defended retributive punishment by appealing to sentiments that show the "inherent rightness" of imposing harsh treatment on those who have broken the law. There is no doubt in my mind that all of us harbour sentiments of that sort, sentiments approving of the imposition of suffering on someone who has inflicted suffering on another, and there is no doubt in my mind that such sentiments are, up to a point, useful, at least in our day-to-day affairs. But it goes too far to suppose that a political institution might properly be founded upon those sentiments. Such an institution would itself be an evil thing, and although the most appropriate way to treat competent offenders is with the imposition of limited and proportional harsh treatment, the need to employ it should always be a matter of regret.

C

Correction is a kind of paternalistic approach to crime, it is true, but the sense in which it is paternalistic is not pernicious. The paternalism involved is not the sort that guides our treatment of the mentally ill and the incompetent, who are – at least temporarily – beyond the reach of reasoning and threats. It is instead the optimistic paternalism of the sort that guides our treatment of children. The child who has endangered herself or others may be sent to her room by a loving but angry parent, not because she deserves it but in order to help her to understand that what she has done is wrong. The state is not our parent, of course, and we are not children. But the optimistic use of correction should be the same.

22 For the argument that without desert and retribution there is no punishment, that desert and retribution are part of the meaning of punishment, see Corrado (2001).

There are thus similarities between a correction theory and theories proposed by Herbert Morris and others (Morris 1981; Hampton 1984). It rests its justification for imposing harsh punishment in part on the promise that the offender will learn something from his incarceration. There are two things, however, that distinguish correction from a moral education theory of punishment. First of all, it is not the education itself that justifies. There is no guarantee that the offender will take the harsh treatment to heart. The justification lies rather in the benefit to the offender, in the chance the offender is being given to change his behaviour. To see this as a benefit, we must understand it against the background of the state's right to protect the peace. The other instrument for combatting crime that the state has in its arsenal is the draconian one of enforced therapy and indefinite detention, and it is in insulating the competent offender from that sort of treatment that we find the justification for the harsh treatment.

The other thing that distinguishes correction from an education theory of punishment is that it is not about punishment. In my view punishment is essentially a matter of retribution and desert, and those notions are tied up inevitably with a sense of outrage against the offender, and a sense that the imposition of pain upon those who have caused pain is a good thing. However much we would like to cleanse the theory of punishment of those implications, they are inextricably tied up with it.

Pereboom argues against such theories:

> [W]here punishment might be successful in morally educating children, it is typically administered in the context of a caring environment. Punishment outside such a context arguably tends to create resentful attitudes and behavior rather than moral improvement.
>
> (2001: 163)

How appropriate that an instrument that some believe is rooted in the sentiment of resentment should provoke a response of resentment in those who suffer under that instrument. Is it too much to hope that an instrument not rooted in resentment might be more effective, an instrument rooted, if not in love, at least in good will toward the offender?

What would a system of harsh treatment rooted in good will look like? Forging correction into a plausible theory will, I admit, require a lot of work, but one further thing that it has in its favour is that it gives the right result for those who reject the usefulness of the concept of desert. Unless something like correction can be made to fly, unless there is some alternative to punishment (with its inescapable attachment to retribution and desert), a person in my position who does not believe in responsibility will find it hard to avoid rejecting proposition IT and settling for what so clearly seems to be inappropriate behaviour.

D

It is not my object here to say any more about the details of the theory (see Corrado 2013a), but rather to address some questions about what I have said so far, and some obvious objections to it.

First of all, if correction (laid out as it is against the background of the state's power to detain indefinitely and to insist upon therapy) is indeed a benefit, what obligates the state to offer this benefit to the offender? Why would the state not be justified in withholding this benefit? The answer, I think, lies in precisely those things that make detention and therapy inappropriate for competent human beings. Call it respect; call it what you like. My starting point here is the fundamental intuition that leads Hodgson to insist upon responsibility and retribution. But Hodgson's solution is wrong; responsibility and retribution are not suited to satisfy the requirements set up by that intuition, if indeed they have any application in the real world at all.

There is also a question on the other side of this: Is the correction regime to be imposed willy-nilly upon competent offenders, or should they be given a choice between correction and prevention? It's not hard to see that leaving it a choice might invite abuse, by both offenders and officials. On the other hand, it would help to keep the state honest. It would guarantee that the option of correction really was a benefit to the offender. Although in general correction should be more appealing than preventive measures, offenders would be inclined to accept correction over prevention only if correction really did count as a benefit: if the penal sentences were not excessively long, if prison treatment were not barbaric. (I assume that a sound system of prevention, aimed as it is at the general good, would require the state to compensate the detainee whose freedom is taken for the general good, and that is something that complicates this question.[23])

And finally, where do we place the psychopath in this system?[24] I have argued, in another paper, that since the psychopath is assumed to be capable of sound reasoning, and since nothing prevents him from implementing his conclusions in action, he should be subject to something like correction (Corrado 2013b). However, if the essential characteristic of the psychopath is his inability to understand the suffering of others, the question arises whether the psychopath has what it takes to make use of corrective harsh treatment. Until that question is answered, the theory has nothing to say about the psychopath.

There are also some obvious objections. The first is this: A theory like this one would not justify the application of harsh treatment to those who do not have a character manifestly in need of correction, or to those who committed crimes in circumstances unlikely to arise again. We might imagine someone who, though in every other way a stellar citizen, takes the opportunity one night to murder his fiancé with an axe. Or imagine someone who reacted with violence to a situation highly unlikely ever to recur. The damage done is unfortunate, but there is no reason to think that in either case the offender would benefit by the application

23 See Corrado (1996) and Smilansky (2011). But see also the discussion by Markel (2013).

24 On the problem the psychopath presents for the system of punishment, see Kiehl and Hoffman (2011), Slobogin (2003), Morse (2008), Litton (2008), Levy (2007), Kennett and Fine (2004), and Corrado (1996). Stephen Morse's other contributions on this topic are too numerous for me to try to mention all of them. Three earlier philosophical efforts to deal with the problem were Murphy (1972), Schoeman (1979), and Floud and Young (1981).

of harsh treatment, and so he should be released. Another way to put this is that we should not try to correct someone whose crime is out of character.

The answer in both cases is the same: The willingness to break the law in those limited circumstances shows a character flaw, one that needs to be corrected. The offender should not be willing to commit a similar crime even in the unlikely case in which those circumstances recur. Moreover, lack of dangerousness is not a defence since correction is not aimed at his dangerousness but rather at his willingness to break the law. Someone who is willing to break the law under extremely rare (but not exculpatory) circumstances is not dangerous, but does have a character flaw. Someone who is violent by nature but resists breaking the law may be dangerous but does not have a character flaw of the appropriate sort.

And a second possible objection of the same sort: Why wouldn't the theory justify pulling people in need of correction off the street, even if they have not committed any crime? The answer, I think, lies in the notion of benefit that justifies the imposition of harsh treatment; part of the benefit of a correction regime is precisely the guarantee that this sort of arbitrary detention will be ruled out for those who qualify for correction.

The most serious question that can be raised, however, is of a different sort: What would such a theory say about the "persistent" offender, one who can but will not over time reap the benefit of correction? Must society release the competent but persistent offender after he has served his limited term of imprisonment, only to watch him wreak havoc before he can be apprehended once more?

This is no more of a problem, notice, for the proposed theory of correction than it is for a theory of retributive punishment, given the collapse over time of the line between retribution and prevention, and perhaps less of a problem. The theory of desert either provides no protection against the post-sentence detention of *any* offender, or, if called into service as the only justification for the physical restraint of competent offenders, would simply disallow it completely. Because correction is based upon benefit and not desert, on the other hand, there are practical questions to be answered. For one thing, how much recalcitrance must society countenance in order to guarantee the benefits of correction, including freedom from preventive restraint?

For minor crimes, society's patience and trust should be virtually unlimited; but the patience for vicious crimes will have a limit. The period of correction for a vicious crime will be longer and require a greater investment, and there comes a point at which we may be justified in supposing that the criminal not only won't but can't benefit from limited correction. He simply lacks the cognitive and volitional capacities to make use of what he is given.[25]

25 The existence of psychopaths – if they exist, and if they are anything more than persistent criminals (that is, competent persons with a profound tendency to choose to commit crimes) – may require a modification in what we require of someone before he can be considered suitable for correction: It may be that the correctable person will be one who can not only reason more or less correctly and act more or less accurately upon the conclusions he reaches, but understand the suffering of others. See Litton (2013) and Corrado (2013b).

This point should not come too early, at the risk of undermining the trust upon which the benefits of the system depend. On the other hand, it may be that identification of an individual as a psychopath (if there is such a thing) would warrant the state in concluding that in spite of an ability to reason and an ability to implement his reasoning in action, he is nevertheless unable to benefit from correction. It may be that the ability to empathize with the suffering of others is a necessary condition for correction to work.

Conclusion

Hodgson is quite right to suppose that it is inappropriate to subject competent individuals to a regime of therapy and preventive detention. I would claim that he is wrong, however, about two things. He is wrong to suppose that desert and responsibility succeed in protecting us against a world in which coerced therapy and preventive detention may be used against competent individuals. And he is wrong as well to suppose that if desert and responsibility do not do the job, then we are doomed as rational beings to accept the application of the prevention and therapy, all for the general good. I am confident about the first of these two claims, and I remain optimistic about the possibility of demonstrating the second.

References

Bosanquet, B 1919, *Some Suggestions in Ethics*, MacMillan and Co., London.

Caruso, G and Pereboom, D 2017, 'Hard-Incompatibilism Existentialism: Neuroscience, Punishment, and Meaning in Life', in G Caruso and O Flanagan (eds), *Neuroexistentialism: Meaning, Morals, and Purpose in the Age of Neuroscience*, Oxford University Press, New York.

Corrado, ML 1996, 'Punishment and the Wild Beast of Prey: The Problem of Preventive Detention', *Journal of Criminal Law & Criminology* 86: 778–814.

Corrado, ML 2001, 'Abolition of Punishment', *Suffolk University Law Review* 35(2): 257–276.

Corrado, ML 2013a, 'Why Do We Resist Hard Incompatiblism? Some Thoughts on Freedom and Determinism', in T Nadelhoffer (ed), *The Future of Rehabilitation and Punishment*, Oxford University Press, New York.

Corrado, ML 2013b, 'Some Notes on Preventive Detention and Psychopathy', in K Kiehl and W Sinnott-Armstrong (eds), *Handbook of Psychopathy and Law*, Oxford University Press, New York.

Corrado, ML 2013c, *Presumed Dangerous: Punishment, Responsibility, and Preventive Detention in American Jurisprudence*, Carolina Academic Press, Durham.

Corrado, ML "Chapter Two: Retribution and the Limits of Criminal Justice," *After Responsibility* (in progress), available June 2016 at SSRN, http://ssrn.com/abstract=2771325.

Corrado, ML 2017, 'Insanity and Free Will: The Humanitarian Argument for Abolition', in M White (ed), *The Insanity Defense: Multidisciplinary Views on Its History, Trends, and Controversies*, Praeger, Santa Barbara.

Craven, C 1932, 'The Report of the Departmental Committee on Persistent Offenders', *Howard Journal of Criminal Justice* 3(3): 69–72.

Ferri, E 1908, *The Positive School of Criminology*, trans. E Untermann, Charles H. Kerr and Company, Chicago.

Ferzan, KK 2011, 'Beyond Crime and Commitment: Justifying Liberty Deprivations of the Dangerous and Responsible', *Minnesota Law Review* 96: 141–193.

Floud, JE and Young, W 1981, *Dangerousness and Criminal Justice*, Heinemann, London.

Goldman, A 1979, 'The Paradox of Punishment', *Philosophy & Public Affairs* 9: 42–58.

Hagen, Lynda, New Zealand Law Foundation, 'Government Rethinks Post-Sentence Treatment of High Risk Offenders', 11 April 2014, www.lawsociety.org.nz/lawtalk/lawtalk-archives/issue-839/government-rethinks-post-sentence-treatment-of-high-risk-offenders.

Hampton, J 1984, 'The Moral Education Theory of Punishment', *Philosophy and Public Affairs* 13: 208–238.

Hodgson, DH 2012, *Rationality + Consciousness = Free Will*, Oxford University Press, New York.

Kaufman, WRP 2012, *Honor and Revenge: A Theory of Punishment*, Springer, Dordrecht.

Kennett, J and Fine, C 2004, 'Mental Impairment, Moral Understanding and Criminal Responsibility: Psychopathy and the Purposes of Punishment', *International Journal of Law & Psychiatry* 27: 425–443.

Kiehl, KA and Hoffman, MB 2011, 'The Criminal Psychopath: History, Neuroscience, Treatment and Economics', *Jurimetrics* 51: 355–397.

Landecker, W 1941, 'Criminology in Germany', 31 *Journal of Criminal Law and Criminology* 31: 551–575.

Levy, N 2007, 'The Responsibility of the Psychopath Revisited', *Philosophy, Psychiatry, & Psychology* 14(2): 129–138.

Lewis, CS 1953, 'The Humanitarian Theory of Punishment', *Res Judicatae* 6: 224–230.

Litton, P 2008, 'Responsibility Status of the Psychopath: On Moral Reasoning and Rational Self-Governance', *Rutgers Law Journal* 39: 349–392.

Litton, P 2013, 'Criminal Responsibility and Psychopathy: Do Psychopaths Have a Right to Excuse', in KA Kiehl and WP Sinnott-Armstrong (eds), *Handbook on Psychopathy and Law*, Oxford University Press, New York.

Mannheim, H 1935, 'The German Prevention of Crime Act 1933', *Journal of Criminal Law and Criminology* 26: 517–537.

Markel, D 2013, 'Compensation, Takings and Preventive Detention for Failure to Appear and Dangerousness', *PrawfsBlawg*, web blog post, viewed 3 March 2018, http://prawfsblawg.blogs.com/prawfsblawg/2013/10/compensation-takings-and-preventive-detention-for-failure-to-appear-and-dangerousness.html.

Moore, M 1984, *Law and Psychiatry: Rethinking the Relationship*, Cambridge University Press, New York.

Morris, H 1968, 'Persons and Punishment', *The Monist* 52: 475–501.

Morris, H 1981, 'The Paternalistic Theory of Punishment', *American Philosophical Quarterly* 18: 263–271.

Morse, SJ 2008, 'Psychopathy and Criminal Responsibility', *Neuroethics* 1: 205–212.

Murphy, J 1972, 'Moral Death: A Kantian Essay on Psychopathy', *Ethics* 82: 284–298.

Murphy, J 2007, 'Remorse, Apology, and Mercy', *Ohio State Journal of Criminal Law* 4: 423–453.

Pereboom, D 2001, *Living Without Free Will*, Oxford University Press, New York.
Radzinowicz, L and Hood, R 1979, 'Judicial Discretion and Sentencing Standards: Victorian Attempts to Solve a Perennial Problem', *University of Pennsylvania Law Review* 127: 1288–1349.
Schoeman, F 1979, 'On Incapacitating the Dangerous', *American Philosophical Quarterly* 16: 27–35.
Slobogin, C 2003, 'A Jurisprudence of Dangerousness', *Northwestern University Law Review* 98: 1–62.
Smilansky, S 2011, 'Hard Determinism and Punishment: A Practical *Reductio*', *Law and Philosophy* 30: 353–367.
Walen, A 2011, 'A Unified Theory of Detention, with Application to Preventive Detention for Suspected Terrorists', *Maryland Law Review* 70: 871–938.

10 Why capacity matters

Is it fair to treat people like that, like that, for that?

Nicole A Vincent

David Hodgson thought that responsibility requires what he called "plausible reasoning", which is reasoning that is not only sound, but also and importantly not completely law-governed. Otherwise, he thought, whether our choices were formed through the operation of natural laws or through the operation of reason's laws, in both cases our choices would be made for us rather than us choosing those things.

Given this view, the compatibilist idea that responsibility requires the possession of the right kinds of mental capacities in the right degree – on one prominent account, mental capacities required for "moderate reasons-responsiveness" (Fischer and Ravizza 1998) – must have seemed decidedly un-compelling to Hodgson.[1] After all, when a capacitous and an incapacitous person – that is, a person who satisfies the compatibilist mental capacity requirement for responsibility and one who does not – both act wrongly, the law-governed nature of each of their psychologies means that on that occasion neither could actually have acted better.[2] And since on any given occasion when a capacitous person does something wrong, they could no more have done the right thing than an incapacitous person, this raises the question of what difference in the compatibilist's own view psychology is supposed to make for responsibility – or, as I put it in this chapter's title, why mental capacity matters.

Since this is the topic on which this chapter will focus, I will state this worry another way. Given that on any occasion when a capacitous person does something wrong, their superior psychology gives them no advantage vis-à-vis choosing differently over an incapacitous person, what reason is there to think that capacitous people are more responsible for their acts of wrongdoing (and perhaps more deserving of blame and maybe even punishment) than incapacitous people? What difference is psychology supposed to make for responsibility in the compatibilist's view, in virtue of which compatibilists believe that they do

1 This is, at least, the impression I had from the few conversations I was fortunate to have with David, and those conversations are indeed what motivated giving the talk on which this chapter is based.

2 Further below, I explain why the reply that with the right analysis of "could" (e.g., a counterfactual analysis) compatibilists can deal with this concern, will sound less compelling to someone who is not already sold on the compatibilist message.

not also need that further requirement which Hodgson thought was needed – namely, that reasoning must not only be sound, but also not be completely law-governed?

This chapter takes up the challenge of trying to explain why, from a compatibilist perspective, mental capacity matters to responsibility. It also aims to do this in such a way that a jurisprudentially minded libertarian like Hodgson might find this explanation satisfying. After sketching the concerns that led Hodgson to claim that responsibility requires "plausible reasoning", and explaining how I think this translates into what I shall call "Hodgson's Challenge", I then propose a solution to this challenge. Namely, I argue that mental capacity matters because the justification of holding someone responsible for what they did in any given situation derives from whether it would be fair for a system of responsibility[3] to treat people like that (with that kind of psychology), like that (by reacting in that manner to them), for that (for what they did). I also argue that the question of this system's fairness need not in turn be thought of as a matter of whether that person could have acted otherwise, which would again re-introduce the same problem that my approach was intended to solve, but rather such things as whether this system would treat like cases alike, treat different cases differently, and be even-handed in how it treats different categories of cases right now and over time.

On my compatibilist account – an account which, as I shall explain, differs from what compatibilists like Fischer and Ravizza and others who have developed their views propose – it thus takes two steps to understand why mental capacity matters, even though on any given occasion people's psychology (i.e., their mental capacities) can be exercised only in whichever way they actually are exercised (or, if we are talking about an indeterministic system, *they* are not the ones who indetermine how their psychology will be exercised). First, how a *system* of responsibility takes account of people's psychology, in the way that it responds to people on account of the sorts of things that they do, bears on that system's fairness. Second, the justification in any *specific* case for holding a given person responsible for what they did in a given way is derived from the justification of the system as a whole under which doing that would be a practice. Mental capacity thus matters for the justification of *systems* of responsibility, and at this level it does not matter that on specific occasions *individuals* cannot exercise their mental capacities differently. But once a system of responsibility is deemed fair, there is no further justificatory question that a compatibilist needs to address regarding why they treat capacitous and incapacitous (or sub-capacitous) people differently. There is, of course, still the question of how to accurately assess what the given person's psychology actually was like

3 My use of the word "system" in the locution "system of responsibility" is not intended to imply that I am talking only about the justification of, e.g., a given legal system's response to criminal offenders, which would still leave the further matter of moral responsibility (whether what that legal system does was also morally justified) un-addressed. Rather, the locution "system of responsibility" is intended to refer to any systematic justification for claims about people's moral responsibility.

on the occasion of concern when they acted as they did. This is by no means a trivial matter – to assess what a person's psychology actually was on some given occasion – but it is not the same as the problem of trying to explain why a psychology that on any given occasion can be exercised only in the way that it is exercised (or, yet again, if we are talking about an indeterministic system, why a psychology that is not indetermined in how it is exercised by the will of the person whose psychology it is) can provide a sound normative foundation for distinguishing people from one another qua fully responsible versus less than fully responsible.

Before proceeding, here are three notes, and then a brief outline of what follows in this chapter. First, I will use the locutions "why mental capacity matters" and "why psychology matters" interchangeably, and I will also use interchangeably pairs of terms like "capacitous and incapacitous", "sane and insane", "mentally sound and mentally unsound", and "moderately reasons-responsive and not moderately reasons-responsive". Second, I shall refer to compatibilist views like John Fischer's as "capacitarian". Responsible people on Fischer's account are those who have the mental capacities required to recognize and respond appropriately to reasons – those whose actions issue from moderately reasons-responsive mechanisms – not those who, e.g., have the metaphysical power or ability to act differently holding fixed the actual history and laws of nature, or who are genuine sources of their own actions, or anything else of a similar ilk. I call such views "capacitarian" because they predicate responsibility (among other things) on how much of which kinds of mental *capacities* people have.[4] Third, because from my compatibilist perspective the problems for responsibility under determinism and indeterminism are almost identical – whether my actions are determined or undetermined by the laws of nature, either I could not have done otherwise, or if I could have then not I but indeterminism would have seen to that – I will therefore treat the challenges posed by determinism and indeterminism as practically the same challenge. And here is this chapter's outline. In the first section I recount what I take to be Hodgson's understanding of the threat that determinism (and equally indeterminism) is thought to pose to responsibility; his understanding of the main features of the capacitarian compatibilist strategy for responding to that threat; and his reasons for finding fault with this strategy. The second section re-formulates and builds on Hodgson's critique with the aim of explaining why, as a compatibilist, I find his concerns forceful and worthy of being re-formulated as "Hodgson's Challenge" to compatibilism. Finally, the third section develops an approach I have sketched out elsewhere (Vincent 2013), according to which the justification of treating differentially capacitous

4 Other things also matter, not just mental capacity – for instance, whether that capacity was the agent's own, or if it is an incapacity, whether the person concerned is responsible for that, just how much of which kind of capacity they need, and precisely how their contribution to the causal chain of events in the world played itself out; I discuss these things later – but mental capacity is clearly a core component of this (as I call it) capacitarian picture. Also see note 7 and the surrounding text.

people differently vis-à-vis their responsibility resides not in features of narrow moments or synchronic time frames, but in features of whole systems of responsibility that can be gleaned only when we examine how those systems operate diachronically.

Hodgson's take on responsibility, determinism, and compatibilism

David Hodgson begins the first chapter of his book with an evocative example:

> In *Red*, the final film of Krzysztof Kieslowski's *Three Colours* trilogy, neighbours throw a stone through a retired judge's window, and the judge muses, "I wonder what I'd do in their place." After a pause, he says, "The same thing." The girl who's with him asks, "You'd throw stones?" The judge replies, "In their place, of course. And that goes for everyone I judged. Given their lives, I would steal, I'd kill, I'd lie. Of course I would."
>
> (2012: 3)

This example, I believe, is meant to elicit one way in which determinism threatens responsibility – namely, by straight-jacketing every aspect of our lives, creating only one path for us to tread. Here is a judge who, with the luxury of hindsight and time to reflect, confesses that if he had had precisely the same upbringing and experiences and been faced with precisely the same circumstances as the people whom he had judged, often harshly, throughout his career, he too would not have acted any differently. With everything tied down like that – with all of the variables filled in with precisely the same values as those people – he too would perceive the very same things that they had perceived, he too would learn what they had learned, he too would make the same judgements that they had made, he would choose the very same things that they had chosen, he would have acted as they had acted, and assuming that everything in the physical world around him was indeed also the same as what it was for them, the outcomes of his actions too would have been identical. He would be little more than a passive occupant/observer – presumably like what they were, even if they took themselves to have been active – doomed to do the same things as them. With the benefit of hindsight, the judge thinks that he would have been – and that they were – doomed to do those things as well. They possessed no more freedom in their own shoes than the judge would have possessed if he had occupied their shoes, given that all those variables were set like they were.

Or, if determinism threatens responsibility at an even more fundamental level – by making no room for anything resembling actions, and thus no room for agency and hence for agents – then there wouldn't even be an occupant to occupy anyone's shoes, nor anyone for that matter in whose shoes they were in the first place. After all, under determinism human actions become swallowed up into the category of mere events, squeezed out of existence on one side by the antecedents to our choices, and on the other side by the consequences of those choices.[5] If that is the right way to look at it, then all there'd be is just a cold physical world transforming itself from moment to moment from one state to the next in accordance with the automatic mechanical operation of completely impersonal laws of nature. Indeed, in explaining how in some people's view a scientific understanding of the world presents a similar kind of problem, what Hodgson says next deftly bridges these two ways of understanding determinism's threat to responsibility. He writes:

> There are those who think [that] science shows that we human beings are physical systems that change over time in accordance with the laws of nature that govern all physical systems, and thus [that we] cannot do other than as determined by those laws. According to these views, whatever we do is either the inevitable product of our genes and our circumstances, or of chance occurrences, or of some combination of the two; and there can be nothing in our genes or circumstances (or indeed in chance or the laws of nature) for which we can be *ultimately responsible*. Thus, *everything flows from things that happened before we were born* or are otherwise *outside our control*, so that we cannot have free will in any meaningful sense and cannot be truly responsible for our decisions and actions.
>
> (2012: 3, my emphasis)

Agents and their choices vanish from this picture. In this picture we are not entities distinct from the world that surrounds us, but, at best, we are features of that world, and what we do is better characterized as what happens – i.e., part of the history of the world, not part of our history.

In my view, Hodgson's *Three Colours: Red* example captures the intuition that in a deterministic universe *we lack freedom* or elbow room, whereas the second passage quoted captures the different idea – but equally troubling for free will and responsibility – that in a deterministic universe *we are not genuine sources* of our choices.[6] And without *freedom* or *sourcehood* – ideas that are both prominent in the sprawling literature on determinism, free will, and responsibility – people cannot be responsible for what they do.

Earlier compatibilist attempts to shield responsibility from determinism's threat included such things as *counterfactual analyses* of what it means to say that a person could have done otherwise, or the claim that responsibility requires

5 This way of framing the problem that determinism (and equally indeterminism) poses to responsibility is suggested by Thomas Nagel's discussion of moral luck (Williams and Nagel 1976).

6 That Hodgson worried about sourcehood as well as freedom also comes through clearly in this passage: "John Fischer has written that 'our behaviour may well be "in the cards" in the sense that we simply have to play the cards that are dealt us'. This has drawn the apt comment from philosopher Kip Werking that it (perhaps somewhat misleadingly) suggests there is a *player of the cards* distinct from the hand that is dealt, whereas in truth human beings simply *are* the cards that are dealt them by genes and environment, and the cards just have to play themselves" (Hodgson 2012: 165).

neither sourcehood nor an absence of causation, but rather an absence of *coercion*, *compulsion*, or *impediments*. For instance, consider Ayer: "to say that I could have acted otherwise is to say, first, that I should have acted otherwise if I had so chosen; secondly, that my action was voluntary in the sense in which the actions, say, of the kleptomaniac are not; and thirdly, that nobody compelled me to choose as I did" (2009: 117). In a similar vein, Taylor writes: "I am sometimes free to move my finger this way and that but not, certainly, to bend it backward or into a knot. But what does this mean? It means, first, that there is no obstacle or impediment to my activity [and] that nothing constrains or forces me to do one thing rather than another" (1963: 42).

More recently, though, a number of compatibilists – in particular those whom I have elsewhere called "capacitarians"[7] – have made use of the observation that the way we normally distinguish people who are fully responsible for what they do (e.g., most adults) from people who are less than fully responsible for what they do (e.g., children, or people with intellectual disability or mental disorders) is by reference to their psychology. Here is how David Hodgson describes the central idea behind this compatibilist approach to defending responsibility from the threat of determinism:

> [C]entral to most contemporary compatibilist positions is the idea that what is necessary for responsibility is that a person have the *capacity* to recognize and respond to good reasons for conduct, and to control his or her conduct accordingly. . . . A leading compatibilist philosopher, John Fischer, has characterised what is necessary in this respect as a *mechanism* that has moderate-reasons-responsiveness. And . . . on this approach . . . it is sufficient that [in virtue of having that mechanism] the person have what Fischer calls guidance control, so that what the person actually does is caused by the person's exercise of his or her *rational capacity*.
>
> (2012: 169, emphasis modified)

A change of focus from causation to *psychology* is the most prominent feature of this contemporary compatibilist position.[8] Predicating responsibility not on whether the universe operates according to deterministic laws, indeterministic laws, or some other laws, but rather on people's psychology, capacitarian compatibilists suggest that people are responsible for what they do only if at the time of acting they possessed a sufficient quantity of the right kinds of mental capacities,

7 For instance, see Vincent (2013). A natural contrast to capacitarian theories are *quality of will* theories according to which actions are worthy of praise or blame to the degree that they express good or ill qualities of will respectively (e.g., Arpaly 2007). Alas, there does not appear to be terminological uniformity about how to refer to these contrasting theories. For instance, Neil Levy (2007) refers to capacitarian and quality of will theories respectively as *volitionist* and *attributionist* theories, and Jason Benchimol (2011) refers to them respectively as *will-centred* and *non-will-centred* theories. In this chapter I limit my discussion to capacitarian compatibilist theories.

8 Sections of this paragraph are borrowed from Vincent (2015).

and if their actions indeed issued from their exercise of those capacities.[9] In my view, what John Fischer and Mark Ravizza's (1998) compatibilist account does is to re-deploy this very same idea, though they give mental capacities physical form since on their account we are responsible for those actions that issue from our own moderately reasons-responsive mechanisms. Roughly speaking, in Fischer and Ravizza's framework moderately reasons-responsive mechanisms implement, embody, or instantiate mental capacities required for moral agency. Fischer and Ravizza also emphasize two further points: (i) that incapacities for which we are responsible do not exculpate (the "tracing" condition); and (ii) that those mental capacities must be our own (the "ownership" condition). An absence of impediments, coercion, duress, compulsion, and other ways of being forced to do things also remains important in the capacitarian compatibilist picture, but at the core of that account lies the familiar and intuitively plausible idea that responsibility tracks mental capacity – that responsibility hinges on what psychology a person has, not on such things as sourcehood or being uncaused.

What is appealing about this change of focus from causation to psychology is that having the right psychology[10] is indeed what seems to enable some people to navigate the world without trouble, whereas others whose psychology is significantly compromised navigate the world in ways that get them and others into trouble. Intuitively, those of us bestowed with the right psychology notice what's there to be noticed, we take these things into account in our reasoning in the right way, and then we act in accordance with the dictates of our judgements, but the same cannot be said of people whose psychology is compromised.

However, in Hodgson's view this compatibilist solution is still inadequate because the psychology with which even the lucky among us (i.e., the responsible ones, the ones with a sufficient quantity of the right kinds of mental capacities) are imbued is inflexible in a problematic way:

> [T]here is a sense in which [a chess-playing] computer [also] makes a decision, on a rational basis, between alternatives that are open, namely the moves that are possible according to the rules of chess. In that sense, the computer rationally controls its conduct, is free to make one move rather than another, and is responsible for making one move rather than another. But when one considers the physical construction of the computer and the

9 The suggestion that responsibility requires a *sufficient* quantity of the right kinds of mental capacities calls forth the view that responsibility is a *threshold* concept. For instance, that once a person has enough of that kind of mental capacity, more of that mental capacity won't necessarily make them more responsible for what they do (or don't do), but if they do not have enough of it, then they won't even be responsible. A somewhat different view is that responsibility is a *scalar* concept, such that with a greater amount of the required mental capacities, one becomes more responsible, and with less of those mental capacities, one becomes less responsible. For the present discussion, nothing of particular note hinges on whether we take it that responsibility is a threshold or a scalar concept, but for discussion see Bernard Berofsky, "The luck argument against libertarianism", Chapter 5 of this volume.

10 Setting aside the question of precisely what *the right* psychology might be.

> program according to which it operates . . . there never is more than one move possible [and] I don't believe anyone would attribute free will or responsibility to a chess-playing computer.
>
> (2012: 155–156)

What the chess-playing computer lacks in Hodgson's view – precisely because of its "physical construction", which means that its operation is governed by the laws of nature – is a certain kind of flexibility. Its rules make its decision-making rigid. It has no room for being *influenced* in its decisions. Rather its decisions are completely determined (or indetermined, if the universe is indeterministic) by the rules of its program, by its physical implementation, and by the setup of the chess board. Similarly, Hodgson thought that if human psychology were implemented in physical mechanisms governed by deterministic (or whatever other kinds of) natural laws, then regardless of precisely what psychology was implemented in any given person – be it the sub-capacitous psychology of a madman or the capacitous psychology of a judge – both of their psychologies would make their decision-making equally inflexible since given any situation each could make only the very same decisions that they actually make.[11] The madman and the judge would both be equally inflexible, constrained by their different but equally inflexible rule-governed psychologies, and so both would equally fail to be responsible in Hodgson's view.

What Hodgson wanted from compatibilists was an explanation for how the requisite flexibility could be purchased with a psychology that is rule-based and rigid, wholly implemented in physical mechanisms, and ones that operate according to natural laws. To see that this is indeed what he sought, pay attention to the words "influenced" and "determined" in the next quoted passage, which appears just after the *Three Colours: Red* passage I quoted at the top of this section:

> Is it . . . that everything we do is the inexorable playing out of the role in life given to us by our genes and our circumstances, by nature and nurture? Or . . . that our actions and our lives are not entirely *determined* by the luck of our genes and circumstances, but are *influenced* by decisions we can freely make and for which we are truly responsible?
>
> (2012: 3, my emphasis)

Intuitively, when your decisions are *influenced* by considerations, there is still something left for you to do, a decision for you to make, something over which you have say. There is leeway or elbow room or something of this sort. On the other hand, when your decisions are *determined* by considerations processed

11 Or, to provide another example, if the universe operates according to stochastic laws, then although different decisions might be made, which decisions are made would not be determined by the person but by those laws of nature. I return to the question of why different analyses of "could" or "capacity", such as counterfactual analyses, do not properly address the concerns that I think Hodgson had in mind in the second half of the second section later in this chapter.

by a physically implemented psychology – a psychology that, in virtue of being implemented in a law-governed substrate (of a deterministic or perhaps an indeterministic variety), is itself governed by the laws it implements – regardless of what psychology it happens to be, those considerations are, in an important sense, making up your mind for you. Or perhaps, similar to the way in which I framed Hodgson's sourcehood concerns earlier, there is not even a *you* to make up your mind, but only a mind that gets made up by the considerations. Yet, when we consider how Fischer and Ravizza's agents would make their decisions, what we seem to get is not people being *influenced* by reasons but rather people being determined by reasons. What we get is not people being *guided* by reasons but rather – due to the physical implementation of whatever psychology or rationality they possess – people being pushed or dragged around by those reasons. This leads Hodgson to write that "the central problem of free will and responsibility is not whether they can be reconciled with determinism, but . . . *whether rational processes are or are not rule-determined*" (2012: 172, italics added). This concern about not being rule-determined or law-governed is what lies at the root of Hodgson's concern about the compatibilist's strategy for staking out room for responsibility within a deterministic or indeterministic universe.

Flexibility in rationality, in decision-making, is what David Hodgson thought was thus needed to underwrite responsibility, and for the reasons outlined earlier in his view the capacitarian compatibilist strategy fails to deliver such flexibility. It is precisely this role for the self – a role that is more substantial than a mere number-crunching machine, a machine that takes reasons in as input, processes them using physically implemented mechanisms that operate according to natural laws or rules, and spits out "choices" – that David Hodgson wanted to carve out with his libertarian approach that postulated a human capacity for "plausible reasoning", informed by conscious experiences of gestalts, which was meant to be a form of reasoning that left room for genuine choice. He writes:

> In this book I [argue] that, while the engagement of our genes and our circumstances with laws of nature makes an enormous contribution to the way we are and the way we behave, we nevertheless do make real decisions that are not themselves wholly determined by that engagement and/or by chance, but are in a fundamental way truly *down to us.* [T]hese choices are *influenced* by input from our conscious experiences that is not determined by laws or rules of any kind, but rather is the exercise of a capacity that our consciousness gives us . . . As regards . . . the nature of human rationality . . . I argue that essential to this rationality is the ability to engage in *plausible reasoning*; that is, in reasoning in which the premises or data do not *entail* the conclusions by virtue of applicable rules for good reasoning, but rather *support* them as a matter of reasonable albeit fallible judgment.
>
> (2012: 4–5, emphasis altered)

Consciousness, in Hodgson's view, presents us with gestalts of the world which are reflective of who we are. These gestalts are branded or coloured by features of our cognitive and perceptual machinery through which we experience the world, and so, on account of this, Hodgson thought that our choices reflected us after all. As I have argued elsewhere, "what Hodgson is eager to show with his . . . talk of [consciousness and] gestalts is . . . that there is something unique and irreducible about the subjective, individual, unitary conscious experience of the world, [and] that such a conscious experience plays a [sourcehood-like] role in human rational action and decision-making" (Santoni de Sio and Vincent 2015: 640).

However, in my view Hodgson's attempt to offer a libertarian solution does not work. What his strategy delivers is, at best, only expressions of individuality rather than genuine sourcehood. And, perhaps more problematically, at the end of the day "[o]ne may wonder [w]here do gestalts come from" (Santoni de Sio and Vincent 2015: 641) anyway if not from the operation of deterministic or indeterministic mechanisms in which we are implemented? Hodgson at best delivers an account of uniqueness or individuality but not sourcehood, and responsibility just can't be purchased with that currency. Nevertheless, I do think that the general thrust of his *attack* on compatibilism is insightful, and so in the next section I will re-cast his concerns in a way that I hope other compatibilists will find poses an important challenge for compatibilism.

Responsibility, capacity, and moments in time – a synchronic approach

As I understand Hodgson, his concern is that the capacitarian compatibilist merely swaps the tyranny of utterly inflexible laws of nature for the tyranny of equally inflexible rule-based rationality. And if what was meant to threaten responsibility in the first place was the lack of elbow room (or lack of sourcehood) entailed by determinism[12] – for instance, the lack of genuine alternatives, or the fact that we are nothing more than mere effects caught up in an impersonal mechanical causal chain – then it would not be clear how any more elbow room (or sourcehood) would be purchased by swapping (meta)physical constraints for (psycho)logical constraints. If the problem that compatibilism was meant to address was that the uncompromisingly inflexible laws of nature either leave no elbow room or write us out of the picture, then it is not clear how swapping uncompromisingly inflexible laws of nature for equally inflexible rules or rationality solves anything. Both seem like a kind of straitjacket, and for this reason I think that Hodgson was right to call capacitarian compatibilists out for offering a quasi-solution.

The way in which the responsibility question is often pre-theoretically posed is whether at the pertinent moment in time – for instance, when a person perceives something, when they make their judgement, when they settle on a choice, or when they act upon their decision – the person concerned could have done otherwise. Capacitarian compatibilists attempt to capture the same concern but with a question about whether at that moment in time the person's actions issued

12 . . . or indeterminism, the laws of nature, or whatever other rule-governed or law-governed universe we are asked to imagine.

from the right kind of psychology – a psychology with the right (kind and degree of) mental capacities. But Hodgson's worry was precisely that in such moments, whatever our psychology might be – be we capacitous or incapacitous; be we the judge or the madman – we will still perceive, judge, decide, and act only as is dictated by the constraints of our particular psychology, which is itself implemented in physical matter governed by laws of nature. When two people – one capacitous, the other sub-capacitous – both do the same wrong thing, in a completely law-governed or rule-governed universe given each one's psychology neither actually could have acted differently on that occasion. To the extent that capacitarian compatibilism attempts to cater for the same concern as the pre-theoretical way of posing the responsibility question, this means that that question is effectively left un-addressed. Furthermore, given the role that our conclusions about responsibility often play in practical settings, like the legal questions about guilt, blame, and punishment that would have been of concern to Hodgson, one would hope that the capacitarian compatibilist strategy would provide answers to responsibility questions that will support broadly the same sorts of attributions of blame, guilt, and punishment decisions that our pre-theoretical responsibility intuitions would suggest. But yet, turning back to the capacitous and sub-capacitous person, one receives blame and punishment, while the other's blame and punishment are attenuated. What use then is having that superior psychology? Why do we, the capacitous ones, get treated more harshly than sub-capacitous people? It's not as if we really could have perceived, judged, decided, or acted in a better way. It's not as if we really could have made better choices.

Another way to understand Hodgson's Challenge is that capacitarian compatibilists merely substitute one set of modal notions (e.g., alternative possibilities, being able to have done otherwise, etc.) for another set of equally modal notions (e.g., mental capacities, moderately reasons-responsive mechanisms, etc.) without actually explaining how any of that modality (inherent in the word "capacity" of mental *capacity*, and "moderate" in *moderate* reasons-responsiveness) is meant to make a real difference to anyone stuck in a moment of decision-making in a deterministic universe. John Fischer maintains that there *is* a sense in which capacitous people *can* make better choices, a sense in which their actions issue from mechanisms that really have the property of moderate reasons-responsiveness, a property in virtue of which they have the requisite mental *capacities*, regardless of the fact that those capacities did not manifest themselves on the given occasion. Fischer writes:

> one can *make sense* of modal or dispositional properties (at least in part) in terms of . . . non-actual possible worlds . . . to specify the sorts of properties that must be exemplified by the actual-sequence mechanism that issues in the behavior in question. . . . If the . . . purpose of [looking at] alternative scenarios [had been] to establish that one has genuine metaphysical access to alternative possibilities, then I grant that only . . . scenarios with the same past and laws as the actual world [would have been] relevant . . . But . . . the purpose of the assessment of ranges of non-actual possibilities is to establish the

> nature of the properties that are in fact (actually) exemplified in the sequence of events leading to the behavior under consideration.
>
> (2005: 147–148, my emphasis)

Fischer's idea is that a given mechanism from which a person's action issued might be such that in a sufficient number of hypothetical scenarios that mechanism will respond to reasons which were present – i.e., that mechanism has the property of being moderately reasons-responsive, or, put another way, it has sufficient capacity for receptivity and reactivity to reasons. And even though on a specific occasion that mechanism might not actually respond to the reasons that were present, in Fischer's view that does not entail that this mechanism lacks the property of moderate reasons-responsiveness, of having the capacity to respond. That mechanism is moderately reasons-responsive – it has the capacity – but the capacity did not manifest. Hence, Fischer looks at what the mechanism does in non-actual worlds to ascertain what properties the mechanism has in this world.

Neil Levy provides an analogy with another dispositional property – fragility – to explain what Fischer is doing:

> The fragility of the vase is constituted by the bonds between its molecules. Fragility is a property the vase possesses right now, *while it sits on the shelf* . . . We test for fragility . . . by asking how it would behave in a world in which the vase was dropped . . . We ask about that world because so doing is the best way to understand the properties the vase has in this world. Similarly, in assessing whether an agent is responsible for a decision or an action, we ask *how the mechanism upon which she actually acts would respond in a world in which the agent was presented with sufficient reason to do otherwise* . . . We ask about that world because this is the only way to understand the capacities of the relevant mechanism in this world. In each case, the counterfactuals are relevant not because we are interested in what happens in alternative scenarios, for the sake of such alternatives, but because we are interested in the properties of the actual sequence.
>
> (2008: 227–228, my emphasis)

Levy's analogy with fragility – in particular his claim that even while it sits on the shelf the vase possesses the property of fragility – nicely explains why Fischer thinks that it is relevant to consider what happens in other possible worlds – namely, to capture a *sense* in which we might have capacities even in a deterministic world, but not because he thinks we actually have access to those other worlds in the actual world. Put another way, Fischer is offering us an explanation of the sense or meaning of "capacity" in claims like "This mechanism has capacity X". The sense in which the mechanism – the mechanism from which the actions of the party in question issued – has sufficient capacity is that it will respond to the reasons that are present sufficiently often.

However, although I appreciate the subtlety of what Fischer and Levy are doing by explaining the sense in which mechanisms still possess capacities – in which these are properties of those mechanisms even when those properties do not manifest themselves in the operation of those mechanisms on a given occasion – I can also see how, especially from the perspective of our non-compatibilist interlocutors, the ones whom we are trying to convince after all, this borders on disingenuous word play rather than genuine engagement with their concerns. Telling our non-compatibilist interlocutors *what we mean* by "could have" or by "capacity" – and in particular where what we mean still does not make it such that on that occasion in time the person concerned had access to that capacity – merely invites the following sort of response: "But why, precisely, does having that property *in that sense* matter? How does it address my worry that actually all capacities are doomed to be exercised in the very same way that they actually are exercised on any given occasion? Or that, if indeterminism obtains, and those capacities are not doomed to manifest in any particular way, then we are still nevertheless not the ones who indetermine how they will be manifested? How does what you mean by 'capacity' change anything?"

Evidently, what matters to us when it comes to responsibility is having the right psychology. However, as David Hodgson pointed out, regardless of our psychology – that is, regardless of whether we are capacitous or sub-capacitous, whether we have the psychology of the judge or of the madman – in a deterministic universe at any given moment in time we only "could" have perceived, judged, decided, or acted in the way that we did. Sure, for some clever analysis of the word "could" or "capacity", we "could" have made morally better choices. But really, we could not have made better choices. We had the "capacity" to act better but not the capacity to act better.

I acknowledge that in response Fischer might offer the following example: that even when a piano player is not currently exercising their capacity to play the piano – indeed, even if they will never again get to exercise their capacity, perhaps because of an untimely early demise – they nevertheless still retain that capacity, even when they are not playing, and even if they will never play piano again. They may never again get an opportunity to exercise that capacity, but they still surely have that capacity, and would what I said earlier not commit me to the counter-intuitive view that unless a capacity is being exercised it is non-existent?[13]

In my view there are at least two problems with this kind of reply. First, this reply shifts the problem from one modal notion (capacity) to another (opportunity). The question that we asked, after all, is whether at the given moment in time the person concerned could have done otherwise. The response is that they could have – they had the capacity, but just not the opportunity to exercise it. But since determinism does to opportunities precisely what it does to capacities – we are doomed to have the opportunities that we actually get and no more – our response to Fischer should still now point out the cosmic unfairness of blaming and punishing a person who lacked the opportunity to exercise their capacities. As far as the justification of responsibility is concerned – and any implications

13 I credit John Fischer with this example, which he raised in response to what I said earlier at a workshop organized by Maureen Sie in late 2011 in the Netherlands.

for blame and punishment – why does it matter that a person had capacity on a given occasion when determinism made it such that they lacked the opportunity to manifest it?

Second, my point is not that under determinism there can be no capacities other than those that manifest themselves. For instance, I am not denying that the piano player retains the capacity to play the piano even when they are not manifesting it and even if they will never again manifest it. In some sense they retain that capacity. My point is not that determinism is inhospitable to capacities, but rather that only some senses of "capacity" can play the right role in staking out room for responsibility, and for justifying responsibility-based practices like blame and punishment. The problem that non-compatibilists want to address is not addressed merely by telling them what we mean by "capacity", unless that sense of "capacity" can stake out room for responsibility and perhaps also justify differential blame and punishment of capacitous and sub-capacitous offenders. But yet, it is far from clear how having a capacity in a sense that makes me no better off on a given occasion than the madman, for instance, should make a difference to my blame.

As I argue elsewhere (Vincent 2013: 183), there are many senses of "capacity" that a deterministic universe can accommodate, but it is hard to see how any of those senses makes a difference as far as the justification of blame and punishment is concerned if the responsibility question that we ask focuses on the moment at which the person acted, chose, decided, or perceived whatever they perceived. As the past turns into the future, at any given moment in time I have the capacity to take the as-yet-untaken steps that I will eventually take in that future. This is an *unfolding* sense of capacity. Neil Levy has a *dispositional* sense of capacity in mind when he says that wine glasses are fragile since they will probably break if they are exposed to a shock. In a *strength* sense, given my musculature I have the capacity to lift a 40 kilogram box. In a *stress* sense, given how they are built bridges have different capacities to withstand different loads. In a *volumetric* sense, different sized glasses have the capacity to hold different volumes of beer. And in an *ability* sense, I have the capacity to speak English, Polish, and some Dutch. In a deterministic universe, things and people would clearly have capacities in all of these different senses. However, under determinism nobody would have capacities in the sense of genuine access to alternative possibilities, and that seems to make a difference to responsibility.

Yet again, I do not deny that evidently what matters to us is psychology. We want people to have the right *mental capacities*, *competencies*, *capabilities*, *abilities*, *skills*, *powers*, *potentials*. We care about what a person *can* do, what they *know how to do*, what's *possible* for them to do, or what they *could have* done or had the *opportunity* to do given their psychology. The italicized words in the two preceding sentences all have a ring of modality. But these psychological aspects will soothe the minds of those who worry about the threat of determinism only if we (compatibilists) can tell a compelling story about why in virtue of having superior psychologies (even ones that can't be exercised differently on any given occasion) capacitous and sub-capacitous people are differentially responsible when they do something wrong. But this can't be done merely by providing an analysis of "capacity" for the very same reason why an analysis of "could have done otherwise" never sufficed to stake out ground for responsibility in a deterministic or indeterministic universe.

Part of my own concern as a compatibilist is that as compatibilists we have honed our skill of genuinely failing to understand what problems others see with our solution. Not understanding why hard determinists or libertarians just don't get it that we have capacities has become a fine art. I am a compatibilist, and until recently I practiced this fine art too. However, I would like my own and my compatibilist colleagues' theories to be compelling – not just *for us*, but to actually convince our non-compatibilist colleagues that we have struck upon a solution. Consequently, I value the fact that like the child in Hans Christian Andersen's "The Emperor's New Clothes", Hodgson manages to so clearly point out that our current capacitarian compatibilist approach just does not deliver what it was meant to deliver, or at the very least that it has a flaw which needs to be addressed. My aim is not to abandon ship on the compatibilist project, but to give the best reading to the concerns voiced by our critics, and few do a better job at pointing out the faults with capacitarian compatibilism than Hodgson.

Compatibilists need to explain why having a sufficient quantity of the right kinds of mental capacities – what I have also referred to as the right psychology – is enough to stake out sufficient ground for responsibility under determinism or indeterminism. This is what the next section will attempt to do – to explain *why capacity matters* even if it can't be exercised differently on a given occasion.

Responsibility, capacity, and fairness – a diachronic approach

As I argued earlier, at any given moment in time in a deterministic universe we can do only what we actually do, and in an indeterministic universe we are still not the ones who indetermine what we end up doing. This applies equally to everyone across the board. Judges can do only what they do at any given moment. And madmen too can do only what they do at any given moment. In a deterministic universe, during moments of perception, judgement, choice, or action, the modal properties of people's respective psychologies do not put capacitous wrongdoers in a better position than sub-capacitous wrongdoers. Both are on an equal footing, equally doomed to do what they do, and similarly troubling problems arise under indeterminism. For this reason, when I confine my focus to narrow time frames, to moments, I see no reason to treat capacitous and sub-capacitous people differently, and I doubt that we will find anything lurking in those narrow time frames that is capable of justifying differential responsibility judgements and correlated treatment of people with different psychologies.

But if the justification for responsibility, blame, and punishment is not to be found within those moments, then where else can we look? Anywhere? Does mental capacity make any difference? And if so, then how and where?

My answer springs from Tony Honoré's observation that *psychology matters to how well people do in a given society* – or, as he puts it, under a given system of "outcome responsibility" (Honoré 1999: 14–40 and 121–142).[14] Over time, people with certain psychologies stand to fare better living under certain systems of responsibility – that is, under certain systems that treat *people like that* (with that kind of psychology) in a given manner in response to them having acted in a given way – than do people with different psychologies. But systems of responsibility are not natural orders – they are things we put into place[15] – and so the reactions we have (including our judgements of responsibility) and the legal regimes we put into place are things that require justification. And my suggestion, again in line with Honoré's idea, is that one way to justify such systems is on grounds of *fairness*. Put in my own Honoré-inspired terminology – terminology that appears in this chapter's sub-title – mental capacity matters to the justification of such things as attributions of responsibility or blame, or pronouncements of guilt and punishment decisions, because of the role that mental capacity plays in assessments of whether a given system of responsibility would be fair when it treats people like that (i.e., people with a particular psychology), like that (i.e., in a given way), for that (i.e., for doing what they did). Before formalizing my approach, the next three paragraphs offer examples to demonstrate how in my view psychology makes a difference to blame and punishment. I anticipate that these examples will resonate with compatibilists and incompatibilists alike.

For instance, imagine a system much like our own – the systematic way in which we come to make responsibility judgements, the informal social system of blame, or the formal legal system that also punishes and imposes liability – that treated *2 year old children* no differently to adults. That is, a system that held both to the same behavioural standards – that imposed the same expectations on both, and that viewed breaches of those expectations as morally on a par regardless of whether the adult or the 2 year old behaved in that manner – and that in

14 Honoré's approach, which I'll be drawing upon, seems to place more emphasis on overt social systems – e.g., on such things as *legal systems'* responses toward people – than my own focus, which is more on systems of thought or of justification. In the first instance, my own aim is to stake out ground for responsibility – and thus my focus is on systems of thinking that warrant claims about responsibility in a law-governed universe – and only then to connect this to overt responses like, e.g., people's or legal systems' pronouncements of blame, guilt, or punishment practices. However, Honoré's approach, when generalized so that "system" refers to a system of thinking rather than literally to any particular legal system, appears to offer a promising approach to explaining why differential responsibility judgements of capacitous and sub-capacitous wrongdoers might be justified, even if the capacitous wrongdoer's psychology was evidently of no benefit to them on any given occasion of their wrongdoing.

15 For instance, it is not a *natural* consequence that in response to a given behaviour or transgression we react in such-and-such a manner (e.g., that we have certain reactive attitudes like blame that not only reflect our judgements about that person's responsibility, but maybe even express something to them and others about our disapproval), or that a particular legal consequence is visited upon someone (e.g., legal punishments like fines and imprisonment). By contrast, asphyxiation is a natural consequence of oxygen deprivation, and destruction is a natural consequence of a tornado.

reaction to those breaches imposed precisely the same treatment on both. Two year old children would clearly fare badly under such a system, a lot worse than adults, and I view this as a good reason to maintain that this particular system would be unfair.

Here is another example. Imagine a system, yet again much like our own, except that it would *execute insane people* who kill other people (while under the influence of psychosis, not in a moment of clarity) as well as sane people who do likewise. Because insane people are unlikely to think straight, perceive things accurately, or be deterred by the fact that such a harsh punishment is visited on people like them when they act in that manner, by comparison to sane people insane people would stand to fare very badly under such a system. I view this as a good reason to maintain that this particular system would also be unfair. On the other hand, a system that *executed only non-insane adults* for that same transgression would be less unfair. Perhaps, all things considered, it would still be unfair, but it would not be as unfair as a system that executed insane people for this transgression.[16] An all-things-considered judgement about what would be a fair systematic practice of holding people responsible would need to take into account a great many things including (but not limited to, see further discussion) how other people who engage in similar wrongdoing are treated.

Now compare that to a system that *imprisoned non-insane adults* for murder. Depending on how "non-insane" was parsed (i.e., who would qualify for being found to be insane), what exactly qualifies as "murder" (e.g., rather than manslaughter), and precisely how long the prison terms would be, it is plausible that such a system could be fair. But note that if we again changed just one variable, such that now under this system *insane* adults (or *2 year old* children) were also imprisoned for murder, then again we may find that such a system would be unfair – perhaps because we think that neither insane adults nor 2 year old children can be expected to control themselves (even though it would be nice, and certainly a lot better, if they did), or because we think that their proper place is in mental health facilities or in special juvenile facilities designed to help steer them away from a life of crime, not in prisons. Or if we change yet another variable, such that now the transgression for which people would be imprisoned was petty theft, then again our fairness intuitions might shift.

Our fairness intuitions in the preceding examples are crucially affected by three factors – *the person's psychology*, what *expectation they breached*, and *our reaction* (e.g., punishment) – and I surmise that our judgements of fairness will probably be heavily influenced by our own views about fittingness or propriety of (as I put it in the sub-title of this chapter) treating people like that, like that, for that. For instance, sometimes it might seem unreasonable to have those sorts of expectations of those sorts of people (this would be an *expectation–psychology* mismatch). "She is just a child", we might say, "How could you honestly have expected her

16 I do not endorse execution – in my view it is always a disproportionate response – but I recognize that this as a substantive political judgement about which different people may have differing views.

to do that? She has insufficient capacity". Other times the lack of fittingness might relate to the treatment being inappropriate, perhaps arbitrary, given the kind of transgression (this would be an *expectation/breach–reaction* mismatch). One might imagine someone saying, "But why would scraping chewing gum off the bottom of school desks be a fitting punishment for calling someone a bad name at school?" Alternatively, our sense of fairness might be disturbed by the fact that that sort of treatment is appropriate only to some people (e.g., sane adults) but not to the person who now stands before us (e.g., a child, or an insane person). This would be a *psychology–reaction* mismatch – for example, because we hold out the hope that the little human before us can still be reformed since they are still in the process of growing, developing, and being formed, whereas we might suppose that the older person is now set in their ways and that attempting to reform them is pointless. And finally, at yet other times the lack of fittingness or propriety may relate to how the *three* things sit together (this would be a *psychology–reaction–expectation/breach* mismatch). For instance, we might say, "It might be fair to treat a sane adult that way for that transgression, but a 2 year old child? You've got to be kidding!", and presumably the person who says this could offer intelligible reasons of the sort I have mentioned earlier to explain their dumbfoundedness.

On my account, the reason why we care about people's psychology – about mental capacity – is because of the role it plays in such fairness assessments. Psychology is one of three factors that needs to be considered when arriving at a judgement about whether a given system of responsibility would be fair if it treated people like that (with that kind of psychology), like that (by reacting in that manner to them), for that (for what they did). Thus, to decide if a given person is responsible for what they do, whether they are blameworthy, and perhaps whether they should be punished – and, importantly, if so then how (in what way, and to what degree) they should be punished – for what they have done on a given occasion, we should:

1 Ascertain their psychology at the time when they transgressed – i.e., from what sort of mechanism their action issued, what mental capacities they had.
2 Ask if it would be a fair system that held responsible this kind of person, in this way, for that transgression – i.e., if it would be fair to treat people like that, like that, for that.

There are two differences between my and Honoré's approaches that warrant further comment. Namely, while for Honoré fairness is a matter of whether *this person* would stand to *gain more than they lose*, my approach focuses on *groups*, not individuals – my question is whether it would be fair to treat this *kind* of person in the proposed manner – and I also adopt a *pluralist* stance on what factors affect fairness.

About the second difference (I return to the first difference three paragraphs later), I see no reason to confine an investigation of fairness to, e.g., a narrowly utilitarian-style calculus. I think Honoré is right in suggesting that the sort of considerations that he raises bear on the fairness of a system.[17] However, lots of other things might also be relevant to our fairness investigation than just whether people would be better or worse off living under such a system, and by highlighting the three things that I highlighted earlier I do not intend to exclude other considerations from the fairness calculus. For instance, I said earlier that sometimes it may strike us as unreasonable to have those sorts of expectations of those sorts of people – i.e., that our judgement would stem from an *expectation–psychology* mismatch. However, what it is reasonable to expect of people – for what things it is reasonable to expect them to take responsibility – might itself be something that changes with advances in knowledge, with what technology is available, and with what resources are made available by society to people. For instance, if an adult person starts finding themselves sexually attracted to minors (Burns and Swerdlow 2003), in a modern society which has doctors available and perhaps effective medications to treat this predicament, we may think it reasonable to expect the person to seek help from a doctor rather than to hide it. Or, once it comes to a person's attention (once they know) that they have a weak spot for alcohol (or again, for young children), then it may be reasonable to expect of them that they take a route that avoids walking past pubs (or school playgrounds).

Also, how *others* are impacted by the given reaction may also affect what judgements we come to about the fairness of treating a person like that, like that, for that – for instance, because others may be future victims of this particular person, or of others like them; because unless we lock them away then they will continually impose an amount of fear on everyone (Nozick 1974); or perhaps because the given judgement does not sufficiently denounce the offender's action or affirm solidarity with the victim and those to whom they are (or were) dear.

Another factor that impacts on fairness is whether like cases are treated alike and whether relevantly different cases are treated differently.[18] A distinct advantage to explicitly recognizing this *comparative* aspect of fairness enquiries is that it provides us with another moral criterion by which to justify differential treatment of people, one which is unaffected by the truth or falsity of determinism, or indeterminism, or any other way our universe may be. After all, even if determinism were true, it would still be the case that similar cases should be treated similarly, and that different cases should be treated differently. And even if determinism were false, it would still be the case that we should treat similar cases similarly and different cases differently.

I believe that these two differences between Honoré's approach and my approach will make my approach more attractive in general (because I do not confine fairness to a narrow utilitarian calculation), and in particular attractive

17 A feature of his approach that I find very attractive is that it is unlikely to ever warrant imposing extreme punishments on people – e.g., life without parole, or capital punishment – since some people would indeed be worse off living under such a system.

18 This point explains why there is that first difference that I mentioned earlier between Honoré's approach and my approach – i.e., why I focus on *groups* rather than on individuals, why I ask whether it would be fair to treat *people like that*, like that, for that.

to compatibilists and incompatibilists (of either the libertarian or the hard determinist stripe) alike. Lots of things might matter to fairness; however, what it is important to notice is that what need *not* be taken into account is whether that person really could have done otherwise on that occasion. We do care about what psychology was in play when a person acted as they did – what mechanisms or mental capacities generated that action – and this is what makes my approach into a *capacitarian* approach. But the reason why we care about this is not because we suppose that during those moments in time, given that psychology, that person really could (or could not) have done better than they did. We need not suppose that unfairness necessarily stems from not being able (in a robust sense) to do otherwise. Rather, unfairness can reside in the fact that that sort of response for that sort of action would be grossly disproportionate, inappropriate, unfitting, or whatever else when applied to that sort of person, or that it involves not treating them like we treat others in their class, or treating them as if they fell into a different class. The fact that my account offers a justification for responsibility and blame attributions, and perhaps for punishment decisions, regardless of the truth or falsity of whether the universe is deterministic, indeterministic, or some other way, is what makes my approach a *compatibilist* approach.

Admittedly, my approach is thick with irreducibly normative and political judgements (rather than metaphysical claims or empirical findings), and I acknowledge that this might be viewed as a distinct disadvantage.[19] After all, there will surely be many normative disagreements about such things as *what kind* of capacities a person needs to have to be fully responsible, *how much* capacity they need to have, *what expectations* are unreasonable when imposed on various kinds of people, and what is proportionate as opposed to disproportionate – and undoubtedly a plethora of other things. However, not only do I think that this is as it should be – that it is better to acknowledge the inherent normativity of responsibility judgements, and that they involve what are ultimately and unavoidably contestable substantive evaluations as well as norm-setting rather than just fact-finding (Vincent 2011) – but that it is wrong-headed and futile for the reasons that I cited earlier to expect metaphysical or factual matters (e.g., whether anyone ever *really* can do otherwise) to settle responsibility questions.

Also, epistemic problems with the measurement of a person's capacity at the time when they acted would still abound. Because what we care about is the person's capacity – their psychology – at the time when they acted, and we do not have access to a time machine to conveniently inspect them at that time, we will inevitably have to contend with relying on proxy judgements informed by, e.g., a psychiatrist's assessment at some stage later in time, or historical records of how they were known to behave prior to the incident. However, this is not a specific problem with my approach since it applies to any capacitarian system, and in any case what I take myself to be doing is specifying the conditions under which someone is responsible for what they do, when they are blameworthy, and

19 My views on the complex relationship between facts and norms are discussed in Vincent (2011).

perhaps when punishment is justified, not providing a method for ascertaining whether those conditions have or have not been satisfied.

Furthermore, just how wide a time frame should we consider when we investigate what *kind* of psychology that person's action issued from? A 5 minute time-span? Or a 5 second time-span? Or something else? Although I do not yet have a fully worked-out answer to this question, the idea that people can at times be acting from a compromised psychology – for instance, under the influence of a disease or disorder of the mind – seems to offer one attractive response. However, I suspect that our views about pathology – about whether a person's action can be traced back to the influence of a disease or disorder of the mind – are more an *expression* of our presuppositions regarding where to draw the line between a person and their pathology, rather than pathology being a genuine premise in a determination of responsibility. Hence, I suspect that this is yet another norm-setting task, rather than a fact-finding mission, but as with what I said two paragraphs earlier, I again think that this is how it should be. And, naturally, the consequences of where we decide to draw the line between a person and their pathology – e.g., that certain kinds of people may be locked up, treated as patients in need of treatment, or whatever else – may also need to be taken into account in our fairness investigation.

Finally, I recognize that there may be many fair and unfair systems under my approach. After all, a given system might drop its mental capacity threshold for full responsibility from that possessed by an average 18 year old to that of an average 15 year old, and remain fair as long as the expectations that it now imposes on the nominally fully responsible people are less demanding – after all, those expectations would now apply to 15 year olds as well. Or perhaps it can remain fair under this scenario as long as the punishments that it inflicts are made less harsh, or altered in some other manner that accommodates that we will now hold responsible 15 year old people. And there are clearly also many ways for systems to be unfair – e.g., by imposing varying kinds of (perhaps increasingly) unreasonable expectations on given groups of people, or by imposing increasingly unreasonably harsh (kinds of) punishments onto people given their particular transgression. I do not, however, see this as a problem with my approach – e.g., that it exposes some kind of moral relativism – since there is nothing objectionably relativistic about recognizing that there are different ways to arrange society in a good way.

Elsewhere (Vincent 2013) I have offered an explicitly diachronic analysis of the notion of "capacity". On my account there, whether someone has sufficient capacity is not a matter of whether at a given moment in time, in other possible worlds, the mechanism from which their action issued issues in the right action. Rather, it is a matter of whether the mechanism from which their wrongful action issued on this occasion issues in the right action on a sufficient number of other occasions in relevantly similar scenarios. Although I still think that my analysis of capacity is superior for reasons that I outline there (see Vincent 2013: 189–190 for a list of some of the advantages), and indeed its diachronic focus meshes with the sort of argument that I have presented in this section, in a way

I now think that it does not matter terribly much how we understand the notion of "capacity", what analysis of capacity one adopts. As long as that analysis faithfully captures a plausible meaning of the term "capacity", and as long as we have a way of ascertaining how much capacity people have – from what psychology their actions issued – then we will be in a position to move along to the normative task that I have discussed in this section – namely, to assessing whether it would be fair to treat a person like that, like that, for that. To justify attributions of responsibility and blame, and perhaps related impositions of punishment, what we have to show is *not* that capacities exist even in a deterministic universe, since as I said in the previous section, there are many senses in which even a deterministic universe can accommodate capacities. Rather, we have to explain why having sufficient capacity or a particular psychology is morally significant in regard to responsibility, blame, and perhaps punishment – i.e., *why capacity matters* to responsibility, blame, and perhaps punishment – and that is what I have tried to do in the present section.

Addressing David Hodgson's challenge

In my view the immense value of David Hodgson's last book was the clear way in which he explicated the problem that capacitarian compatibilists have not in my view addressed, by highlighting the feature of *plausible reasoning* that he thought was needed to warrant blame and punishment – namely, its not being rule- or law-governed, or rule- or law-constrained. I see this as an immensely valuable contribution to the debate about free will, determinism, and responsibility precisely because it draws attention to the fact that the capacitarian compatibilist strategy has not completely delivered on what compatibilists may have hoped that it would deliver – i.e., something that would give capacitous people an edge over sub-capacitous people during moments of perception, judgement, decision, and action, in virtue of which we can hold them (but not sub-capacitous) people responsible for what they do. When we restrict our focus to such moments in time, swapping utterly inflexible rules of nature for utterly inflexible rules of psychology is cold comfort to capacitous individuals who engage in wrongdoing. In those moments, their capacitous psychology bestowed upon them no advantage over their sub-capacitous wrongdoing buddies. Both did the only thing they really could have done.

David Hodgson clearly captured the problem with the capacitarian compatibilist strategy, but as I commented briefly, his own approach does not give those people whom we call "capacitous" an advantage during moments in time over those whom we call "sub-capacitous". I take the failure of theories that have a synchronic focus – synchronic in terms of where we look for the justification of responsibility, blame, and perhaps related practices of punishment; namely, in narrow *moments* of perception, judgement, or control, where we may have hope some free will or elbow room might lurk – to provide an adequate account of how blame and punishment can be justified, as a good reason to look elsewhere for features that might justify these responsibility practices.

And things change radically when we broaden our focus and start considering how different psychologies make a difference to people's lives over longer stretches of time. When we ditch *synchronic* questions like, "Was P responsible *on that occasion*?" in preference for a question like, "Is P a person *with undermined responsibility*?" that can be understood from a *diachronic* perspective, it becomes easier to explain why having a capacitous psychology is advantageous. Even a rigid, rule-governed, and synchronically inflexible psychology of someone like you or me – a capacitous psychology – places us in an advantageous position when compared to people with a sub-capacitous psychology. Because of your and my psychologies, it is fair to expect more of us and to treat us more harshly than what it is fair to expect of sub-capacitous individuals and how it is fair to treat them. Capacity or psychology makes a difference, but to see it you have to move further away from the page to see its diachronic significance.

On my account, the justification of genuinely backward-looking reactive attitudes – those that are meant to reflect attributions of responsibility – and related responsibility practices like punishment should not be sought in analyses of "capacity", nor in features within moments of perception, judgement, decision, and action, that distinguish the capacitous person from the sub-capacitous person. Rather, the justification of such things resides in diachronic considerations that draw our attention to the importance of assessing whole systems of responsibility on grounds of fairness. On my account, the reason why mental capacity matters – specifically in regard to responsibility, blame, and possibly related practices of punishment – is because of the role that mental capacity plays in assessments of whether a given system of responsibility would be fair when it treats people like that, like that, for that.

David Hodgson's challenge to compatibilists who claim that the universe could even be deterministic but still have room for responsibility, was to explain why even if nobody could exercise their capacities differently to how they actually exercise them, we may still be justified in treating people differentially given their different psychologies. I hope to have met David Hodgson's challenge by explaining why even if our rule-based psychologies are rigid and inflexible in the sense that he described, we may still be justified in treating people with some psychologies more harshly when they do something wrong than how we may treat people with other psychologies. On my account, psychology matters because of its role in the fairness enquiry – whether a system of responsibility that treats people like that, like that, for that, is fair – and in my view this compatibilist approach should also be palatable to incompatibilists of different stripes.

References

Arpaly, N 2007, 'Unprincipled Virtue – Synopsis (of Sorts)', *Philosophical Studies* 134(3): 429–431.

Ayer, AJ 2009, 'Freedom and Necessity', in D Pereboom (ed), *Freedom and Necessity*, Hackett Publishing Company, Indianapolis.

Benchimol, J 2011, 'The Moral Significance of Unintentional Omission: Comparing Will-Centered and Non-will-centered Accounts of Moral Responsibility', in NA Vincent, I van de Poel, and J van den Hoven (eds), *Moral Responsibility: Beyond Free Will and Determinism*, Springer, Dodrecht.

Burns, JM and Swerdlow, RH 2003, 'Right Orbitogrontal Tumor With Pedophilia Symptom and Constructional Apraxia Sign', *Archives of Neurology* 60: 437–440.

Fischer, JM 2005, 'Reply: The Free Will Revolution', *Philosophical Explorations* 8(2): 145–156.

Fischer, JM and Ravizza, M 1998, *Responsibility and Control: A Theory of Moral Responsibility*, Cambridge University Press, Cambridge.

Hodgson, DH (2012) *Rationality + Consciousness = Free Will*, Oxford University Press, New York.

Honoré, T 1999, *Responsibility and Fault*, Hart Publishing, Portland.

Levy, N 2007, 'The Responsibility of the Psychopath Revisited', *Philosophy, Psychiatry & Psychology* 14(2): 129–138.

Levy, N 2008, 'Counterfactual Intervention and Agents' Capacities', *The Journal of Philosophy* 55(5): 223–239.

Nozick, R 1974, *Anarchy, State and Utopia*, Basic Books, New York.

Santoni de Sio, F and Vincent, NA 2015, 'Rationality + Consciousness = Free Will by David Hodgson', *Criminal Law and Philosophy* 9(4): 633–644.

Taylor, R 1963, 'Freedom and Determinism', in R. Taylor (ed), *Metaphysics*, Prentice-Hall, Englewood Cliffs.

Vincent, NA 2011, 'Legal Responsibility Adjudication and the Normative Authority of the Mind Sciences', *Philosophical Explorations* 14(3): 315–331.

Vincent, NA 2013, 'Blame, Desert and Compatibilist Capacity: A Diachronic Account of Moderateness in Regards to Reasons-Responsiveness', *Philosophical Explorations* 6(2): 178–194.

Vincent, NA 2015, 'Assessment and Modification of Free Will via Scientific Techniques: Two Challenges', in W Glannon (ed), *Free Will and the Brain: Neuroscientific, Philosophical, and Legal Perspectives*, Cambridge University Press, Cambridge.

Williams, BAO and Nagel, T 1976, 'Moral Luck', *Proceedings of The Aristotelian Society, Supplementary Volumes* 50(9–11 July 1976): 115–135, 137–151.

11 Mitigation is difficult

A moral evaluation of a mitigation practice at sentencing

Allan McCay

At the sentencing of those who have been convicted of criminal offences, pleas in mitigation sometimes focus on agency-related issues such as difficult formative circumstances, intellectual difficulties, and mental illness. Defence lawyers sometimes make such pleas in order to present the offender as a deficient agent, in order to reduce the court's assessment of their blameworthiness.[1] This is done with the hope of reducing the punishment imposed by the court.[2]

In some legal systems, this practice has resulted in case law which addresses these mitigation issues.[3] Legislatures have also sometimes passed laws which impact upon how these matters are addressed.[4] However, one might ask whether such legal doctrine has any independent moral justification, and if the law picked out a morally arbitrary issue as being worthy of mitigation, or if a more significant factor was omitted, this would be disconcerting.

In this chapter, in order to address the question of moral justification (or otherwise) for legal doctrine pertaining to agency-related mitigation practices, I use the philosophical work of Dana Nelkin and David Hodgson, to develop a moral theory of agency-related blame assessment. This moral theory is intended to have general application across a range of jurisdictions, but as a case study, I use the theory to evaluate some mitigation practices of a particular criminal justice system, one with similar punitive aims to those of many other common law systems – that of New South Wales (NSW), Australia (the legal system in which David Hodgson was an appellate judge).[5]

1 It is possible that an unrepresented offender might also make such a plea.

2 Here is not the place for an overview of mitigating factors at sentencing; however, it is worth noting that not all mitigating factors draw attention to agency-related issues with a view to presenting an offender as being less blameworthy for what they did. Thus a plea mitigation that is based on an early plea of guilty, or good prospects for rehabilitation, would not present an offender as being deficient and less blameworthy for what they did. Such pleas are recognized as having merit in at least some jurisdictions (e.g., NSW – see the *Crimes (Sentencing Procedure) Act 1999* (NSW) s21A (3) (h) and (k)).

3 Where juries are involved in sentencing, they do not give reasons for their decisions and thus do not produce such case law.

4 One such law will be discussed later in the chapter.

5 For a discussion of blameworthiness in the context of American sentencing practice see Kelly (2017: 585–587).

The moral theory developed here focuses on the difficulty that was faced by an agent in complying with a norm they have infringed, as a factor in blame assessment. In response to Hodgson's work on free will, it takes a diachronic approach to difficulty (rather than an approach similar to that of Nelkin which appears to envisage all of the relevant difficulty as being present at the time of the infringement of a norm).

According to my moral theory, in order to assess the degree of blameworthiness deserved for failure to comply with a norm, one must ask how much compliance difficulty was present at the time of non-compliance. One must also ask how the history of the agent has created difficulties related to the non-compliance. One's assessment of the degree to which an agent is blameworthy should be informed by an *overall* assessment of the difficulty of compliance (comprising both aspects of difficulty). An implication of my theory is that competent and accurate blame assessment is a complex and very challenging task.

I argue that some (but not all) of the NSW mitigation practices considered here find some moral support from my theory. While this support is not decisive in considering whether the practices should be endorsed, all things considered, the support of a plausible moral theory of blame assessment is a factor in favour of them.

I note that a more precise theory would need to be more complex. However, acceptance of this complexity might raise questions about human capacity (and thus the capacity of courts) to competently assess degrees of blameworthiness. It may also raise further doubts for those who, like me, are concerned that there may be insufficient moral justification for the retributive practices found in many, or perhaps all, legal systems.

Agency-related pleas for mitigated blameworthiness

The first step in my argument involves the development of a moral theory of degrees of agency-related blame assessment. This is required in order to theorize about the presentation of an issue of agency as a factor that is purported to mitigate blameworthiness. But what kind of pleas are under consideration?

My concern is with pleas which present the agency of a wrongdoer as problematic, with a view to demonstrating that they are *less* blameworthy than an agent with less problematic moral agency who did the same thing.

I will be attempting to develop a theory that can evaluate claims like these:

1. I *deserve* less blame and punishment for what I did because my adverse formative circumstances had a role in my offending.
2. I *deserve* less blame and punishment for what I did because my brain damage had a role in my offending.
3. I *deserve* less blame and punishment for what I did because my genetic constitution had a role in my offending.
4. I *deserve* less blame and punishment for what I did because I have a mild mental illness which had a role in my offending.

I call these "pleas for agency-related mitigation", and will first attempt to find a principled way of morally evaluating such claims, before going on to evaluate the sentencing practice.

The motivation for the development of a moral theory of agency-related blame assessment

In order to explain the motivation for the chapter, it is useful to refer to my Australian case study. It is clear that NSW, like many other criminal justice systems, has a retributive aim (aiming to give offenders what they *deserve* for their criminal conduct), which operates alongside other consequentialist aims such as deterrence, incapacitation, and rehabilitation.[6]

Blameworthiness is an important consideration in retributive justice.[7] According to legal doctrine which will be discussed later in this chapter, when sentencing, NSW judges must consider what might be thought of as a legal analogue of blameworthiness, the "moral culpability"[8] of the offender, and in so doing, consider pleas in mitigation relating to some characteristics particular to the offender. These include difficult formative circumstances, cognitive disability, and/or mental illness. Appellate judges may also be required to consider whether a sentencing judge has erred in the assessment of moral culpability.[9]

The term "moral culpability" is thus a concept that is regularly discussed in NSW courts, and legal doctrine (some of which will be discussed later) maintains that moral culpability varies in degree from case to case, contingent at least in part on the agency-related issues mentioned in the last paragraph. When one bears in mind the retributive aim of the NSW practice, it is the concept of moral culpability that most clearly provides the legal means to address agency-related pleas for mitigation of blame.

From the perspective of retributive theories of punishment, the NSW practice's concern with agency and blame makes sense, as retributivists generally think

6 See *Veen v R* [1979] HCA 7 and *Veen v R (No 2)* [1988] HCA 14 which relate generally to sentencing in Australia. Section 3A of the *Crimes (Sentencing Procedure) Act 1999* (NSW) details the statutory purposes of sentencing. It is useful to set out the whole range which runs as follows:

> *(a) to ensure that the offender is adequately punished for the offence, (b) to prevent crime by deterring the offender and other persons from committing similar offences, (c) to protect the community from the offender, (d) to promote the rehabilitation of the offender, (e) to make the offender accountable for his or her actions, (f) to denounce the conduct of the offender, (g) to recognise the harm done to the victim of the crime and the community.*

Some of the subsections seem to be retributive (for example, (a), (e), (f), and maybe (g)).

7 As Fine and Kennett point out "[i]t is surely necessary to retributivist justifications that punishment be morally *deserved*" (2004: 433) and that the agent must be blameworthy (2004: 433). In a discussion of American criminal law, Kelly notes that "retributive punishment grounds punishment in blameworthiness and desert" (2017: 577).

8 For a discussion of the significance of moral culpability in the context of American capital punishment jurisprudence see Levine (2001).

9 See *Yucebsoglu v R* [2015].

that it is important for legal systems to consider the culpability of an offender as a factor when imposing punishment.[10] If it turned out that a criminal justice system (NSW or another) had an agency-related mitigation practice that significantly diverged from offenders' blameworthiness, this would be troubling from a retributive perspective. Thus those who endorse retributivism have an interest in morally evaluating mitigation practices.

As noted earlier, NSW has adopted a range of punitive goals insofar as it pursues both retributive and consequentialist aims. This range means that any failure of the mitigation practice to track offenders' blameworthiness would not settle the question of whether the practice should be endorsed, given *all* of the aims of the system. Thus a person who supported a mixed view of criminal justice (a view which embraces both retributivism and consequentialism) would need to consider consequentialist concerns as well as blameworthiness, when morally evaluating a mitigation practice.

However, to the extent that they supported the retributive aim, the way that a legal system assessed blameworthiness would be of some significance, and consequently the way issues of moral agency affected such an assessment would also be significant (albeit not decisive) in any overall evaluation.

So if one endorses retributivism, whether as the sole proper aim, or as part of a mixed theory of sentencing, moral evaluation of agency-related mitigation practices matters. Because it would be good to have a principled way of undertaking such evaluation, the construction of an evaluative theory is the first aim of this chapter.

It is worth noting that although much moral theory has focused on determining what kind of agents, if any, can be morally responsible and blameworthy for their wrongs, there is little theory which focuses on the ways in which issues of agency affect *degrees* of blameworthiness. However, a contribution from Dana Nelkin does have this focus, and can be used as a starting point in the development of my theory.

While I will retain core aspects of Nelkin's theory (her focus on the difficulty of complying with a norm) in the development of my own moral theory, I will argue that her theory needs to be modified and made more complex, using diachronic insights relating to self-formation from Hodgson's work, in order to better evaluate sentencing practices.

Constructing a moral theory of agency-related blame assessment: Nelkin's account

Prior to addressing Nelkin's work, it is useful to briefly say something about an influence on her view that comes from the legal philosopher H. L. A. Hart, who also focuses on the significance of *difficulty* in relation to mitigation (2008: 15).

Speaking of legal mitigation (Hart was not attempting to develop a moral theory of mitigation), Hart said that "difficulty" in complying with the law

10 Many retributivists argue that the degree of punishment should be affected by both harm and culpability (Duff (2001: 135), Von Hirsch (1993: 29).

underpins mitigation. In his book *Punishment and Responsibility* Hart comments as follows:

> [t]he special features of mitigation are that a good reason for administering a less severe penalty is made out if the situation or mental state of the convicted criminal is such that he was exposed to an unusual or specially great *temptation*, or his *ability to control* his actions is thought to have been impaired or weakened otherwise than by his own action, so that conformity to the law which he has broken was a matter of special *difficulty* for him as compared with normal persons normally placed.
>
> (2008: 15 italics added)

For Hart, mitigation is due in the following circumstances:

1 Where temptation was significant
2 Where ability to control was diminished otherwise than by the offender's own action[11]
3 Where either or both of these factors led to a special difficulty in complying with the law

According to Hart, the benchmark for the assessment is "normal persons normally placed", and thus mitigation is a comparative enterprise.[12] He sets out principles that underpin a legal practice of mitigation, and Nelkin's account (2016) follows on from Hart in regarding the issue of difficulty as significant. Her approach to the assessment of blameworthiness is in the context of moral theory, rather than legal theory, and thus her work is of assistance in the development of the evaluative moral theory that is the aim of the first part of this chapter.

While she has a broader aim, Nelkin's approach to difficulty is the focus here.[13] She sees the issue of difficulty in "doing the right thing" (2016: 357) which would appear to include difficulty in complying with norms, as significant in the assessment of

11 Later in the chapter I will argue for a diachronic approach to mitigation, but at this stage it is worth noting that Hart's formulation has a diachronic aspect insofar as point 2 refers to a historical action of the offender. Hart does not solely focus on the time of the offence.

12 It is interesting to consider whether Hart is right about the legal benchmark. So do the courts in England actually compare wrongdoers with "normal persons normally placed", or do they in fact compare with the normal *offender* in a normal *situation of wrongdoing* (if there is such a thing)? Is it the same in other jurisdictions such as NSW? There is no need to answer these questions in this chapter.

13 Nelkin's broader aim relates to debates about free will and moral responsibility. She first notes that existing theories in the moral responsibility literature fail (without supplementation) to accommodate *degrees* of blameworthiness, and by way of example she demonstrates this by focusing on prominent theories of moral agency. She argues that consideration of questions of degrees of blameworthiness and praiseworthiness may help make progress on the free will problem, suggesting that her analysis lends some support to compatibilist views (views that claim that moral responsibility is compatible with determinism). Her argument is that the specifically indeterministic aspects of libertarian free will are not significant in matters of mitigation. This finding is said to lend some support to the view that responsible agency does not require indeterminism and is thus a contribution more broadly to the free will debate that is supportive of compatibilism (2016: 374).

blameworthiness, but sees difficulty as subdividing into two subcategories: the degree of *effort*, and the degree of *sacrifice*[14] needed to do the right thing (2016: 357).

Nelkin does not argue the following, but in order to better understand the role of difficulty in non-compliance with a norm, it is worth noting that difficulty could have a role in at least two ways. An agent might experience difficulty in trying and fail to comply as a result of the experience of difficulty, or they might envisage difficulty and fail to try because of anticipated difficulty.

Efforts and sacrifices, whether actual or imagined, are generally things that are experienced.[15] This seems to suggest that for the blaming party to assess mitigation claims, Nelkin is committed to the view that they would need to attempt to assess some subjective states of the agent whose action is being assessed, namely, those involving envisaged or actual effort, and envisaged or actual sacrifice. This would seem to require knowledge of something of the agent's cognitive world (for example, what was envisaged), and affective world (for example, how much something was valued).

In order to evaluate blameworthiness, her theory would ask how difficult it was to comply with a norm, given a purported mitigating factor. It would ask how much effort and how much sacrifice would have been needed to comply.

To the extent that an action or omission requires significant effort and/or sacrifice it is indeed difficult, and that would seem to be the case for compliance with norms. However, Nelkin does not claim that difficulty is the only factor to be considered in relation to blameworthiness. She says that, all other things being equal, the more difficult it is to act well, the less blameworthy an agent would be should they fail (2016: 372). I am also not committed to the view that difficulty is the only factor in determining blameworthiness, but like Nelkin, I do assume that it is a factor.

Nelkin's account focuses on the "quality of opportunity" that an agent has to comply with a norm (Nelkin 2016: 370). On her analysis, the fairer[16] the

14 An example that Nelkin gives of a great sacrifice is that of a soldier who jumps on a grenade to save her fellow soldiers (2016: 357). If the soldier had refrained from jumping on the grenade, because it would have led to the end of her life, the action of jumping on the grenade could be said to have been difficult, not because of the effort, but because of the great sacrifice involved in losing her life. In her paper Nelkin also discusses the relevance of difficulty to assessments of praiseworthiness, and this example seems to relate to the role of difficulty in assessing a praiseworthy action.

15 Later in the chapter I will raise the possibility of what I call "epistemic difficulties". These are impediments to moral knowledge, and it is not clear that there is necessarily an experiential aspect to such difficulties. I do not wish to suggest that all difficulties are subjectively experienced.

16 Of fairness, Nelkin asks:

> [w]hat can it mean to say that opportunities can be more or less fair in a non-legal context? One answer is that the more reasonable it is to expect or demand that one take it, the more fair it is. And so the more blameworthy one is for not taking it and the less praiseworthy one is when one does. This suggestion might very well be correct, but it does not follow that considerations regarding fairness or reasonableness are fundamental. I believe that what makes it reasonable to make particular demands of agents in particular situations is the quality of the relevant opportunities, determined by the agents' capacities and the features of their situations.
>
> (2016: 371)

opportunity of compliance, the more blameworthy an agent is for failure. But the capacities of the agent and the features of the situation that they are in affect the quality of their opportunity.[17] In a paper co-written with Brink (2013) she also sees features of the situation as interacting with the agent's capacities. Thus "[t]wo people in a similar situation might have quite different opportunities that depend on their differing capacities" (Nelkin 2016: 377).

One important thing to note about this view of mitigation is its near synchronic nature. What appear to be significant are the capacities of the agent and features of the situation *at the time of the wrongdoing* (she makes no reference to historical situations). She says:

> what determines blameworthiness is whether one has a fair opportunity to avoid wrongdoing, where whether one has such an opportunity depends on both one's capacities and one's situation.
>
> (2016: 370)

This factor in blame assessment does not appear to be diachronic because any agent would have had a variety of capacities over time (from birth to their current stage in life) and would have experienced a variety of situations. The reference to the "situation" seems to be most sensibly understood to be the situation at the time of wrongdoing, and the same goes for the reference to "capacities".

In her 2016 paper, Nelkin does not consider mitigation in respect of difficulties that an agent may have encountered in forming a self with greater capacity to act appropriately in the situation of wrongdoing, and/or difficulties in the formation of a self that was more motivated to exercise their capacity to act appropriately.

However, it is not clear that such difficulties are inconsistent with her theory, or that it could not be adapted to embrace and specify this historical dimension. In the next section I will argue for the moral significance of these difficulties, and I will argue that there is merit in explicitly incorporating them into a moral theory of degrees of agency-related blame assessment.

Nelkin's theory is more fine-grained than Hart's as to what constitutes a difficulty – she makes it explicit that both the need for effort and sacrifice create difficulties in complying with norms. Her moral theory of degrees of blameworthiness was my starting point in developing a still more fine-grained moral theory, with the ultimate intention of putting this new theory to use to evaluate mitigation practices in the law. I will now continue Nelkin's nascent project of specifying difficulties in complying with norms in greater detail, by attending to the historical dimension of difficulty.

Why is there merit in increasing the specificity of the theory? Whether in a legal or non-legal context, if one is serious about assessing degrees of blameworthiness, and knowledge of difficulties is thought to be useful in performing such assessment, then it is going to be important to consider as many morally relevant difficulties as possible.

17 It seems that the fairer the quality of the opportunity, the better quality it is.

Of course, there may be considerations other than accurate assessment of blameworthiness that are at play in deciding what to do about a wrongdoer. Thus in a legal context these might include the limitations of time available for judgement, the legitimate demands of a victim, or the consequentialist aims of punishment. Some of these concerns may also apply in a non-legal context, but wherever possible, it would be a good thing to know, as precisely as possible, how blameworthy the wrongdoer is. A theory that draws the attention of a blame-assessor to a wider range of difficulties than a more restrictive theory should thus be of more assistance in attaining accuracy. This is because by drawing attention to the various forms of difficulty, it can reduce the chances of omitting relevant difficulty (difficulty in complying with a norm that one has failed to comply with) and thus bolster the accuracy of the assessment of blameworthiness.

Why does this matter? The negative impact of overestimating blameworthiness could be great, particularly when the estimation is linked to retributive action in a criminal justice context. It might also have a negative impact in a non-legal context if an overestimation were to lead to an excessive blaming act. In either a legal or non-legal context if blame assessment were thought to be important, there would also seem to be something problematic about underestimating it.

The project here might be thought of as one that tries to minimize negligence, or worse recklessness, in blame assessment by adopting a morally conscientious[18] and rigorous approach. However, it will be seen later that this moral conscientiousness and concern for rigour lead to a challenging task for the blaming party. It is a task that, by drawing attention to epistemic problems in determining how blameworthy wrongdoers are, may start to call into question the legitimacy of action taken based on assessments of degrees of blameworthiness.

Once one starts to take precision in matters of blame seriously and to acknowledge the epistemic problem of proportionate blame, doubt is cast on our capacities as assessors of degrees of blameworthiness, and somewhat paradoxically this doubt might even lend support to the claims of those who have general misgivings about blaming and retributive practices, and would prefer to abandon them.[19]

Why is the historical dimension to agency-related blame assessment important?

As has been mentioned earlier, according to Nelkin's theory, one's blame-assessor should consider the fairness of one's opportunity to comply with the norm with which one has failed to comply.

18 I use Double's term here. He uses it in the context of a discussion of libertarian free will, and blame and punishment (2002).

19 I am grateful to Robert Anderson for coining the phrase "the epistemic problem of proportionate blame", in response to a draft of this chapter.

But how could one have complied with a norm with which one has in fact failed to comply? Hart uses the language of temptation, and one way of complying would have been to resist the temptation to do wrong (perhaps by resisting temptation to throw a punch or to steal something), at the time of wrongdoing. Of course, one's capacities and one's situation may have made resistance difficult, and such difficulty is a factor, which may reduce blameworthiness on Nelkin's view.

However, if one widens the temporal frame (as is the case in accounts of moral responsibility that rely on tracing),[20] then resisting the temptation to do wrong, *at the time of wrongdoing*, is not the only thing that might have led to compliance. Perhaps earlier in one's life one might have taken steps to augment one's capacities or to affect one's motivation such that one was not the kind of person who was likely to be tempted, or to succumb to temptation. If anger management was a factor in wrongdoing, one might have taken steps to join an anger management programme, and thereby augment capacities relevant to compliance. If addiction was a factor in wrongdoing, one might have taken steps to rid oneself of the addiction, thereby diminishing one's motivation to perform the non-compliant act.

One might think of these steps as self-formative acts, and the question of whether one has attempted such self-formation seems to be relevant to degrees of blameworthiness. If one has not, it seems to matter why not. There seems to be a moral difference between someone who has failed to take up a self-formative intervention that would have been easy and someone who has failed to take up an intervention because it was difficult (albeit possible), and so questions of difficulty now take on a diachronic aspect. In an unmodified form, it is not clear how Nelkin's theory can accommodate these moral differences, and this provides the motivation to look beyond her theory, as I will in the next section.

But first, and in order to further illustrate the diachronic aspect of the difficulty of compliance with norms, I will use a hypothetical example. This example involves a 20 year old offender with issues of alcohol addiction and anger management (Sean). Sean is from a disadvantaged community, and has committed a drunken assault on Ben. Sean's peer group has a strong focus on binge drinking, and his neighbourhood environment is one of gang violence.

In order to avoid the assault on Ben, Sean could have made more effort to control himself at the time of the assault. On Nelkin's view it would be important to consider how difficult that was – how much effort and/or sacrifice would have been required to walk away.

But surely, being aware of his anger management issue, Sean should have tried to control his drinking earlier in the evening. Perhaps that may have been somewhat difficult given his alcohol addiction, but if successful it could have averted the wrong.

However, Sean might also have taken steps earlier in his life that could have averted the attack on Ben. He might have resisted the peer pressure that initially

20 Vargas explains tracing to be:

> the idea that responsibility for some outcome need not be anchored in the agent or agent's action at the moment immediately prior to outcome, but rather at some suitable time prior to the moment of deliberation or action.
>
> (2005: 269)

led him to start drinking, thereby forming an adult self without a drinking problem. Later on he might have participated in an anger management programme and/or engaged in alcohol counselling, both of which might be thought of as self-formative acts which may have averted the assault on Sean.

However, these self-formative acts may have involved significant effort and significant sacrifice, perhaps through ostracism from peers, loss of status or protection in a violent community, or even becoming a victim of violence from peers. They might have been difficult steps for Sean to take.

As mentioned earlier, there might be reasons relating to other considerations that make it appropriate for a blame-assessor to ignore this diachronic aspect of blameworthiness; however, there seems be no reason *related to blameworthiness* to fail to take a diachronic approach. Nelkin does not address this issue, but there is no apparent reason why the *timing* of preventative effort or sacrifice carries great moral significance. This seems to be a reason to widen the temporal frame.

An attempt to assess the degree to which an agent was blameworthy would benefit from a diachronic approach insofar as it was concerned with greater precision about degrees of blameworthiness, and it will be seen later that some aspects of NSW sentencing law take something like this diachronic approach to difficulty. Prior to evaluating the legal practice it is useful to return to the project of theory construction, and examine the moral theory of David Hodgson, who was both a philosopher and a judge, and thus a professional assessor of the legal analogue to blameworthiness: moral culpability.

Hodgson's work is useful for the purposes of constructing a moral theory of agency-related blame assessment because it suggests the way for the theory to take note of the agent's *past* as well as features of the agent's capacities and situation, at the time of the wrong. It points the way to a diachronic approach to difficulty through a discussion of self-formation.

Constructing a theory: self-formation and difficult self-formative tasks

Before examining Hodgson's approach to self-formation and mitigation in respect of self-formative difficulties in his philosophical work, it is useful to very briefly provide the broader context for the parts of that work that are of most significance to the current discussion. This involves saying something more general about punishment and free will in his philosophical theorizing. This context sheds light on his interest in the themes of this chapter, and provides background that is explanatorily useful in order to understand the comments that are relevant to blame assessment.

While Hodgson aims to show how generally we are free and can be morally responsible for what we do, his project has specific relevance to the law insofar as he attempts to put forward a view of moral agency that could provide a justification for the retributive aim that operates within the criminal law's mix of aims.[21]

21 For a discussion of the role of his theorizing in supporting retributivism see Hodgson (2012: 213).

There are a number of steps in his theorizing, and it is not easy to distil them into a short form, but he argues that we are free because we can engage in plausible reasoning, and rationally respond to gestalts[22] in a way we control. We have free will and control over what we do (rather than what we do just being a matter of luck) because *alternatives are truly open*, albeit limited by the way we are, as governed by the laws of nature. Though our choices are undetermined, Hodgson argues that we can respond in a way that is not random, but rational, and we can put our selection into effect by voluntary action. This has implications for responsibility, and because we have libertarian[23] free will, we have some control. As a result of this we have responsibility in a "robust sense" (Hodgson 2012: 157), and we bear some ultimate responsibility for what we do. We can deserve punishment (that is, retributive punishment) because we are responsible (Hodgson 2012: 210).

However, and of great relevance to this chapter, factors outside our control, such as genes and environments, reduce our responsibility (but do not normally eliminate it) (Hodgson 2012: 158). As a result of this we are "partly responsible" for the way we are and what we do, and we increase our responsibility for the way we are by engaging in *self-formation* (Hodgson 2012: 177). This affects our responsibility for what we do. So we can make good or bad choices and thereby become better or worse people, and through these self-forming choices and actions become progressively more responsible over time for whom we are. This increases our responsibility for what we do.[24]

It seems possible under Hodgson's view that we could engage in self-formation that would have the effect of increasing our capacities as a moral agent and/or the likelihood that we would exercise those capacities we do have, in a way that is consistent with moral and/or legal norms.

For Hodgson there can be two contributions to responsibility for a wrong, and I will call them "direct" and "indirect". He says that an agent is responsible for a wrong:

1 to the extent that it is caused by the agent's non-rule-determined response to gestalt experiences, and

22 Hodgson argues that agents experience sets of circumstances as gestalts – the whole experience being greater than the sum of the parts. This experience of the circumstances as a whole, rather than merely a series of component parts, influences agents' decisions. For the present purposes it is not necessary to further consider the role of gestalts in his theorizing, but see chapter 5 (Hodgson 2012).

23 In the free will debate those who argue that we can make undetermined choices which we control are referred to as libertarians (this is unrelated to political libertarianism). Hodgson's view is thus a libertarian view of free will.

24 Other thinkers in the contemporary debate highlight the moral significance of self-formation. In this volume, another libertarian, Robert Kane, is an obvious example, particularly as he is a philosopher with whom Hodgson's work has engaged (2012: 159), but it is important to note that one does not have to be libertarian to regard self-formation as morally significant. For a compatibilist perspective on self-formation see Roskies (2012).

2 to the extent that it is caused by the agent's character, to the extent in turn that the agent's character has been caused by self-forming decisions or actions, and those decisions or actions were caused by the agent's non-rule determined response to gestalt experiences.

(2012: 175)

Direct contributions are contributions derived from the way we respond *at the time* of a wrong, and point 1 addresses direct contributions. Indirect contributions are contributions to character that are accrued through self-forming actions (*earlier choices in our life* that turned us into the kind of person we are). Point 2 relates to indirect contributions.

The value of Hodgson's view in relation to the current project of theory construction is in drawing attention to the direct and indirect contributions to responsibility, and thus making room for contributions from both the time of the wrong, and from the history of the agent.

A composite theory

There appears to be no reason why Hodgson's view of agency could not make room for both direct difficulties in complying with norms that relate to diminished capacities[25] at the time of offending, and indirect difficulties occurring earlier in life that made it harder for the agent either to have superior moral capacities, or to have greater motivation to use those capacities that they did have appropriately. Similarly, as mentioned earlier, it is not obvious that there is anything in Nelkin's view to preclude a diachronic approach to difficulty, or quality of opportunity.

So what would the composite moral theory of agency-related blame assessment, based on the insights of both Nelkin and Hodgson, look like?

According to my composite theory, in order to know how difficult it was to comply with a norm, one needs to know about the agent's *diachronic quality of opportunity* (Nelkin's view of the quality of opportunity was focused on the time of wrongdoing). So in addition to knowing about the way that the wrongdoer's capacities interacted with the situation of wrongdoing to create compliance difficulties, one also needs to be aware of some historical information about the wrongdoer. This further information is needed in order to gauge another aspect of difficulty that is also relevant to the blame assessment: indirect difficulty (the difficulty of forming a self that would have been more motivated to comply, or would have had superior capacities such as would have made compliance easier).

If the blaming party considered all of these difficulties (both direct and indirect), they would be in a better place to accurately assess the degree of blameworthiness of the offender than if they focused only on the time of the offence, and failed to pursue the diachronic approach.

25 Hodgson accepts the moral significance of an agent's capacities (2012: 224).

The examples of pleas raised at the beginning of the chapter can now be considered. For reasons of space I will focus on the first to give an example of the approach to mitigation derived from the composite theory. The first plea runs as follows:

> I *deserve* less blame and punishment for what I did because my adverse formative circumstances had a role in my offending.

According to the composite theory, the blaming party should enquire about the extent to which the formative circumstances made it difficult to form a self that would have been more motivated to comply with the infringed norm, and how difficult they made it for an agent to have formed a self with superior moral capacities such as would have made compliance easier. This would be the indirect contribution to the overall assessment of difficulty.

This indirect contribution would not settle the question of how difficult compliance was. The blaming party should also consider the direct contribution to the overall difficulty of compliance with the infringed norm. They should consider how difficult the interaction of the agent's actual capacities, in the context of the actual situation of wrongdoing, made compliance with the infringed norm.[26]

Knowledge about these two contributions would give them information about diachronic difficulty of compliance, and thus the quality of the agent's diachronic opportunity. Perhaps one kind of effort or sacrifice, on its own, would have led to compliance with the norm, or perhaps some combination of direct effort, direct sacrifice, historical effort, and historical sacrifice would have been needed for compliance. In order get a full picture of the difficulty of compliance with the norm, the blaming party would need to consider all of this difficulty.

Thus they would need to consider difficulty at the time of the offence, and from the history of the offender, in order to gain an *overall* sense of difficulty of compliance and compare it with the overall difficulty of compliance "for normal persons normally placed".[27]

This could well be breathtakingly complex and, ironically, a difficult job, for the blaming party. The complexity would only be increased in situations where an offender had raised a number of different types of agency-related issues in mitigation. It would raise questions about the relative weight of different types of difficulty and how to reconcile them into an overall assessment of difficulty. However, the fact that the task of blame assessment is complex and confusing does not mean that the argument that led to the complexity is flawed.

26 Working out the impact of the difficult formative circumstances on the agent's actual capacities would not be easy as their actual capacities may be influenced by difficulties related to the formative environment, good aspects of the formative environment, non-environmental factors (such as genetic predisposition), and perhaps self-forming actions for which an agent is responsible.

27 See note 12 earlier in the chapter for a discussion of this quote from H. L. A. Hart.

This complexity raises the question of what one should do about uncertainty about the degree to which an agent is blameworthy for what they have done.[28] It is interesting to note that Hodgson accepts that issues of mitigation raise difficult questions in assessing what people deserve for their wrongs, but advocates for retention of the retributive aim in punishment despite the problems (2012: 215–216). He does not consider the implications of these problems for blame assessment outside of the legal context.

However, another approach might be to conclude that the uncertainty about the degree to which agents are blameworthy is so great that the whole notion of blame should be removed from responses to wrongdoing. While this would entail a rejection of blaming practices it would not amount to a rejection of the view that humans have free will, are generally morally responsible for what they do, or can be blameworthy – the suggested change to the practice would take place because we cannot ***know*** how blameworthy wrongdoers are with sufficient precision.[29] It is worth noting that this is a form of empirical rather than normative uncertainty – the blame assessment problem derives from impediments to knowing about efforts and sacrifices (both actual and counterfactual).

A conclusion as radical as a total rejection of our blaming practices may need more support than is provided by what has been said thus far. Assuming, as I now will, the practices remain intact, the complexity would mean that a blaming party should accept that full comprehension of the import of the plea in mitigation may require more information than they have available, and could even be beyond their capacities as an evaluator. This would mean that the epistemic basis for any blaming action is likely to be rather weak. The extent to which a blaming party should be concerned about accuracy might be contingent on factors such as the seriousness of the wrong for which mitigation is being sought.

At this point it is worth briefly summarizing the composite theory. The theory argues that when assessing the blameworthiness of an agent, one must take a

28 When considering the blameworthiness of the murderer Robert Harris, Watson notes that on hearing about his dire formative circumstances, our judgements about blameworthiness become more "ambivalent" (2013). The theory sketched here suggests the possibility that epistemic uncertainty about facts concerning Harris' level of difficulty in complying with the criminal law may have a role in unsettling judgements of blameworthiness. Perhaps before hearing about Harris' background we presumed it was fairly easy for him to have refrained from what he did. After hearing of his formative circumstances, we start to wonder about self-formative difficulty and begin to have doubts about the overall ease of compliance, but because of our epistemic problems, remain unsure about questions of difficulty, and thus blameworthiness.

29 For a paper that considers the implications of epistemic uncertainty about moral responsibility (without a focus on mitigation) see Rosen (2004). Rosen argues that epistemic issues about the subjective states of particular agents mean that "it would be unreasonable to repose much confidence in any particular positive judgment of responsibility" (2004: 308). My own project suggests that even if we knew an agent was responsible for what they did, it would be very difficult to know how much mitigation is due, and we may sometimes overlook mitigating factors, through ignorance of salient facts about the agent's difficulty in acting appropriately.

diachronic approach to the assessment of difficulty – one which considers the way in which the capacities of the agent interacted with features of the situation of wrongdoing, in order to create difficulties in complying with a norm, and considers how historical factors may have made it difficult for the agent to form a self that had greater motivation and/or greater capacity to comply with a norm that they have infringed.

A virtue of this approach is that the blaming party can approach blame assessment with an understanding of a *range* of things an agent could have done to avoid infringing a norm, and can approach the assessment of the difficulty of compliance with that richer understanding.

The upshot of the composite theory is that blameworthiness is difficult to assess. Does the sentencing practice of the jurisdiction that I have chosen as a case study (NSW) accept any of this complexity?

Evaluating a legal practice of sentencing

As has been mentioned, the practice of sentencing has consequentialist aims, as well as a retributive aim that is concerned with blameworthiness's legal analogue: moral culpability. There is also a political dimension to sentencing, which sees it as a regular site of discussion for tabloid newspapers, shock jocks, and aspirational politicians. Because of the diversity of aims and the political dimension, perhaps there are reasons to think that sentencing might not be a place in which complex and challenging evaluations of degrees of blameworthiness are likely to thrive.

Nonetheless it does seem that NSW practice often recognizes some of the complexity of blame assessment discussed earlier – it is at least sometimes attuned to both the direct and indirect difficulty of compliance with the criminal law, in relation to matters of mitigation.

With the composite moral theory in place, it is now possible to look to the legal practice of assessing moral culpability in order to consider how well it fits with the moral theory that I have sketched earlier. This moral evaluation of a sentencing practice asks whether given the composite moral theory outlined earlier, one would have reason to be morally concerned about particular actual practices of NSW sentencing law, or alternatively given the theory, one could find some moral reassurance.

Practices that could find some support from Nelkin's contribution to the composite theory

I will start with Nelkin's contribution to the composite theory, which focuses on the way the capacities of the agent interact with the situation of wrongdoing to create difficulty in complying with a norm.

In NSW sentencing law one can easily find evidence of a focus on the capacities of the offender at the time of the crime, and the features of the situation of wrongdoing. This seems consistent with Nelkin's views on the assessment of an agent's opportunity to act appropriately at the time of wrongdoing. For example, the High Court of Australia has made it clear that the capacities of the offenders are significant in the assessment of moral culpability. In *Muldrock v The Queen* [2011], a decision involving the sentencing of an offender for child sex offences, the court noted of those with a "mental handicap" that the:

> lack of capacity to reason, as an ordinary person might, as to the wrongfulness of the conduct will, in most cases, substantially lessen the offender's moral culpability for the offence. The retributive effect and denunciatory aspect of a sentence that is appropriate to a person of ordinary capacity will often be inappropriate to the situation of a mentally retarded offender and to the needs of the community.
>
> (para 54)[30]

This decision focused on intellectual disability, but a similar form of reasoning in relation to capacities occurs with respect to mental illness.[31] Thus in the New South Wales Court of Criminal Appeal decision *R v Hemsley* [2004] Justice Sperling stated that:

> where mental illness contributes to the commission of the offence in a material way the offender's moral culpability may be reduced; there may not be the same call for denunciation and the punishment warranted may accordingly be reduced.
>
> (para 33)

These cases demonstrate the significance of the moral capacities of the offender, but features of the situation in which the offence is committed are also of significance in sentencing decisions. So, for example, some form of duress, which is not sufficient to amount to a full defence, may mitigate punishment.[32]

Thus far it seems that the actual mitigation practices are to some extent consistent with Nelkin's quality of opportunity view, and could be supported by her contribution to the moral theory of blame assessment developed here. While the legal doctrine does not explicitly mention the concept of difficulty, it does focus

30 If a person *completely lacked* the capacity to reason about the wrongfulness of conduct it would seem unjust to hold them responsible. The most charitable understanding of these comments would see them as referring to people who can reason about wrongfulness, but for whom, as a result of their diminished capacities, it is more difficult and requires more effort.

31 Like many other jurisdictions, NSW has a mental illness defence, but where this defence is not used, or is unsuccessful, mental illness can be relevant to mitigation at sentencing.

32 An example of an Australian approach to duress as a mitigating factor is found in NSW legislation. See s21A (3)(d) of the *Crimes (Sentencing Procedure) Act 1999* (NSW).

on capacities and situations, and if one embraced Nelkin's view or the composite theory, one need not object to the practice. This would be something in favour of the practice when seen from the perspective of a person who endorsed the retributive aim of sentencing (and thus was interested in assessing moral culpability), and found Nelkin's views persuasive.

However, sentencing judges do not concern themselves only with the capacities of the offender at the time of the offence, and features of the situation in which the offence took place. There is also a diachronic aspect to legal blame assessment in NSW that could find support from the self-formative element derived from Hodgson's contribution to the composite theory.

Practices that could find some support from Hodgson's contribution to the composite theory

An important Australian High Court case, *Bugmy v The Queen* [2013], demonstrates the significance of a diachronic approach to mitigation. There is a strand in Australian criminal law that addresses particular concerns about Aboriginal social disadvantage and their significance for sentencing. While this case focuses on the conditions in Aboriginal communities, the principle is applicable more generally to those who are socially disadvantaged (para 38), and will be used to underscore the actual sentencing practice's diachronic nature (and concordance with the self-formative aspect of the composite moral theory).

The case involved an already incarcerated Aboriginal offender who assaulted a prison guard, and the High Court affirmed a long-standing thread in Australian jurisprudence that said that adversity in the formative circumstances of offenders is a factor that may be taken into account in sentencing. The court noted that adversity is likely to affect the offender's moral culpability (para 40) and may lead to mitigation. The court also stated that the availability of this form of mitigation does not diminish with increasing age or increasing criminal record. It was also said that such a background "may leave a mark on a person throughout life" (para 43) and that "among other things" it "may compromise the person's capacity to mature and to learn from experience" (para 43).

Such adversity needs to be proved with evidence relating to the offender's background (para 41).[33] There is thus a requirement for historical evidence of social disadvantage which, if it were to "compromise the person's capacity

33 Perhaps it might be argued that a reason to mitigate punishment of those who are socially disadvantaged flows from issues with the legitimacy of the punishing authority. In relation to the status of Indigenous communities or others who are socially disadvantaged there may be questions relating to the standing of the courts, but if such questions have bearing on punishment, this would not relate to the moral culpability of a particular offender but to the legitimacy of any response to a wrongdoing. The courts do not cite standing as their reason for mitigation (perhaps this would be too frank an admission), and in any case, if the issue is standing, this seems to go to the legitimacy of the courts rather than to questions of mitigation.

to mature and to learn from experience", would seem to make prosocial self-formation more difficult.

The historical dimension to this form of mitigation thus makes it distinct from that considered in the last section (which was focused on the time of the offence). The reasoning in *Bugmy* is consistent with the idea of mitigation being available to those with self-formative difficulties in complying with the law; indeed the High Court referred to the "grave social difficulties" faced by Aborigines (para 40). However, these difficulties relate to an offender's formative environment, and so the comments are *not restricted to difficulties present at the time of the offence.*

This can be thought of as a diachronic approach to difficulty and quality of opportunity, and because of the historical and self-formative dimension, this analysis of the legal doctrine could be supported by Hodgson's contribution to the composite diachronic theory of moral-agency-related blame assessment.

According to this way of thinking, the adverse formative environments that are of concern to the court create difficulties with complying with norms that are not merely present at the time of a wrong performed in adulthood, but are present *at earlier stages in life.* One might think of these as difficulties of self-formation – for some it may have been more difficult to form a self that would be likely to have the motivation to use their capacities in such a way as to comply with a legal norm that they have infringed, or to have superior capacities than they actually had at the time of the offence such as would have made compliance easier than it actually was. Where self-formative difficulty has made compliance more difficult, this diminishes moral culpability for failure.

Taken jointly, the legal doctrines relating to capacity and difficult formative circumstances could thus find some moral support from the composite diachronic theory developed in this chapter.

However, as suggested earlier, it is not clear that emphasis on complexity is a popular strategy among participants in sentencing's political environment, and it must be noted there are aspects of NSW criminal law that firmly reject a complex diachronic approach to mitigation. Perhaps the clearest example is the following piece of mandatory sentencing legislation.

A sentencing practice that jars with the theory

In 2011 the NSW Parliament legislated to make the murder of a police officer in the course of duty, or later and in response to actions performed in the course of the officer's duty, an offence that attracts a mandatory life sentence. There are two exceptions to the scope of this law. One is where the offender was under 18, and the other is where they "had significant cognitive impairment" other than a temporary self-induced impairment at the time of the offence.[34]

This means that if an adult offender, without significant cognitive impairment, offends in the way envisaged by the section, there can be no mitigation. So in

34 *Crimes Amendment (Murder of Police Officers) Act 2011* (NSW).

respect of such a murder (and contrary to both the moral and legal approaches to mitigation described earlier) mild cognitive impairment, dire formative circumstances, a difficult situation of offending, or a combination of all three *cannot mitigate*. Parliament has directed judges to ignore all of these difficulties in complying with the criminal law. An offender who has experienced these difficulties is to be treated in the same way as one who has not.

This legislation has faced criticism from some quarters including from the former NSW Director of Public Prosecutions, Nicholas Cowdery (2011). A criticism consistent with the approach to mitigation argued for in this chapter is that it radically disconnects punishment from accurate assessments of the degree to which offenders are blameworthy for what they have done. It facilitates this disconnection by telling judges to ignore some difficulties of compliance with the law that are morally, and were formerly, legally relevant, thus offending against both Hodgson's and to some extent Nelkin's contribution to the diachronic moral theory.

If retributivism is concerned with giving offenders what they deserve, and the degree to which they are blameworthy is a factor in such determinations, one reason why this form of mandatory sentencing is unjust is that it flouts retributive concerns. On this view despite its harshness, the *Crimes Amendment (Murder of Police Officers) Act 2011* (NSW) could be thought of as a profoundly anti-retributive law.

If the composite theory in this chapter is in some way concordant with the intuitions of the legal community, it is perhaps not surprising that a law which tells judges to ignore all indirect, and some direct, difficulties has caused some disquiet.

While it is true that at least some mandatory sentencing laws[35] appear to fly in the face of the moral theory developed here, it is worth noting such laws are rare in Australia. It is more common for judges to be able to follow a diachronic approach to moral culpability-assessment in a way that could find some support from the evaluative theory developed in this chapter.

Further complexity; beyond capacities and self-formation

It is worth noting what has happened in the process of construction of my evaluative moral theory, which has been applied to aspects of NSW sentencing law in the last few sections. Nelkin added further specificity and a little complexity to Hart's mitigation formulation. By drawing on Hodgson, I have added yet more specificity and complexity to Nelkin's formulation. But any comprehensive moral theory of agency-related blame assessment may need to go further.

The views of Nelkin and Hodgson give pointers as to some elements that might go into a more comprehensive theory of mitigation. But with precision as an aim,

35 Difficulties come in many forms, and there may be reason to think that it will not be easy for a legislator to envisage them all, and to build them into a just mandatory sentencing regime.

any such theory may need to be more fine-grained. So, for example, a difficulty of self-formation might be subdivided into:

1 Epistemic difficulty (difficulty in knowing it is important to engage in self-formation in order to make compliance with norms more likely, or knowing how to go about such self-formation)
2 Non-epistemic difficulty (difficulty in taking the necessary measures in order to self-form in a way that is more likely to lead to compliance with norms)

It may also need to take into account more dimensions. For example, perhaps those with diminished capacities and/or difficult self-formative tasks could *structure their lives*[36] around these difficulties to increase the chances of compliance. This adds a further diachronic aspect to the theory.

Such a mitigation project would also need to attempt to try to find a principled way of weighing efforts as against sacrifices and epistemic difficulties, and then to decide what to do about the complex temporal interplay of various difficulties in order to arrive at an overall assessment of difficulty.

The aim (and much more work needs to be done here) would be to enable a blame-assessor to engage in a principled critical analysis of initial judgements about blameworthiness – one that recognizes the complexity of morally evaluating different people, with different histories, in different situations.

Earlier it was suggested that the diachronic approach to difficulty creates a challenging task for the blaming party. Now because of the further sub-division, and burgeoning historical dimension, the task seems to have become even more difficult. This raises the question of whether humans have the epistemic capacities and can obtain sufficient information such as to participate, *even moderately competently*, as assessors of blameworthiness in just retributive practices. Even if it is not necessary to be an ideal epistemic agent,[37] a lot of knowledge about the person who has infringed a norm is needed, and the task of applying mitigation theory to such knowledge seems daunting. One might wonder whether humans could ever know of, and mentally process, the winding concatenations of ease and difficulty involved in competent moral evaluation of the acts and omissions of those who infringe norms.

If blaming practices were influenced by my theory (other than by ending them as a result of practically insurmountable problems in knowing about degrees of blameworthiness), it seems possible that some agents would receive less blame than they would have, but for the revision to the practices. However, it might turn out that other agents would be viewed as more blameworthy (perhaps those with great difficulty in complying with norms at the time of the offence, but who could have easily had less difficulty at the time of the offence had they taken earlier

36 Perhaps by moving away from a pub if alcohol was a factor in their risk of offending.

37 Some religiously orientated writers have argued that humans should not attempt to assess moral culpability, but leave that to an omniscient deity. See Levine (2001) from a perspective of Jewish law and philosophy.

steps to engage in prosocial self-formation or structuring of life). Thus application of the theory would be likely to lead to some re-ordering of blame assessments.

Conclusion

Mitigation is difficult. It seems that in order to evaluate pleas properly, one needs to consider the agent's capacities and their situation at the time of the offence. One must also consider the agent's history including their formative years. Competent evaluation of a plea in mitigation requires an enquiry into their overall difficulty of compliance with the norm that has been infringed, in light of all of these factors.

Insights from Nelkin and Hodgson point the way to a composite diachronic theory, focused on the overall difficulty of compliance with norms, which lends moral support to some sentencing practices. There is a complexity to the theory that is to some extent paralleled in the criminal law (at least in the jurisdiction picked as a case study in this chapter).

However, further reflection shows the need for an even more complex theory – one that might unsettle judgements of blameworthiness by highlighting the demanding nature of the epistemic task of the blaming party. Ultimately such a theory may thereby raise questions about the epistemic justification for retributive practices found in Australia and elsewhere.[38]

References

Brink, DO and Nelkin, D 2013, 'Fairness and the Architecture of Responsibility', *Oxford Studies in Agency and Responsibility* 1: 284–313.

Cowdery, N 2011, 'Mandatory Life for Cop Deaths', *Bar News: The Journal of the NSW Bar Association* Winter 2011: 43–45.

Double, R 2002, The 'Moral Hardness of Libertarianism', *Philo* 5(2): 226–234.

Duff, RA 2001, *Punishment, Communication and Community*, Oxford University Press, Oxford.

Fine, C and Kennett, J 2004, 'Mental Impairment, Moral Understanding and Criminal Responsibility: Psychopathy and the Purposes of Punishment', *International Journal of Law and Psychiatry* 27(5): 425–443.

38 I am grateful to Michael Sevel, Jesse Cunningham, Steve Mathews, Neil Levy, Bruce Waller, Nicholas Cowdery, Andrew Martin, Andrew Haywards, Paul Dower, Nicole Vincent, Michael Proeve, Jonathan Pugh, Hanna Maslen, Kei Hiruta, Mary Walker, Charles Foster, Julian Savalescu, Joshua Shepherd, John Gardner, Ilina Singh, Paul Hutchins, Jeanette Kennett, Daphne Brandenburg, Adam Piovarchy, Dorothy Economou, the participants in the Julius Stone Institute of Jurisprudence conference *Rationality + Consciousness = Free Will: Legal and Philosophical Reflections* (2013), the Australian Catholic University, *Philosophy Research Seminar Series* (2015), the Centre for Applied Philosophy and Public Ethics, *Seminar Series* (2015), and the Sydney Law School's *Criminal Responsibility and Criminal Law Theory* workshop (2017) (in particular my respondent Phillip Quadrio), for help in developing the ideas in this chapter. I am also grateful to Macquarie University's Centre for Agency Values and Ethics for support in the development of these ideas.

Hart, HLA 2008, *Punishment and Responsibility: Essays in Philosophy of Law*, 2nd edn, Oxford University Press, Oxford.
Hodgson, D 2012, *Rationality + Consciousness = Free Will*, Oxford University Press, Oxford.
Kelly, E 2017, 'Free Will and the Criminal Law', in K Timpe, M. Griffith, and N Levy (eds), *The Routledge Companion to Free Will*, Routledge, New York.
Levine, SJ 2001, 'Playing God: An Essay on Law, Philosophy, and American Capital Punishment', *New Mexico Law Review* 31: 277–297.
Nelkin, DK 2016, 'Difficulty and Degrees of Moral Praiseworthiness and Blameworthiness', *Noûs* 50(2): 356–378.
Rosen, G 2004, 'Skepticism about Moral Responsibility', *Philosophical Perspectives* 18(1): 295–313.
Roskies, AL 2012, 'Don't Panic: Self-authorship Without Obscure Metaphysics', *Philosophical Perspectives* 26(1): 323–342.
Vargas, M 2005, 'The Trouble with Tracing', *Midwest Studies in Philosophy* 29(1): 269–291.
Von Hirsch, A 1993, *Censure and Sanctions*, Oxford University Press, Oxford.
Watson, G 2013, 'Responsibility and the Limits of Evil: Variations on a Strawsonian Theme', in P Russell and O Deery (eds), *The Philosophy of Free Will: Essential Readings From the Contemporary Debates*, Oxford University Press, Oxford.

Cases

Bugmy v The Queen [2013] HCA 37.
Muldrock v The Queen [2011] HCA 39.
R v Hemsley [2004] NSWCCA 228.
Veen v R [1979] HCA 7.
Veen v R (No 2) [1988] HCA 14.
Yucebsoglu v R [2015] NSWCCA 226.

Legislation

Crimes (Sentencing Procedure) Act 1999 (NSW).
Crimes Amendment (Murder of Police Officers) Act 2011 (NSW)

12 David Hodgson's theory of plausible legal reasoning

Christopher Birch

Introduction

David Hodgson produced a substantial body of published work developing a distinctive libertarian conception of free will. In arguing for that libertarian view, Hodgson places significant reliance on an argument about the nature and importance of plausible reasoning. This chapter will seek to challenge Hodgson's view that plausible reasoning is a ground for accepting the libertarian conception of free will. However, I will argue that Hodgson's work has nevertheless provided an important insight into the nature of rationality.

In his 1991 work *The Mind Matters*, Hodgson discusses the nature of plausible reasoning, which he contrasts with formal reasoning (1991: 114). Plausible reasoning seeks to establish reasonable beliefs. It involves the use of more than deductive reasoning. Plausible reasoning extends to all those non-formal modes of inductive reasoning and probabilistic reasoning which go beyond the mere application of the calculus of probabilities. It includes all those methods of inference, from common sense reasoning about matters of daily life, to the reasoning of scientists and other investigators, such as historians, archaeologists, and the like.

The philosophy and methodology of science have been a central area for the investigation of the nature of plausible reasoning. Hodgson builds his account of plausible reasoning on the work of philosophers of science such as George Polya (1954) and Karl Popper (1972a, b) and philosophers of induction such as David Hume. However, his goal is the development of a broader theory than one concerned with scientific knowledge. The general conception of plausible reasoning developed by Hodgson is as applicable to the decision-making of a judge, as it is to the methodological choices of a scientist.

Hodgson contrasts plausible reasoning, or what he also calls informal reasoning, with formal reasoning. The latter includes not just formal logic, based on the propositional or predicate calculus, and any of the other so-called logics, but all mathematical reasoning and probabilistic reasoning, such as that using the Bayesian calculus. This all neatly interacts with the philosophy of mind, because we can construct machines to draw inferences in accordance with any of the formal systems. It remains, at least for the present, an important distinction between formal and plausible reasoning that plausible reasoning is something that can, Hodgson argues, be engaged in only by conscious minds (1991: 163).

Apart from the claim that the ability to engage in plausible reasoning is a capacity of conscious minds, Hodgson makes two other important claims about plausible reasoning. First, that it is rational. Hodgson treats rationality as pre-eminently concerned with decision-making, but he holds a broad view of its scope and considers the holding of beliefs to be within the field of matters to which rationality applies. Further, in describing rationality as concerned with making reasonable decisions, holding reasonable beliefs, or drawing reasonable inferences, Hodgson is speaking about the ability to weigh up reasons, especially where they conflict, and to produce judgements or decisions.

Where we are concerned about the rationality of our beliefs concerning things of which there is a truth or fact of the matter, the starting point, and frequently the finishing point, of rational appraisal of such beliefs will be a concern with the extent to which our beliefs reliably track truth. Hodgson accepts that rational appraisal may also apply to practical and not merely epistemic concerns, and in practical contexts rationality extends beyond a narrow means/ends prudential calculus, since we may rationally appraise our ends and our desires, and reasonableness can apply to our beliefs about what we should value.

Hodgson argues that plausible reasoning produces reasonable beliefs because it could not be the case that the outcomes from engaging in plausible reasoning are no more favourable than we could obtain from outcomes determined randomly. It may at first blush appear circular to suggest that plausible reasoning produces reasonable beliefs, if we have only plausible reasoning itself to warrant its level of success. However, this objection can be met in part by recognizing that plausible reasoning, like science, involves a temporal aspect, and in a loose sense both prediction and confirmation. Hindsight provides an opportunity of judging the degree of success of plausible reasoning, in precisely the fashion in which, in scientific enquiry, the same assessment process is continuously undertaken.

Hodgson concludes that from our capacity to engage in plausible reasoning, we derive reasonable beliefs, or what some philosophers have called knowledge. This could not be produced simply by the mechanical application of conclusive rules (2012: 39). Our conscious minds thus give us the capacity to engage in a form of reasoning which, in turn, produces reasonable beliefs, or knowledge, that could not be obtained in any deterministic fashion. This then becomes an argument for the possession of a form of libertarian free will; indeed it becomes something of a description of libertarian free will.

It is not a co-incidence that in propounding these philosophical arguments in regard to the nature of mind, David Hodgson spent the greater part of his working life as a lawyer, first as a barrister and then for thirty years as a judge, initially as a Judge of the New South Wales Supreme Court, and then a Judge of Appeal.

At many points David Hodgson's work discusses the reasoning of judges in order to make good his claims about the nature of plausible reasoning and human minds (2012: 27, 38). Judicial decision-making provides an excellent case study for exploring the nature of plausible reasoning. Like scientific methodology, but unlike normal common sense reasoning in everyday life, judicial decision-making involves a self-conscious exercise of legal reasoning, in which judges lay out, sometimes at great length, the reasoning processes that they have undertaken. Further, the exercise is not a purely theoretical one. The purpose of judicial reasoning is to arrive at a judicial decision which is practical in the most full-blooded sense of the word. The judicial decision culminates in a verdict or orders directed to legal officials and citizens as to what must be done on pain of a sanction.

Legal cases are almost paradigmatic instances of matters for judgement in which the evidence or reasons point in different directions. A crucial aspect of judicial decision-making is the weighing and reconciliation of these conflicting reasons (Hodgson 1991: 138 and Hodgson 2012: 38). Legal reasoning usually involves some reasoning about matters of fact, as to which there will be a truth of the matter. Most legal decisions also include some reasoning about law, which may involve legal interpretation and conceptual analysis. Jurists would be divided as to whether there is necessarily a truth of the matter in regard to these legal and conceptual issues. These two aspects of legal reasoning are not isolated from each other, and both constitute reasons for the ultimate judicial decision.

It is necessary, at this point, to enter a qualification. Much legal reasoning, of the sort we read in the judgements of courts and tribunals, represents examples of plausible reasoning. Nevertheless, one might take a completed judgement by a court and translate that judgement into a set of propositions that are, in turn, capable of being viewed as logically valid deductive arguments (see, for example, Tammerlo 1978 and Schauer 1988). Reconstruction of legal reasoning as deductive argument is, however, possible only because the court that has produced the judgement has already made a number of important decisions and choices about what to treat as relevant, and what to treat as premises for the justification of its conclusions. Any such reconstruction may also need to postulate further premises where these have been suppressed in the reasoning of the court. Such a reconstruction may demonstrate that the court has not violated the laws of logic in reaching its conclusion. It does not demonstrate that the laws of logic alone would have permitted the court to arrive in the first place at the conclusion, from the evidence and established legal principles.

I will argue that David Hodgson's claim that plausible reasoning is rational is defensible for many of the reasons that he gives. It can give rise to reasonable beliefs arrived at through the weighing of reasons and reconciliation of conflicting reasons. Hodgson argues that such reasonable beliefs are rational in large part because they enjoy a sufficient measure of success. This concept of success is ultimately a pragmatic conception looking to the extent to which our reasonable beliefs allow us to interact with the world in a fashion which at least partially satisfies goals and desires.

I will use legal reasoning as an example of plausible reasoning to examine Hodgson's claims. I will argue that plausible reasoning may, at least in many instances, be rational, and that is because it enjoys success in Hodgson's sense. However, I will argue that this success, and hence rationality, can be explained deterministically, and it is not therefore ultimately an argument that establishes the existence of libertarian free will. I will, however, argue that the success Hodgson attributes to plausible reasoning as a rational activity depends upon the capacity of conscious minds to bring forth new ideas or hypotheses (which I shall refer to as the "creativity thesis"). The creative capacities of conscious minds could possibly emanate from a libertarian free will; however, this need not necessarily be so, and the creativity thesis alone does not establish the possession of libertarian free will.

Using legal reasoning as an example, the chapter will examine how one may describe plausible reasoning as successful in Hodgson's sense. Nevertheless, the chapter will also seek to show that this success does not depend upon assuming the existence of libertarian free will. Also borrowing from the philosophy of science, this chapter will argue that all activities involving the accumulation of reasonable beliefs or knowledge must be understood as practices operating through time with a history, and evolving in a fashion akin to natural selection. Once viewed from this perspective, the success of plausible reasoning ought not to surprise us, nor call for any assumptions regarding the existence of free will.

Plausible legal reasoning

Lawyers frequently distinguish between reasoning about law and reasoning about fact. This is a notoriously difficult distinction to consistently maintain. Whether the meaning of a word is a question of fact or a question of law is a perennial problem. Nevertheless, it is clear that when one is concerned with factual issues concerning whether or not people are engaged in particular conduct, different reasoning tools are deployed to cases where one is concerned with ascertaining law through an interpretative process such as resolving a conflict between legal rules or principles, or seeking to determine the ambit of a legal doctrine.

In regard to facts, law does not generally deploy any special legal methodology, but rather, relies upon the same modes of inference that might loosely be called common sense reasoning about facts (Hodgson 2012: 34ff.). What distinguishes legal reasoning about facts is a set of technical rules of evidence governing what matters can be admissible reasons, and a concern for teasing out and testing inferences with greater care than most of us would use for everyday matters. However, there are in contemporary Anglo-Australian law virtually no rules governing the types of inferences that may be drawn from evidence, or to put it slightly differently, the weight that might be attributed to evidence. This is left to the intuition of the judge or tribunal member. For example, rules requiring corroboration of particular matters have virtually all been repealed. Consequently, there is little difference between the reasoning processes that would be deployed by a judge upon the admissible evidence, in determining a set of facts, and those that would be relied upon by an investigative journalist, or a member of any other profession or occupation, engaged in detailed consideration of factual circumstances.

Law is usually concerned with ascertaining what happened on a specific occasion, rather than looking for deep underlying patterns of the sort investigated by the natural sciences. It might be thought that statements of legal proof, as to whether a fact in issue or a legal conclusion has been established on the balance of probabilities or beyond reasonable doubt, are not amenable to the statistical analyses of mathematical probability. This view is increasingly rejected by contemporary jurists who accept that the subjective interpretation of mathematical probability permits even the probability of a unique event to be expressed within the calculus.

While deploying the subjective interpretation of mathematical probability, which some jurists have come to call Bayesian probability, offers the prospects of formalizing some part of the process of drawing inferences concerning factual matters; nevertheless, as David Hodgson argues (2012: 43–45), to deploy Bayes' theorem requires one to have made estimates of the prior probabilities of what is going to count as evidence for one's conclusion, and an informal estimate of those probabilities will therefore be necessary before one gets to apply Bayes' theorem. Only in very unusual cases, where the only matters in dispute are amenable to some form of precise probabilistic calculation, could one avoid the need for a preliminary phase of plausible reasoning. Even in those cases, the reasoning process rests on assumptions in turn derived from more general theories which have, in turn, been founded upon plausible reasoning.

In regard to reasoning about law, as opposed to fact, lawyers and legal philosophers have brought forth a substantive body of theory, some of which purports to be uniquely about the problems of reasoning about legal rules and concepts, although generally such theories could be used in regard to reasoning about many other rule systems.

These theories of legal interpretation, in turn, often seek to resolve whether the law consists of rules, principles, or overarching interpretative theories. This sort of legal theory frequently uses a theory of legal truth, according to which there may be a right legal answer in regard to some or all issues, or alternatively that law is indeterminate or that the concept of legal truth is simply inapposite.

So much legal reasoning about the law involves conceptual or interpretative questions, whether or not in the sense conveyed by Ronald Dworkin, that it is difficult to envisage how it could be amenable to formalism. Expert legal systems have sought to create what might loosely be called "legal diagnostic systems", which can be run on computers. Even the keenest supporters of such expert systems accept that there are important interpretative issues that need to be resolved by those designing the systems, and, in any event, their usefulness does not lie in their ability to totally formalize the process of reasoning about law, or to produce judicial decisions (Susskind 2010).

Legal reasoning contains many examples of what lawyers would describe as discretionary judgements. An example, which I will consider in further detail later, would be a sentencing decision in criminal law. Determining the appropriate sentence for someone convicted of an offence will involve drawing together disparate relevant factual matters concerning the offence and the offender, and applying those rules and principles which govern the determination of a sentence. I argue later that this form of reasoning is the least reducible to rule-based reasoning, and hence the most resistant to any formalization. This difficulty in formalizing the reasoning processes about matters such as sentencing explains in part the criticisms often made of so-called grid sentencing, an approach to sentencing which has had some popularity in some parts of the United States in the last few decades.

Despite the difficulties that will be discussed later regarding the formalization of legal reasoning around matters such as sentencing, it remains the case that experienced criminal defence counsel can, and frequently do, make reliable predictions about the sentences that will be given to an offender for some specific offence, and sentencing decisions frequently form strong patterns. This also requires explanation.

Is plausible legal reasoning successful?

David Hodgson argues that human beings are possessed of rationality in the sense of a capacity to discover truths about the world and make sound judgements about what to believe (2012: 26). Hodgson accepts this ability is fallible, subject not only to *ad hoc* error, but to an ever present danger of systematic error through bias, cognitive illusion, or the like (2012: 29).

Insofar as our beliefs concern matters about the state of the world or the universe, then Hodgson believes, in accordance with the correspondence theory of truth, that our beliefs are capable of having at least degrees of truth. Our rational capacity for reasonable beliefs about the universe thus involves us aiming to hold beliefs that are true through correspondence with reality (2012: 21). Further, Hodgson recognizes that our capacity for rationality in holding reasonable beliefs will extend beyond merely those intellectual pursuits where our beliefs may have a truth value through a correspondence with reality, and will extend to reasonable evaluative judgements (2012: 26). Ultimately Hodgson contends that the human capacity for rationality extends to the whole field of beliefs. Clearly what contributes to the reasonableness of a belief will vary, so that the reasonableness of a scientific belief may depend upon one's degree of confidence that the belief possesses a measure of truth about some aspect of the universe, while an evaluative belief (such as what ought to be the degree of punishment inflicted on an offender) will depend upon the extent to which the belief properly applies our moral and legal frameworks, and the extent to which our moral and legal frameworks themselves have a reasonable basis.

Hodgson's principal concerns are not epistemological nor about the formulation of some specific theory of value. Nevertheless, he does not take for granted that we possess a capacity for rationality, and in his 2012 work takes some time to deal with those who advocate radical scepticism regarding our capacity for rationality. The arguments for the existence of our rational capacity are themselves examples of plausible reasoning, and that capacity will in turn apply plausible reasoning to produce reasonable beliefs. It will, of course, be aided where possible by formal reasoning.

For Hodgson, rationality and plausible reasoning are intimately linked. Our capacity for acquiring reasonable beliefs is usually exercised by engaging in plausible reasoning. Nevertheless, that it is rational to hold beliefs arrived at by a process of plausible reasoning is because of the extent to which plausible reasoning establishes beliefs that are frequently true, or frequently possessed of the appropriate nomic value of the discipline or framework within which we are conducting enquiries. These arguments of Hodgson support the claim that plausible reasoning is successful in giving rise to reasonable beliefs.

Apart from arguing that plausible reasoning is successful in the sense of giving rise to reasonable beliefs, and displaying the rational capacity of human beings, two other aspects of plausible reasoning are important. As already described, it is of its nature non-formalizable. I have already referred to a number of the points Hodgson makes in this regard. His critics have not generally suggested that plausible legal reasoning is a covert formalizable system that Hodgson and other philosophers have simply failed to decode. A more potent criticism is the suggestion that to the extent plausible reasoning is not formalizable, it is explicable by causal determination or random elements in the inference drawing processes of the plausibly reasoning subject. Hodgson suggests that the success of plausible reasoning would be inexplicable if its non-formal aspects were simply the result of random processes (Hodgson 2005). This contention appears still to be held by Hodgson in his 2012 work, although it is less explicitly stated (2012: 112).

Hodgson's primary contention as to why plausible reasoning is successful and yet informal lies with his argument that it utilizes a capacity of conscious minds which is indeterministic but allows people to respond appositely when engaged in decision-making. This is Hodgson's theory of the gestalt. This is central to Hodgson's work and involves an analysis of the decision-making process at the intersection between theories of reasoning or rationality on the one hand, and neuroscience on the other. Hodgson is right that this is a field of enquiry that has been underdone by philosophers (2012: 72). Even the theories of legal philosophers that purport to be theories of legal reasoning often stop short of an account of how the judicial mind engages with the relevant body of doctrine to produce a decision on a specific matter.

Chapter 6 of *Rationality + Consciousness = Free Will*, entitled "How Gestalts Promote Rationality", provides the core of Hodgson's account of the way conscious decision-making contributes to rationality. The core of that theory involves a focus on individual judgements, and in regard to plausible reasoning, it is the mind's ability to consciously grasp feature-rich gestalts which, Hodgson argues, contributes to plausible reasoning's success. The task upon which plausible reasoning is brought to bear involves feature-rich wholes, which must be grasped as wholes, or combinations, in order to give rise to a relevant judgement.

Hodgson's approach envisages that a mental act in which a mind consciously grasps a feature-rich gestalt permits, or aids, the formation of a reasonable belief, or the making of a reasonable decision. Assuming that this cannot be redescribed in a way that reduces the mental operation to a causally deterministic process, or a random process, then Hodgson envisages that one can, nevertheless, have a rational belief or judgement arrived at through this process of plausible reasoning. This argument also seems to envisage that we can speak of an individual judgement or belief (as opposed to a series of judgements or beliefs) as being rational, although clearly we may increase or improve our command of the truth, or evaluative success, through a process of judgement or decision-making.

I wish to argue that the success of our plausible reasoning activity in the law, as well as in more mundane common sense fact-finding, is always the success of a sequence of reasoning processes or, more simply, a reasoning practice. Such success can be enjoyed over the course of a practice, even if individual judgements enjoy no more than a random prospect of success. Before turning to explain this point in more detail, it is useful to consider a specific example of plausible reasoning. In order to display what I shall call the fine-grained nature of legal reasoning I have chosen a legal case decided by David Hodgson.

A case study: *R v Mumberson*[1]

R v Mumberson was a decision of the New South Wales Court of Criminal Appeal. The Court was constituted by Justice David Hodgson as the presiding Judge, together with Justice Adams and Justice Hall. Mumberson had pleaded guilty in the District Court to a charge of recklessly inflicting grievous bodily harm. He had been sentenced to one year and eight months' imprisonment, but the sentence had been suspended so that it did not need to be served if Mumberson was of good behaviour for a fixed period. The sentence was appealed by the prosecution on the ground that the sentence was inadequate.

At the time of the offence Mumberson, and the victim, Ms Munro, were in a domestic relationship, although not co-habiting. Following a telephone call, Ms Munro had collected Mumberson and a friend from hotel premises where the two had been drinking, to drive each of them home. During the journey Mumberson, who was significantly affected by alcohol, had made a telephone call which had been upsetting to him, he had become angry and erratic, and he ultimately grabbed the steering wheel, pulling it to the left and causing the car to swerve violently. The victim had lost control, the car had crashed, and the victim had suffered serious injuries, although Mumberson was relatively unhurt. Mumberson had a number of prior traffic offences, but no other prior criminal convictions.

The sentencing Judge found Mumberson to have been a man of very good character, loyal to his family and friends, a hard worker, and that the offence was totally out of character. Mumberson pleaded guilty, and was found to be remorseful and to have accepted responsibility. Importantly, the sentencing Judge found that the case was unique and that, after twenty-seven years of judicial experience, he could gain little assistance by comparison or analogy with other matters in arriving at the correct sentence. A 15% discount was allowed on what the sentence might otherwise have been for the plea of guilty pursuant to sentencing guidelines.

The prosecution appealed against what it claimed was the inadequacy of the sentence, contending that the motor vehicle had been used as a weapon and this was an aggravating factor, that the discount for the plea of guilty was excessive in

1 [2011] NSW CCA 54 (8 April 2011).

light of the guilty plea coming so late in the proceeding, that the Judge had not given reasons for concluding that the objective seriousness was less than typical for such an offence, that viewed objectively the offence was very serious, that the cause of the offence appeared to lay in an un-addressed binge drinking problem, and that there were inadequate reasons to justify the leniency of suspending the sentence.

At the appeal Mumberson essentially relied upon the reasons of the trial Judge, and further suggested that the sentence was within the scope of the discretion available to the trial Judge, particularly in light of his subjective characteristics and especially his good character.

Justice Hodgson gave the judgement of the Court which upheld the appeal. He held that it was a very serious offence involving a deliberate act (grabbing and twisting the steering wheel of the car) knowing that this carried the risk of grievous bodily harm to the victim. He thus found it was an unexplained act of violence, albeit committed intentionally, with knowledge of the risk of serious injury.

Justice Hodgson discounted some of the sentencing Judge's findings on the respondent's good character; the offence appeared to have originated in an episode of binge drinking, and the respondent had not accepted the need to seriously address that.

Hodgson found that the finding of remorse should also be discounted through the respondent's failure to give oral evidence, or make any form of reparation to the victim. Hodgson considered the subjective factors relating to the offender's character were substantial, but insufficient, having regard to the objective seriousness of the offence to justify a starting point, before any discount for the plea of guilty, of the two year period adopted by the sentencing Judge, and the suspension of the sentence was also considered by Hodgson to be overly lenient.

Nevertheless, Hodgson found there were mitigating factors and, while upholding the Crown appeal, considered the circumstances permitted a more lenient sentence than would have been justified at first instance. The Court imposed a non-parole period of fifteen months of imprisonment with the balance of the sentence thus being one year, but also permitted the time served on the good behaviour bond to count toward satisfaction of the sentence, thus creating an effective non-parole period (minimum prison sentence) of nine months.

The sentencing judgement reflects a classic example of the form of plausible legal reasoning engaged in by courts on a daily basis. The reasoning exercise displays many of the characteristics that would not make it easily amenable to any type of formal reasoning. First, while the goal is to establish the correct sentence, it is difficult to suggest that there is a single and precisely ascertainable period of imprisonment that represents the correct answer to the question regarding sentencing. Even if there is a hypothetically correct answer, there will be difficulties in determining it, and difficulties in resolving any disagreement about what it may be.

In Australia the High Court has expressly rejected the suggestion that in determining the correct sentence for a convicted offender, there is any necessary path of reasoning that must be followed by the sentencing Judge, as opposed to the ultimate conclusion merely being a reasonable one, supported generally by the grounds relied upon.[2]

Although the Court expressed some reservations in the *Markarian* decision about using the phrase "process of instinctive synthesis" to describe the manner in which a Judge aggregates the disparate factors that bear upon sentencing, the Court accepted that it was unnecessary to identify the degree or quantum to which each relevant factor contributed in a sentencing decision. Indeed, it recognized there could be a degree of artificiality in seeking to adjust an objective sentence by some mathematical value for each of the relevant specific features of the case. The Court in *Markarian*'s case was clearly wrestling with the difficulty of reconciling the obligation upon Judges to articulate their reasons for decisions on the one hand, with the difficulty of providing any complete account of the weighing and judging process in a discretionary decision such as the sentencing of an offender on the other.

The decision in *Mumberson* involved weighing up reasons, all of which bore weight, not one of which was decisive. The objective seriousness was measured in part by the harm to the victim and the possibly serious harm that was apparent to the respondent at the time of the offence.

Also, having an ambivalent effect on the decision in *Mumberson* is the affectation by alcohol. This undermines the respondent's capacity for rational choice, but on the other hand, it was a result of his having voluntarily engaged in binge drinking. The role of anger in the offence may have undermined its voluntariness, but the respondent's failure to address in his plea his desire to control his drinking and anger undermined his claim of remorse.

Finally, there were many subjective characteristics of the respondent that were treated as mitigating factors by both the sentencing Judge and the Court of Criminal Appeal such as the respondent's prior good character, his devotion to his family and friends, his hard work, and his concern for his children's welfare. The offence appeared to have been an irrational outburst, out of character, and not done from a devious or wicked motive. The sentencing Judge clearly gave greater weight to the subjective factors; Hodgson and his fellow Judges gave greater weight to the objective seriousness of the offence, and saw some of the subjective factors as possessing less weight, or more ambiguity, than did the sentencing Judge.

A common characteristic of legal reasoning, and of much plausible reasoning, is that one appears to be able to go on endlessly elaborating the reasons, making them more precise, and constructing ever more nuanced explanations. For example, it appeared to be a mitigating factor that the offence was an irrational act of violence rather than a scheme. On the other hand, Hodgson considered that it was still committed with knowledge of the high risk of serious injury, and not entirely impulsive, although planned only for a short time. Had the sentencing Judge a right of reply, he may have pointed to the influence of alcohol and anger, and that these render the offence less serious than a plan of harm for

2 *Markarian v The Queen* (2005) 228 CLR 357 at 374.

self-enrichment. On the other hand, there was the respondent's apparent failure to fully address his drinking and anger issues, but against this there was some evidence that the respondent had attempted to drink less. This process of dividing the issues into a more and more finely grained set of considerations makes the ultimate task of weighing the reasons, and deriving a correct sentence, difficult. The criminal law encourages this ever more detailed dissection of causes and motives, with the unintended effect of frequently appearing to dissolve away or undermine responsibility.

The reasoning in a sentencing case like *R v Mumberson* also represents a classic example of legal reasoning in regard to a discretionary matter where the Court is called upon to weigh up a series of reasons which are qualitatively different, although all are being offered because they are thought to be reasons for either increasing or decreasing the sentence. While they may be commensurable to the extent that they can be said to rationally bear upon the sentence length, no formal method of weighing or aggregating these reasons offers itself.

One can make the following reflections upon the reasoning in *R v Mumberson*. Although the appeal was upheld, few lawyers would suggest that the sentencing Judge's decision should be branded irrational, or non-rational. Both he and the Court of Criminal Appeal offered reasons for their conclusions, which appeared to have justificatory weight in regard to their final conclusion on sentence. However, one ought not to draw the sceptical conclusion that it is sufficient to be rational, that one simply has reasons that could be pertinent. Most would accept that a ten year sentence of imprisonment for Mumberson or a $100.00 fine would have both been false answers to the question of what sentence was appropriate. If one moves from the extremes, it may become harder to say what would or would not be a right answer in regard to the question of sentence, but one could envisage models in which the rightness or wrongness of the answer becomes an issue of gradation rather than assuming a single point of correctness with error on either side.

Formulation and justification: two aspects of the creation of knowledge

A detailed analysis of a case such as *R v Mumberson* highlights a lot of the essential attributes of plausible as opposed to formal reasoning. Nevertheless, concentration upon a single case and its line-by-line analysis carries with it a danger for a proper understanding of plausible reasoning, and of its grounds for success. It also goes without saying that the decision in *R v Mumberson* was for all of the legal practitioners involved merely one case in their lifetime's legal work. That lifetime's legal work was in turn a part of an ongoing practice of legal reasoning in which humans have been engaged for as long as they have been arguing and disputing about rule-governed behaviour.

Hodgson saw the literature generated by debates about scientific methodology as an important source of argumentation regarding the nature of plausible reasoning, at least in the scientific context. Debates in regard to scientific methodology sought to grapple with two apparently obvious features of scientific knowledge. First, it appeared to enjoy substantial success in the pragmatic sense. Second, the debate, since the time of David Hume, regarding the nature of induction suggested that scientific reasoning was not formalizable. The attempts at formalization by Karl Popper, and the scientific methodologists who criticized his approach, are discussed at length by Hodgson (1991: 116ff., 2012: 42). However, Popper and the other scientific methodologists offer an explanation for the success of plausible reasoning, without the necessity for postulating a capacity of conscious minds to make rational judgements by the application of an undetermined capacity to make rational judgements.

In understanding the success of plausible reasoning, we should start by recognizing that choices with no better than a random prospect of success may through a long process be aggregated in such fashion as to produce knowledge. Popper's account of science as a process of conjecture and refutation was built upon this principle.

Popper argued that scientific theories had increasing epistemological content or value, even though it could not be shown that any of the particular conjectures at the time they were made enjoyed any particular probability or likelihood of truth (1972b: 255). Popper initially considered that he could provide a formal description of the logic of scientific discovery which overcame the problems that had bedevilled attempts to explain science by a formal inductive logic. However, Popper's approach involved concentration upon the second or justificatory step in the creation of scientific knowledge. The invention or postulation of scientific theories Popper relegated to the field of the psychology of knowledge. This field would examine the wellsprings of scientific creativity and what might have given scientists the inspiration that led to their conjectures. Popper considered this aspect of little interest to anyone concerned with "the logic of knowledge", and for whom all interest focused on the second aspect (1972b: 31).

Popper's early work carried the hope that a single formal principle such as his doctrine of falsificationism would unpack the logic of knowledge. This early formalistic approach suffered its own refutation at the hands of historians and theorists of science who showed that any credible account of the history of science revealed scientific theories were not abandoned when refuted in a Popperian sense; rather they were abandoned only in the light of non-formalizable plausible judgements that it was time to cease working on an old scientific theory and embrace a new one.

In his later work, Popper (1972a) described knowledge as a third world separate from the human mind or the spatio-temporal world. It possessed its own objective qualities reflecting the logical and theoretical relationships between concepts. Further, Popper emphasized, without abandoning falsificationism, that knowledge was the result of a process conducted over time in which the methodology of falsificationism brought about the elimination of error from theories. Popper compared this to the process of Darwinian selection in which the growth of knowledge was seen as a form of evolution. This has the virtue of emphasizing the long term perspective in assessing any advance in the growth of knowledge.

One of the sources for David Hodgson's concept of plausible reasoning was the work of George Polya (1954), referred to at the beginning of this chapter. A pupil of Polya's was Imre Lakatos, whose theory of the methodology of scientific research programmes still remains one of the most persuasive accounts of how science works (Lakatos 1970).

Lakatos outlined a scientific methodology based on his concept of a research programme. Lakatos was keen to avoid the pitfalls of Popperian falsificationism while recognizing the importance of its evolutionary principles in understanding rationality. He saw the pitfalls as lying in part in the demand that a formal criterion could be specified in advance of the test of a theory, specifying the conditions in which it would or would not continue to be rational to support the theory. Lakatos had his own criteria for determining whether a research programme was "progressive" or "degenerating", but eschewed any attempt at specifying a formal criterion for abandonment of a programme.[3]

Lakatos did not offer his theory as a means for assessing and choosing between scientific research programmes. For Lakatos, the success of research programmes was something that could be spoken of only with historical hindsight when one could look back and assess the comparative success of competing theories. From Lakatos' perspective there could be no crucial experiments or critical choices. This brought, in Lakatos' terms, the "end of instant rationality" (Lakatos 1970: 154).

The evolutionary theories of scientific methodology just discussed have analogues in broader fields of decision theory. These might be regarded as attempts at a general theory of plausible reasoning; few, however, are as well-developed as Hodgson's.

Many other philosophers have proposed theories regarding the growth of knowledge in which an indeterminate or random step of theory generation is succeeded by a second step of rational appraisal. Thus, Daniel Dennett proposes a compatibilist theory of decision making in which a consideration generator whose output is undetermined produces a series of considerations subjected to assessment and deliberation by the agent. The process of deliberation is not itself random, and will be determined by the objective structure of the criteria of appraisal (Dennett 1978: 295). Importantly, Dennett does not dismiss the parts of the process prior to rational appraisal as mere psychology. Those considerations that our mind generates in the first place will reflect our prior education and intelligence, and in the elimination of possible considerations without detailed appraisal, these qualities will again be deployed in the preliminary steps of the deliberative process, and will shape the ultimate choices posed for rational appraisal.

Many theorists have proposed theories of choice in regard to the free will debate involving a preliminary undetermined step where ideas are postulated, followed by a determinant process of rational appraisal. None of these theories

3 Some of Lakatos' concepts, such as "explanatory power", reflect virtues of research programmes and have echoes in legal theory; see the recent discussion of "explanatory power" in Lakatos' sense as a model for constitutional interpretation in Aroney (2013).

require us to postulate, in order to explain the growth of knowledge, that conscious minds possess a rational ability to make judgements with a better-than-random prospect of success. The growth of knowledge or of rational choices is explained through the accumulation of judgements that have proven successful, where success is simply measured by a hindsight judgement of success, which then incorporates the successful judgement into the increasing body of knowledge.

This can be explained by an analogy with someone using an algorithm to solve a maze of forking paths; they might apply an arbitrary rule (or make random choices) wherever paths fork, in order to choose a way, but by properly recording the results of each "choice", they will slowly acquire knowledge sufficient to solve the maze.

Such maze-solving techniques are clearly formalizable. However, the production of conjectures, whether as part of a research programme within science, or as part of a developing body of law, is not simply a choice between existing alternatives; rather, it requires the creative production of fresh alternatives. However, these alternatives do not need anything greater than a non-trivial prospect of likely success to become part of an evolutionary growth of knowledge within that practice. The contribution by Neil Levy in this volume argues that even the creative generation of new conjectures can be explained by computational models based on stochastic algorithms without the need for postulating the sort of mental powers proposed by Hodgson.

Legal decision-making and the evolutionary growth of legal knowledge

Legal philosophers have discussed versions of the two-step process in regard to judicial decision-making. Richard Wasserstrom (1961) argues that in regard to a judicial decision there will be a process of discovery reflecting the generation of ideas that may constitute the premises of an argument, and a process of justification in which rational appraisal is brought to bear upon the products of discovery. Wasserstrom, however, like so many of the two-stage theorists (already discussed), focuses on the evaluative stage rather than the creative stage (1961: 27).

One must, however, guard against seeing the idea generation step as a wholly indeterminate phase, prior to and separate from the process of rational appraisal. Just how these two phases should be properly characterized can be better understood by returning to consider the reasoning in *R v Mumberson*.

Episodes of legal reasoning, such as that set out in the decision in *R v Mumberson*, are clearly imbedded within long-standing legal practices. Dworkin has given in his many works a detailed and illuminating account of what might be described as the interpretative practice of understanding law, but a sentencing decision such as *R v Mumberson* demonstrates that legal reasoning involves more than just the sort of interpretative practice considered by philosophers like Dworkin. A decision like *Mumberson* requires the proper characterization and understanding of the facts, the determination of psychological facts, such as the insight or remorse of the offender, the judging of what are essentially sociological criteria, such as the punishment necessary to achieve a deterrent effect and, perhaps, appease public demands for some form of retribution, coupled with the other sentencing criteria which, although embedded within the law, reflect moral principles. These many factors can all be inscribed within an overall theory, or to use Lakatos' term, "research program", of determining how properly to punish offenders.

Each sentencing of an offender is, of course, not merely an experiment in the process of perfecting a wider theory; nevertheless in judging the success of the decisions in individual sentencing cases, it is the success of a long term practice that is judged. Thus, the last forty years have seen many important changes in the approaches to sentencing in Australian and United States legal practice, with the adoption of so-called truth in sentencing legislation, followed by decisions emphasizing retributive and deterrent factors at the expense, perhaps, of rehabilitative factors. The rise of the voice of victims in the sentencing process has had to be integrated into theories of sentencing. Viewed from the perspective of current sentencing law, the decisions of courts thirty years ago might be viewed as having been consistently lenient; consider, for example, the changed tolerance of certain sorts of sexual offence, or domestic violence.

In teasing apart the plausible legal reasoning displayed in *R v Mumberson*, first, it is clear that the legal problem, namely, what sentence to impose, was viewed through a grid of legal knowledge. This can be described as a deterministic process in which the concepts were applied to relevant factual situations simply in consequence of the legal knowledge and training of the judge and advocates involved. Second, the posing of the legal problem does not take place within one single mind. The judge hearing a matter will be presented with alternative cases by prosecution and defence counsel. The judicial mind does not pose the problem as an original problem, but picks up the process already begun by advocates.

No doubt many ideas will occur to a judge during the course of the hearing of a matter, including the consideration of alternative conceptual ways of characterizing the legal choices before him or her, additional to those already posed by the advocates. These alternatives may be generated in a non-rational creative process. They may occur to the legal mind by processes of analogical reasoning, or by recognition of patterns or similarities from past legal problems. However, the generation of these alternative conceptual analyses is merely a presentation to the judicial mind of ways of framing the legal problem that need to be decided. This is an indeterminate process; subconscious influences may cause fresh ways of seeing the legal problem to "pop" into the mind (as gestalts). These processes may also involve an indeterminate element where randomness may produce novel legal solutions. Such tentative conjectures will, however, be viewed through the grid of legal knowledge.

The evaluative stage will allow the judge to rely upon accumulated legal knowledge. Some of this will simply involve the application in deterministic fashion of principles of logical inference. To the extent that the legal mind tracks down paths of logical inference, arguments and concepts may be accepted or rejected on the basis of their consistency with other aspects of legal knowledge.

However, hard cases represent instances where conflicting considerations cannot be resolved by appeal to more general rules and modes of logical inference. These will involve cases that call for the weighing and resolution of conflicting considerations. In a case such as *R v Mumberson* these reflect questions involving the relative weight to be attributed to, for example, subjective factors concerning the defendant's good behaviour as against judgements of his personal responsibility, and still further considerations such as the extent to which the punishment needs to deter future offences. To the extent that there is no possibility of a deterministic evaluative process undertaken in regard to some element in the resolution of the matter, we can postulate that the decision to that extent reflected an indeterminate or random choice, but that does not prevent the case from forming part of a successful practice of plausible legal reasoning.

In describing such decisions as involving random choice, it must be kept in mind that the choices will have been greatly narrowed by the grid of legal knowledge to which reference has been made. The choices are themselves presented within a process of reasoning in which evaluative, deterministic, and formalizable inference drawing has already taken place both by the reasoner and by others involved in the practice.

This view of legal reasoning also reveals the importance of a prized virtue of legal reasoning. Lawyers commend legal reasoning where it displays a fine-grained consideration of the matters to be resolved. The caricature of the slipshod judicial decision is one where a judge is confronted by two diametrically opposed witnesses, and after recitation of their conflicting testimony says, having heard each, he or she prefers witness A and decides the case accordingly. In having failed to identify the multifarious factors that might have led one to conclude that witness A was the more reliable, the reasoning process leaves wide scope for the influence of determinate, albeit non-rational, factors, such as the judicial response to irrelevant aspects of demeanour (a pleasing voice or appearance), or perhaps a judicial mind that found the choice difficult and was oscillating in preference, settling on a final decision that may indeed have been simply the result of randomness at the level of the neurological processes that generated the decision. The more fine-grained the process of legal reasoning the more the elimination of scope for non-rational or random processes to determine the decision. Detailed and fine-grained reasoning does not merely provide the legal audience with a more satisfying explanation of the judicial decision; rather, it reflects a judicial decision in which the scope for irrational determinative processes, and random processes, has been narrowed to the smallest possible compass.

Returning to *R v Mumberson*, how was it a rational decision? I do not believe that it can be described as rational on the basis that it deployed an ability to synthesize the disparate reasons into a conclusion about the correct sentence using a mental ability or faculty that enjoyed a better than random prospect of success, and yet was not determined. The sentencing decision involved the deployment of various factors chosen as relevant because past experience had demonstrated their relevance, and that success could be shown by an appropriate rational reconstruction of the past. However, all this can be explained deterministically. Ultimately,

R v Mumberson was rational if it formed part of a successful practice of sentencing, and this is so even if elements of the decision-making process were random, since the random elements were confined in the manner just explained.

Remaining issues

The argument to this point has sought to show that we do not possess a mental faculty for making plausible rational judgements. However, it is important to understand precisely what is being rejected. Some intellectual tasks will involve assimilating a number of disparate pieces of evidence, and weighing up this material and reaching a conclusion. Some of the mental processes that judges or others would use in making such decisions will be formal modes of inference, whether logical inference or more specialized modes such as mathematical or probabilistic. Those mental processes are capable of a deterministic explanation if and to the extent that they have not been subject to randomly induced errors. However, it is the case that there are many decisions people make which cannot be arrived at solely by such formal modes of inference. Legal reasoning provides one clear example.

Apart from the assistance gained from formal modes of reasoning, in the making of decisions within the wider context of plausible reasoning, accumulated knowledge will profoundly affect the way in which any decision is made. It will frame the questions for decision, and govern, to a substantial extent, what may be considered possible answers. This, however, is likewise capable of a deterministic explanation. It is no more or less than the way in which all events prior to the relevant decision come to bear upon the decision.

When all the deterministic processes, whether inference driven or causal, that may bear upon a decision have been subtracted, what will be left will be those influences which are ultimately random. However, it should not be surprising that despite the fact that our decisions may involve random elements, our plausible reasoning processes result in the making of rational judgements on a significant number of occasions. This apparent paradox is quickly resolved when we appreciate the temporal aspect of practices and the evolutionary processes that generate knowledge, whether in the sciences or other areas, such as law.

Even if the process of gaining knowledge in the law, or any other field, may be explicable from a combination of deterministic and random processes, the account of plausible reasoning still clearly depends upon a conscious mind and, indeed, on the assumptions that I have made that such conscious minds engage in making judgements about feature-rich gestalts, in the fashion that David Hodgson has described. However, what is crucial for the understanding of rationality is not a mental faculty for making rational judgements; rather, it is an ability to proffer or develop theories that can then be tested through experience.

I am not sure how it could possibly be measured, but one imagines that the overwhelming number of potential ideas that could be proffered by random idea generation would be poor ideas. It might, therefore, be suggested that any practice of plausible reasoning, whether legal reasoning or otherwise, will produce overall success only if fresh ideas can be regularly postulated that have a reasonable prospect of aiding the success of the relevant theoretical practice. It might, therefore, be suggested that I have not come up with a serious riposte to David Hodgson's conception, that I have merely substituted for an ability to make plausible judgements that are rational in his sense an ability to postulate theories upon which to work that have a better than random prospect of providing long term success.

I do not believe the possible objection just described is a telling one. There are many factors that constrain or suggest those alternative ideas upon which work should be done, while still leaving choices that might have no better prospect of success than a purely random selection. Further, such constraints can be explained deterministically. For example, past experience provides heuristic constraints and guidelines, but choices within those constraints may be no better than random.

It might also be suggested that knowing only with hindsight that a judgement is successful is simply confirmation of our rational judgement. However, that misunderstands the approach being suggested. Hindsight does not merely allow us to identify what succeeded and what failed in the past. We immediately incorporate the successful characteristics of any successful theory into our next sequence of theories. A successful sequence has an increasing ability to explain the things that matter.

Once again, have we merely displaced the problem of explaining the rationality of individual judgements, to a judgement about the success of a sequence of theories? I do not believe so. There is a difference between explaining past theoretical activity and its success (or lack of success) in producing rational judgements or decisions on the one hand, and the methodological problem of determining which theoretical framework should be deployed in the future. Some in the field of scientific methodology have sought an answer to this second problem. Lakatos eschewed the search for a criterion by which one could decide when rationally one ought to abandon a research programme and adopt a new one. Likewise, there is no reason to believe that we are possessed of a special faculty of plausible reasoning which would allow us to choose between competing theoretical frameworks in a way guaranteed to have more than a random prospect of success, other than those same processes which bear upon and explain the making of individual decisions.

References

Aroney, N 2013, 'Explanatory Power, Theory Formation, and Constitutional Interpretation: Some Preliminaries', *Australian Journal of Legal Philosophy* 38: 1–31.

Dennett, DC 1978, *Brainstorms: Philosophical Essays on Mind & Psychology*, Penguin, London.

Hodgson, DH 1991, *The Mind Matters*, Clarendon Press, Oxford.

Hodgson, DH 2005, 'A Plain Person's Free Will', *Journal of Consciousness Studies* 12(1): 3–19.

Hodgson, DH 2012, *Rationality + Consciousness = Free Will*, Oxford University Press, New York.
Lakatos, I 1970, 'Falsification and the Methodology of Scientific Research Programmes', in I. Lakatos and A. Musgrave (eds), *Criticism and the Growth of Knowledge*, Cambridge University Press, Cambridge.
Polya, G 1954, *Mathematics & Plausible Reasoning*, Princeton University Press, Princeton.
Popper, K 1972a, *The Logic of Scientific Discovery*, Hutchinson, London.
Popper, K 1972b, *Objective Knowledge*, Clarendon Press, Oxford.
Schauer, F 1988, 'Formalism', *Yale Law Journal* 97(4): 509–548.
Susskind, R 2010, *The End of Lawyers? Rethinking the Nature of Legal Services*, rev edn, Oxford University Press, New York.
Tammerlo, I 1978, *Modern Logic in the Service of Law*, Springer-Verlag, Vien.
Wasserstrom, R 1961, *The Judicial Decision: Toward a Theory of Legal Justification*, Stanford University Press, Stanford.

Index

For Product Safety Concerns and Information please contact our EU
representative GPSR@taylorandfrancis.com
Taylor & Francis Verlag GmbH, Kaufingerstraße 24, 80331 München, Germany

www.ingramcontent.com/pod-product-compliance
Ingram Content Group UK Ltd.
Pitfield, Milton Keynes, MK11 3LW, UK
UKHW011005180926
475701UK00004B/567

* 9 7 8 0 3 6 7 6 6 1 4 4 1 *